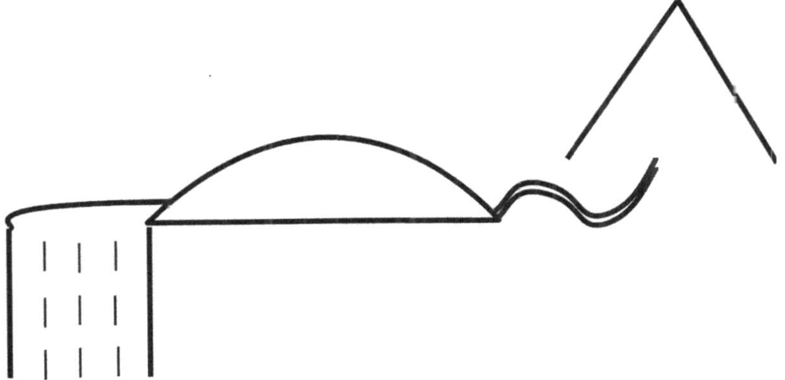

The American Accent Learnway™

Cross the Bridge, Over the Divide

By

Adil Rehman, MA, MSHRM

The Second Edition.
ISBN 979-8-9850855-0-1

For contact and other information,
please see the website: www.americanaccentlearnway.com

Disclaimer:

1. This Course does not state or imply that this Course is a substitute for Dictionaries or any particular Dictionary. It is an independent learning resource in the area of American English Pronunciation and Accent, and complements Dictionary content. Concurrent reference to Dictionary content is recommended.
2. For good reasons provided, this Course does not state or imply that the pronunciation given for word examples are identical with those provided by Dictionaries or any particular Dictionary. For an exact Dictionary pronunciation of any particular Dictionary, it is necessary to refer to that Dictionary.
3. In this Course, the Vocal Fidelity Phonetic System with its Accent sensitive features has been used to closely replicate Accent and pronunciation. Similarly, the content of the Four Lane Route, Vocal Pattern Tables, other Tables and explanation, provide guidance on Accent and Pronunciation. Following a scientific approach toward the development of knowledge, all of these are presented in a manner that is transparent that can be independently tested. No guarantee is offered, nor liability accepted in case of any error.

To my father.

You would have been so happy about this.

To my mother.

You always believed I could.

To my wife.

For being you, with me.

Here it is!

With love and thanks.

I am grateful.

Contents:

Preface.

I remember thinking, sitting in a library, as I was studying a chapter on Linguistics in college when I was in my early twenties – why isn't there something like a dictionary, where you can look up words that share the same vocal rhythms. I also wondered why, notwithstanding dictionaries with phonetic systems and widespread English language education, do people speak English so very differently from each other. I saw that it left a few who spoke a favored Accent as having an advantage which others did not as a problem that needed a solution.

I did not know that almost 40 years later, I would become the person to create that look-up of Vocal Patterns that I had envisaged. And, that I would develop an Accent sensitive phonetic system from the ground up. Life can be so astonishing! Those seeds of thought remained dormant and only sprouted after much weathering and the right conditions came together.

The American Accent Learnway™ is a three Coursebook series, a journey aimed at enabling people to speak the American way – one of two dominant global standards for speaking English. It consists of:

> Coursebook One – "Cross the Bridge, Over the Divide",
> Coursebook Two – "Together, On the Road Inland", and,
> Coursebook Three – "As One, On the Summit".

Coursebook One provides the foundation, via the Four-Lane Route which encompasses Syllabication, Tempo, Voice and Articulation. The Accent sensitive Vocal Fidelity Phonetic System is at its core. In addition, this Coursebook also covers words that are used differently by Americans. It introduces Vocal Patterns and prioritizes the most Distinctive American Vocal Patterns, in the Vocal Pattern Bridge Table. Coursebook One covers most of the journey toward speaking the American way.

Coursebooks Two and Three contain very Distinctive, and, clearly Distinctive Vocal Patterns in the Vocal Pattern Inland and Summit Tables, respectively. Coursebook Two takes you almost all the way toward speaking the American way. Coursebook Three enables the gap to close as the remaining local or foreign elements in your Accent disappear and the less obvious nuances of Accent integrate with the American way of speaking.

Together, the three Coursebooks with their Vocal Pattern Tables, provide a comprehensive look-up of Vocal Patterns. Each of the Tables enable you to make a personal Accent Diagnosis and Development Plan, targeting the specific Vocal Patterns you vocalize differently than Americans. Each of the Vocal Pattern Tables are supplemented by Word List Tables for selected Vocal Patterns so that Accent change progresses in blocks of words at a time, rather than at the rate of single words.

The American Accent Learnway™ is designed to help you get to your destination sooner with less effort. It does so by – prioritizing the presentation of learning content in order of importance – what makes a bigger impact is presented earlier. Also, by enabling you to identify the Vocal Patterns you vocalize differently, you can focus on what you really need to learn.

The development of the Course – including the Four Lane Route, the Vocal Fidelity Phonetic System, and the Vocal Pattern Tables – is the outcome of a scientific process. See Appendix V: Knowledge Creation and Quality, for details.

The Course observes a detailed protocol for consistency in how the different elements of the book are written and laid out, such as with headings, paragraphs, tables, etc. Most of this will appear similar to what is usually encountered in books of a similar genre. Two points need explanation. Firstly – certain words which have been specially defined or explained in the Course are written with the first letter capitalized, as for example with the word "Syllable". By contrast, the word, "word" which is not defined is written normally. Secondly – the Vocal

Fidelity Phonetic System is explained in stages through the Course, to enable you to understand newly introduced Symbols as they are presented. It is also presented in its entirety in the Appendices. It is used as needed to show pronunciation and Accent information of full words or the components of words, within curly brackets or in tables.

The American Accent Learnway™ will enable and facilitate the change you would like to see in the way you speak. It is a journey that will reveal the hidden norms that govern the American way of speaking.

PART 1:
SIZING UP THE LAY OF THE LAND – GETTING READY.

Chapter 1:
What to Expect – The Journey Ahead.

Changing the way you speak a language can be uncomfortable – like, pretending to be someone else!

Your vocal apparatus works differently, you express your emotions vocally in a different way, your voice sounds different!

You have to get to know a strange new you until you become comfortable with an added persona, which also becomes you.

You learn the different ways, first in your mind and then in practice. You repeat them until they become automatic.

You begin to speak according to a different set of principles as you retrain your vocal apparatus. You gain a different sense of how your English should sound!

This course provides new guiding principles and specific directions on speaking the American way.

It is an interesting journey!

Chapter 2:
Knowing the Purpose – Why take a Course on the American Way of Speaking?

This Course was created to serve a certain purpose and fill certain needs. In addition to the main purpose, you may find that a number of the needs are relevant to you.

The main purpose of this Course is to enable English speakers who speak in non-American ways to speak the American way, achieving the best result for effort and time put in, by providing the precise knowledge required, presenting it in priority order, and by being adaptable to individual needs.

To speak English in a way that has global standing and soft influence.

Speaking the American way isn't just for people who live in America or who work with Americans. Across the world, English speakers have a choice of speaking English in a local way or a global way. Those who speak in a global way benefit from advantages in many professional and social contexts. They tend to be received with more acceptance and regarded as more credible. English spoken the American way has long been a global standard. Therefore, those who speak English the American way tend to benefit from these advantages. They feel empowered when they know they are speaking an English that is not just correct but has the sound of an English of global standard.

Part of why English spoken the American way is so positively viewed is because of long held associations with this country. The story of America, its role in the world, and its ideals, have long been an inspiration across the world, over decades – stretching far back. It is also because of its leadership – in the development of knowledge, in the reputation of its universities, and its scientific and artistic achievements. The respect given to this standing transfers inadvertently to the people who speak with the American Accent. Subliminally, the American Accent is associated with liberty, education, leadership, innovation, technology, the arts, and so on.

Students returning from American universities to their home countries, are viewed with respect, not just because of their university education but also for the traces of the American Accent, they imbibe.

For acceptance within America.

If you're new to America and you want to become a part of this society – to be included, trusted and accepted – it really helps to speak the American way. Speaking differently, perhaps more than anything else marks a person out as an "alien". This term has been officially used by Government departments to describe people of other countries. It reflects the way some Americans are inclined to think of foreigners. To avoid being perceived as different, it is specially important to speak like people from here. Speaking the American way will facilitate your inclusion among Americans.

If you have moved to America and you are attending a phone interview for a new job, though laws exist to prevent the interviewer from asking where you've come from – they hear a foreign Accent and may think, "Not from here! This person does not understand how we do things here…". When that view is formed, you will have to overcompensate, somehow shine brighter than others, to be seen as equal. Whether living here or working with Americans, sounding as if you come from an unknown place, makes acceptance harder. Though not always the case, this is certainly how it sometimes is.

The Title of this Coursebook "The American Accent Learnway – Cross the Bridge, Over the Divide" and of the Coursebooks that follow, "The American Accent Learnway – Together on the Road Inland" and "The American Accent Learnway – As One, On the Summit", are about creating unity and integration, through speaking the American way.

By enabling you to speak like Americans, this Course will help you overcome an important obstacle to your acceptance in America, or, by Americans. It will help you feel at home in the American milieu. When you speak like Americans, it will also help others here accept and feel comfortable with you. Speaking the American way has positive implications for your social and work life, for the present and for the future – really, for life as a whole, when you live in America, or work with Americans.

Lots of people who move to America as adults remain glued fast in many ways to the Accents which they learned growing up.

This Course has been created out of the recognition that Accents can be a barrier to self advancement and social acceptance.

To fill the education gap regarding English speaking.

Though English Language is taught the world over, it appears – from the different Accents that proliferate – that insufficient focus has been given to pronunciation and Accent training. It may be because the importance of pronunciation and Accent is treated as secondary to the importance of knowing the language, and therefore compromised. It may also be because there has not been enough phonetic insight and practice provided, in English language education received, to hold firm against local influences that cause slide into a local Accent. Whatever the reason, the outcome is that many people find that they speak in a local Accent – a possible liability for them in professional and global contexts. Clearly, a Course that can reverse local effects and restore a global Accent would be of use for them. This Course addresses their need.

This Course has been designed to fill a void in Accent training that arises from an underestimation of all the challenges involved.

For a clear path to speaking English the American way for those who know English.

It shouldn't be that you have to grow up in America, or to have attended an American University or School, to speak the American way. This Course offers an effective, practical and well defined path for anyone who knows English who wants to speak the American way. It is for those whose English is learned outside America no matter where they live and regardless of their language background.

For adults who learn differently than children.

When children are taught to read, write and speak, they imbibe core speech patterns at an early age, soaking in what they hear, like sponges. If their models speak with a widely accepted or standard Accent, they pick it up. Adult learners do not imbibe language learning and an Accent like children. Their prior experiences come in the way. They need retraining. They need to understand how to vocalize unfamiliar speech patterns. This involves mental and physical aspects. They need to practice new motions of throat, tongue and mouth, to articulate sounds that are strange. This Course provides adults with what they they need to enable relearning.

For the aesthetics in the American way of speaking.

Spoken English of a global standard, such as the American way, has an aesthetic that can be appreciated and enjoyed, just as one enjoys the aesthetics of some form of art. A language well spoken is worthy of admiration and emulation. I see the American way of speaking as bold, elegant and refined. This Course serves to make it accessible to all who know English.

Much like the way we dress or otherwise present ourselves, the way we speak is a big part of how we are perceived and received by others. It plays an important part in our ability to influence others.

Chapter 3:
Two Global English Speaking Standards and Local English Accents.

British English was once the sole English speaking standard.

The very first standard of English, of course, came to us from the English. It was, after all, to begin with exclusively their language. The "Queen's" English – as it is sometimes called, used to be the language of their institutions, their elite, and their educators. At one time, it was the sole model for good English speaking. Though local English Accents exist wherever English is spoken, including in Britain, the Queen's English was upheld in their traditional enclaves – as at universities like Cambridge and Oxford, or old schools, like Eton and Winchester, or in families of the aristocracy. At one time, it seemed to be the only acceptable English Accent for British state media. That has changed as the world has become more inclusive; we now hear a wide range of Accents.

British English dictionaries sustain British English as a global standard – they are referred to, for word meanings and pronunciations, across much of the English speaking world.

Spoken American English is an established global English speaking standard.

Over time, spoken American English has become an alternative English speaking standard for the world. The push in this direction emerged out of America's past, as it forged a separate path from the British. From its separate experience, the remembered words of its own people, its universities and schools, American English developed features distinct from its cousin across the Atlantic.

The Merriam-Webster's Dictionary upholds the American English standard for people across the world who have chosen American English over British English. It clearly distinguishes American English from British English, in spelling and word pronunciation.

Global English speaking standards are clearly different from local Accents.

The large number of local ways of speaking heard in the United States and in Britain or elsewhere are to be distinguished from the American and British standards spoken of above. While often charming, colorful and appealing, their distinguishing characteristics do not have widespread recognition or currency. They are informally perpetuated through social interaction – not through formal education of any form. By contrast, the American and British standards are perpetuated through teaching and educational material as well as by the example of educated people in varied professions. The global standards are the norm for speaking in many institutions, businesses and professions. They are widely spoken among families of the college educated.

> Note:
> While there are many local Accents in America and Britain, there are certain important underlying principles and norms that apply to the American way of speaking in general, clearly identified in the Course.

Other English Language traditions are not global.

Other than the global English standards of America and Great Britain, there are now many other well regarded English language sub-traditions across the globe. These have all in some measure contributed to a broader and richer English language. These include the English of Australia, other erstwhile British colonies such as, of the Indian sub-continent, and countries within Africa. Most of these, display British characteristics, being direct offshoots of the British tradition arising from British historical connections. A few, exhibit characteristics of the American standard emerging through historical connections with America. Their way of speaking do not however have the global recognition, currency, and codified discipline that have elevated the British and American spoken English to the level of global standards.

The relationship between English Accents.

Accents are more closely related to either the American or the British traditions. The closeness of the relationship can be estimated by how similar or different they are to the American and British global standards.

Accents closer to the American global standard are those that are more geographically proximate to the United States, or places that have been more closely engaged with the United States, historically. Accordingly, the English spoken in Canada and Mexico and other North American countries are closer to the American global standard than the British as a result of proximity. To some extent this is true for most of the countries of South America as well, though they are also influenced by the British global standard. Countries like Japan, the Philippines, and South Korea in Asia, Liberia in Africa have had greater historical exposure to the United States and as such, their Accents are closer to the American global standard.

Similarly, Accents that are closer to the British global standard are likely to be found in countries that are geographically proximate to Britain, or that have been more closely engaged with Britain historically. Australia, New Zealand, South Africa and Canada, with many of their people originally from Britain are strongly influenced by the British global standard. While the British influence on Canadian English is strong, it comes across as a bit more similar to the American Accent than the British. Other countries that were associated with Britain over the colonial era also speak an English that shares greater similarity with the British global standard. This includes countries in Asia and Africa. In Asia, countries of the Indian sub-continent, the Middle-East and China; and, in Africa, countries such Kenya and Nigeria, are included. There are other countries such as Guyana in South America and the Falklands close by that also speak an English that is closer to the British global standard because of historical association. The countries of Europe are more similar to the British Accent than the American because of their proximity and their neighbor relationship.

The extent of the relationship between Accents is also influenced by the magnitude and complexity of local influencing factors, such as the number of other languages spoken in the geography and the extent of their diversity. Thus, a local English Accent that is subject to greater local influence is more likely to exhibit greater difference than one that is subject to less local influence.

It is possible to roughly estimate the extent of relative closeness or difference between a particular Accent and the American and British global standards, based on the considerations described above. The diagram below roughly indicates the likely relationship, i.e. extent of similarity or difference, of different local Accents with the American and British global standards. It points to the amount of gap that has to be closed for a local Accent to transition to a global standard.

A View of the Extent of Contrast between Local English Accents Across the World with the American and British Accents

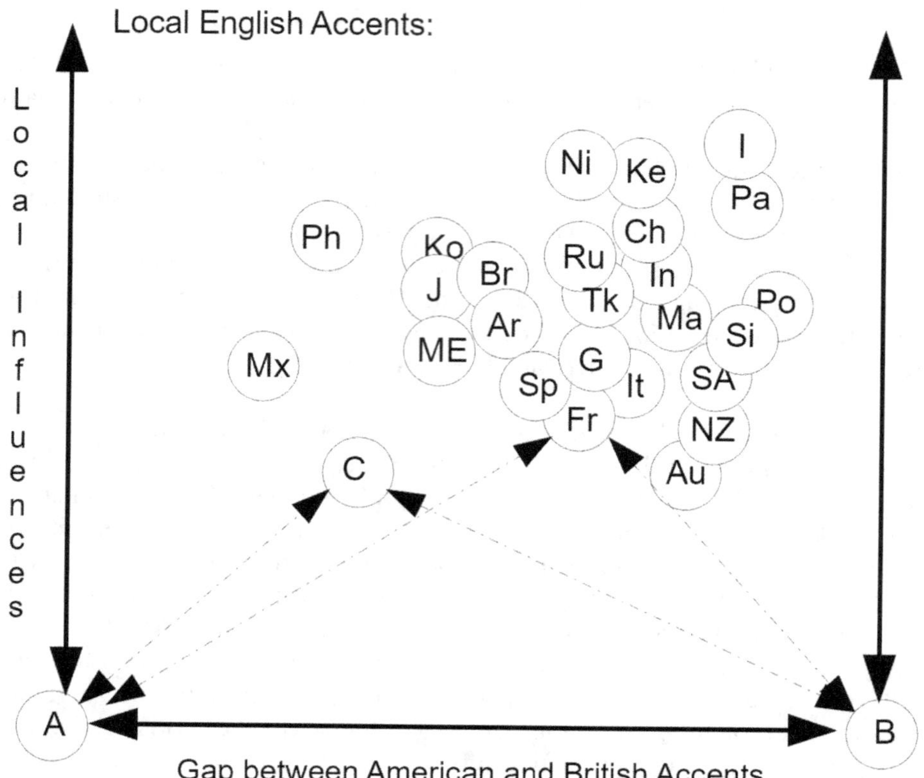

Key for Accents:

A: American
Ar: Argentine
Au: Australian
B: British
Be: Belgian
Br: Brazilian
C: Canadian
Ch: Chinese
F: French
G: German

I: Indian
In: Indonesian
It: Italian
J: Japanese
Ke: Kenyan
Ko: Korean
Mx: Mexican
ME: Middle Eastern
Ma: Malaysian

Ni: Nigerian
NZ: New Zealandic
Pa: Pakistani
Po: Polish
Ph: Phillipine
Ru: Russian
SA: South African
Si: Singaporean
Sp: Spanish
Tu: Turkish

A Cautionary Note:
The diagram is not based on a factual study of these local Accents. Rather, it is based on the logic that Local Accents must be an outcome of influences from:

> -the English source from which the local Accent was originally learned, and the global English standard that is used as a model by the local population – i.e. American or British

-local factors, such as the impact of local languages, culture, etc.
You may, in fact, encounter many local Accents and wonder, what is American or British about a particular local Accent – because the local influence is so dominant. Yet, they will bear traces of the English from which the local Accent originated and the English which they use as their model to follow.

Note:
Remember, there is considerable variation even in local Accents, depending on different factors, such as education and economic & social classes. The impact of global influence will be higher for some segments and the impact of local influence will be higher for others, though all segments will be effected to some extent by both. The diagram provides a rough assessment illustrating the idea of the relationship between Accents. It is not precise or highly accurate.

Note:
Clustered Accents do not necessarily resemble each other in their substantive vocalizations, but are similar in the extent of contrast or similarity with the global standard Accents.

Note:
To estimate the extent of local influence, the number of other languages that are a part of the environment was considered important. Also considered was the closeness of relationship that the local languages have with English, i.e. whether they belong to related or unrelated language families. As pointed out, the estimate does not claim to be precise or highly accurate.

Transitioning to the American way of speaking.

Many people, whether in America or elsewhere in the world, learned to speak an English that was closer to the British tradition or strongly influenced by local factors or both. Of them, there are many who would prefer to speak the American global standard rather than accepting what they learned as a result of circumstance rather than choice.

They may prefer to speak the American way because:

-It sounds good. It is a strong, elegant and refined Accent.
-It is a global standard of speaking English, that is clearly understood and better received than a local Accent.
-It has an important place in the present and the future.
-It helps when living and working in America.
-It helps when working or associating with Americans anywhere.
-It helps when working in the West, in Europe, in English speaking countries across the world, and in the context of international organizations of all kinds.
-It is respected in professional and social English speaking gatherings anywhere.

By rigorous comparison of the differences between the American and British ways of speaking, this Course is able to precisely target the areas of contrast and provide the guidance needed to enable change. It is as if the Course places two mirrors at different angles before an individual, one with information about the American Accent, the other with information about the British, so that an individual can look into both, compare them with his own and make the necessary changes.

The Course encompasses standard American vocalization and includes widely acceptable, popular vocalizations heard in professional, organizational and social settings and by good voice models on audio-visual media.

www.americanaccentlearnway.com

Chapter 4:
Different American Accents and Speaking the American Way.

Different Accents have developed through people of divergent speaking backgrounds who came to America, all influencing each other. Who were these different peoples?

First there were many Native American tribes with their own languages from thousands of years ago. Improbable though it may seem to some – that native American languages had an impact on spoken English, clearly the influence is visible in the names of several places in the United States that exhibit native origin. Similarly, people still display native American art, clothing and jewelry; draw inspiration from their spiritual beliefs, and use their themes in important national symbols.

> Think of place names such as Chattanooga or Sioux Falls. Think of jackets with tassels and moccasins. Think of the bald eagle, a symbol of national pride.

Then, following Columbus's first landing on the islands adjoining the Americas in the late 1400's, people from colonizing countries started arriving in increasing numbers from the 1600's. In North America, the French, the Spanish and the British all had a strong presence. Early on, the French held the most territory, from the deep south around the mouth of the Mississippi where New Orleans is located, advancing up northward on both sides of the Great Lakes and beyond, and eastward nearly up to the Atlantic. The British, then, held the Eastern seaboard, from north of Florida continuing upward, up to and including areas on and off the coast of present day Canada, until they came up against the French, both in the north and toward the west. The Spanish held Florida, Texas, New Mexico and California, and all the territory down to the southern tip of North America, including the region of Central America.

> The Cajun people of Louisiana speak a dialect that is strongly influenced by French.

> Evocative names of towns with Spanish names like Santa Barbara, Santa Margarita, and San Antonio dot the South and Southwest where the Spanish had a presence.

Texas, in fact, was at one time a part of Mexico. Names like San Francisco, and Los Angeles, are just one way in which the influence of the Spanish is evidenced.

There were also smaller colonizers including the Dutch, who established the New Netherlands, which now corresponds, more or less, with New York and New Jersey States. Its capital was named New Amsterdam and was located at the southern most point of the island of Manhattan. New Amsterdam much later morphed into an emerging New York City. Sweden was also an important military power as the New World was being discovered. They created a New Sweden, populated by Swedes and Finns, on the East Coast in the area around Delaware. It was, in time, absorbed by the Dutch.

The British ultimately established themselves as dominant, and English emerged as the primary language across what finally became the United States. Aside from the expansionist initiatives of colonial powers, there were waves upon waves of immigration, starting before American independence and continuing through to the present time. These included not just the English, but other English speakers, from Scotland, Ireland and Wales. There were also groups of Germans, Scandinavians, Italians and others, reaching American shores in successive waves. From the Western Seaboard, Russians, Chinese and Japanese – travelers and immigrants – also came to North America. Much later, with the liberalization of immigration policy, the United States opened its doors to the whole world.

As part of the slave trade, Africans in large numbers were brought to the Unites States, from different regions of Africa. While the languages they brought with them were extinguished through extreme adversity, these would have had some impact on the English they spoke, and traces are likely to have survived. But, like other groups with local Accents within the United States, those engaging with the broader population, integrate their Accents with the broader American way of speaking.

> The Creole dialect spoken by the Creole community in Louisiana is strongly influenced by French and African American speech and culture.

Concentrations of people belonging to a particular background certainly shaped the way the language was spoken in different regions. The legacy for the United States is about half a dozen more broadly spoken local Accents identified in linguistic studies.

With the many local Accents, some question whether there is a mainstream American way of speaking. The answer is "Yes". It is possible to identify many characteristics that span or come close to spanning all these local Accents. Obvious examples include:

-the distinctive 'R' Consonant sound, and
-the Flat-Extended 'O'.

Both are exhibited pervasively, if not ubiquitously, across the country. The Course reveals many other defining aspects, at different levels, associated with the American Accent and way of speaking. As you will see, these are identified, explained and substantiated.

> The intent of this Chapter is to portray what is widely known:
>
> That while the American way of speaking emerged from Britain, it has been touched in different ways by many other peoples, to make it what it is.
>
> Also, that the American Accent and way of speaking is distinguishable and definable.

Chapter 5:
How to View and Approach This Course.

Attitudes about Accent change.

People come to different positions with regard to Accent change. Some think it is best to continue speaking the way they always have. The idea of Accent change may be too daunting. They decide, people should take them as they are, and if they don't, it doesn't matter. They can live with it. As, a result, this category of people remain entrenched in the way they way they always spoke. Others, are more flexible. They are open to the idea that certain changes are desirable. They are willing to make adjustments based on what they observe. As a result, this group, develops. Yet others, are very keen to learn. They are willing to accept that the way they speak needs substantial change. As a result, they go to great lengths to develop. As a consequence, over time, they achieve the greatest self improvement. Younger people often fall into the last category naturally, because of their willingness to accept that they have much to learn and are enthusiastic. Like young people, there are older people, as well, who have the same youthful zest and the willingness to be open to change. As a result, they continue to learn and develop. This is the attitude that is needed to be successful with Accent change.

Anyone can become open to learning. It only requires a little shift: Seeing the advantages to be gained through change; giving oneself time to understand and practice; and, feeling good about achieving progress, can activate and sustain learning.

Motivations for Accent change.

But why might Accent change be needed? Fundamentally, the way you speak effects how you are received. But, it is also about how we see ourselves and how we wish to present ourselves to others. Like we choose to dress a certain way, we choose to speak a certain way. A way that reflects how we think and feel about ourselves. How we choose to dress and speak is very personal. It is not a choice that occurs in a vacuum. It is effected by our circumstances, the roles we play, and the environment. And what we choose has an effect on the way others respond to us. We bear in mind the likely response of others, when we make our choice of how we wish to present ourselves to them.

We may wish to speak in a way that has a certain aesthetic appeal. The global standards for speaking English have polish and style. This has long been true for the American way of speaking as it took its place as a global speaking standard alongside the British way of speaking.

Speaking a global standard is a potent way of communicating readiness for any global stage. It is a great equalizer. For the western world, it provides reassurance, that you belong to their world. Globally, it provides reassurance that you have international exposure. For both, it increases your credibility. By contrast, a local Accent raises questions about whether you can fit in. It may elicit unconscious prejudice or patronizing.

Certain Local Accents, i.e. the Scottish and the Irish English Accents have a nostalgic appeal for many Americans, perhaps because these Accents are a part of their heritage. Their is a feeling of affinity with certain other English Accents, including the Australian, the Canadian and of New Zealand, arising from a sense of shared origins and values with their people. Other local Accents may be viewed with reservation, apprehension, or negatively.

Speaking the American way helps to overcome such barriers that can come in the way of professional growth and social integration in America. Speaking in the way that the rest of a society speaks is probably one of the most important ways of finding acceptance. It opens wide the doors to integration and getting ahead, in America.

The above are some important motivations. There may be others. It is important to identify your particular motivations as they will power your commitment to Accent learning.

The Course journey.

This Course presents the essential factors that underlie the American Accent, in order of importance:

Part 1 discusses why and how to go about learning a new way of speaking. This helps you build the mindset and to follow the right approach to be successful in this kind of learning project.

Part 2 takes you over the Four Lane Route which covers the essential factors that underlie the American Accent. These are described as the parallel "Lanes" of

-Syllabication, i.e how Syllables are formed in the American Accent
-Tempo, i.e the way Americans speed through certain parts of words
-Voice, i.e the characteristics of the American voice, and,
-Articulation, i.e. Vowel and Consonant sounds in the American Accent, described with the Accent sensitive Vocal Fidelity Phonetic System.

The hidden principles, norms and characteristics of the American Accent are made visible to enable you to make deeper level foundational and structural changes first. More detailed, surface level or facade changes are important as well, but these sit true when the foundation and structure are properly set. The details of the facade are addressed in Part 3.

Part 3 details the most Distinctive American vocalizations presented in order of their Rate of Occurrence in what has been named the Vocal Pattern Bridge Table. Thus, those recurring vocalizations that make a greater impact on Accent are covered sooner. The Vocal Pattern Bridge Table is so named because it covers the most Distinctive vocalizations, enabling a crossing of the divide between the American Accent and local Accents learned outside America.

> The Vocal Pattern Tables could also be used by those with local American Accents to realign to a more standard and widely accepted American Accent.

Part 4 covers the American vocalization of commonly used words. The differences that exist would be surprising to many.

Part 5 covers some common English language words, terms and phrases that have different meanings in spoken American English.

Part 6 contains Appendices. These include Tables that provide detailed information regarding essential components of the Accent sensitive Vocal Fidelity Phonetic System developed with this Course. These also include a glossary of words and terms that have been specially defined or explained, essentials on the knowledge creation and quality process, and the bibliography.

The above Parts constitute the first Coursebook of this American Accent Learnway series. The essence of the first Coursebook is visually represented in the diagram below, from the left to about the middle of the diagram.

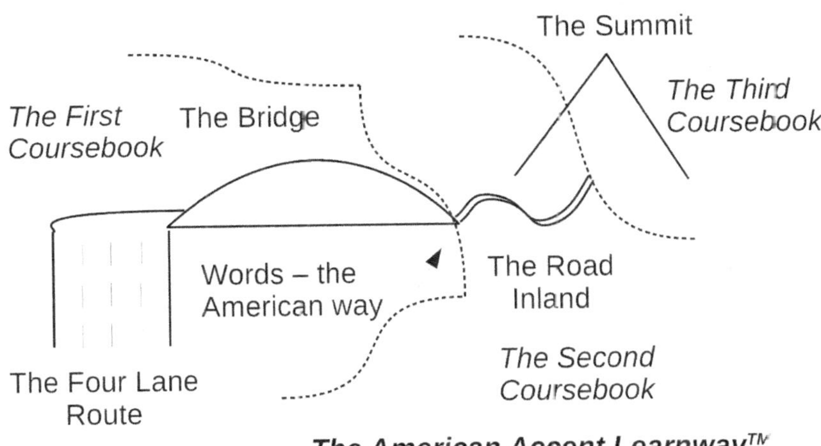

The American Accent Learnway™

As you shift your view toward the right of the diagram, a winding road is shown after the Bridge, which leads to a mountain. The winding road represents the Vocal Pattern Inland Table presented in the second Coursebook, and the mountain represents the Vocal Pattern Summit Table presented in the third Coursebook. These successive Vocal Pattern Tables cover American Accent vocalizations at successively lower levels of Distinctiveness, i.e. more subtly Distinctive vocalizations.

A bit about my personal journey.

As I progressed in my own Accent change journey, I continued to observe and integrate new American forms into my speech, I would read passages out loud to apply and practice my insights. I would listen for errors in my reading and correct them in re-readings. Gradually, I improved my pronunciation – speaking the American way. I continue to have such practice sessions, just as one may practice a golf swing, tennis stroke, or play notes on an instrument.

I remember, I got to a point where I was confident when practicing word lists but still hesitant in my pronunciation when reading aloud. I decided to read the passages without worrying about making errors. This was a leap that enabled me to become free and comfortable speaking in the new way. When I started using the different American word pronunciations in conversation, I began to feel increasingly comfortable speaking the American way. It was like learning a new language.

I recommend, first, going through the whole course relatively quickly so that you have an overview of the entire program. As you understand the different Four Lanes, you will naturally remember more and more of the detail. You will quickly get to a level of familiarity with the material at which you will remember where particular points were covered, so looking back to find something will become easy.

Then, integrate all that you have learned and practice it all together. Keep going back to areas where you remain uncertain, until you understand it all clearly and remember it well.

Do not wait to become perfect with a Lane before you move to the next Lane. Try to improve them all concurrently.

Final thoughts on approaching this Course.

Learning an Accent is a skill that requires internalizing its hidden rules until they become unconscious and automatic. The knowledge and skill elements involved must be tried, practiced and mastered, through repetition in the mind and in action, until they become part of you. With each chapter, you will gain new insights, but these will have to be applied in your speech, and practiced often. Over time, what will at first have seemed strange will become natural for you. You will still need to revisit different parts of this course to remind yourself of the American way of speaking until each aspect of it has become a habit.

If different English Accents are treated like different languages, it is possible to choose to speak one or the other depending on context. However, this can lead to each effecting the other and can slow learning.

Chapter 6:
The Keys to Remembering.

Whether learning a new language or a new way of speaking, being able to remember how a Word Type is to be pronounced is necessary. A Word Type is any set of words which share a pattern of sound in common, and are therefore pronounced in a similar way. Only by remembering and being able to recall these pronunciation patterns is it possible to change one's way of speaking.

To be able to do this, the intent to remember is all important.

> Whenever you encounter a word with an unfamiliar pattern of pronunciation, make a decision to remember it. Back up the decision to lock it into your memory with resolve and conscious effort. Repeat the word as many times as you need, continue to regularly recall it and rehearse it – until it becomes a part of you. Extend the newly learned pronunciation pattern to other words with the same pattern.

Having decided to remember the word, you then act to remember it.

> When remembering a word, focus on the word as if it is the only thing in the world for a few moments, with nothing to distract you. Understand the way it is constructed and its pronunciation logic. Become familiar with its sound and tempo. Repeat it, again and again.
>
> You repeat the word again and again correctly several times – as many times as you need – to register it in your mind. You then recall it shortly afterward – in the next few minutes and then a few times again over the current half-hour, to imprint the pronunciation of the word firmly in your mind. You do this again a few times then in the next few hours. By this time you will have become more familiar with this word. Still, to log the pronunciation of the word in to your long term memory, you will need to recall it again a few more times over the next few days and weeks. Try not only to recall the word but to apply it in a sentence as practice or even better, use it in conversation. By this time your memory of how this word is be pronounced – will integrate into your spoken language.
>
> As you practice on a few some examples of a word type, you will also make changes to your pronunciation of similar sounding words, many of which this course will identify in word lists.
>
> It is important to be alert to recognize words of a word type as they come up in speech so that they are pronounced the American way. Or, to recognize them as they come up as part of your practice when reading a passage, so that you read it aloud correctly. As you use the American pronunciation it becomes a part of your spoken language.

Unlearning entrenched old ways is not difficult or easy.

> Do not underestimate the challenge of changing your way of speaking a language, especially if you already speak it. In fact, because you already know the language, "unlearning" will require some effort, attention, and persistence. You will need to break free of your old way of speaking and supplant it with the new way. Any skill which requires spontaneous competence, as does speaking, requires practice. It is good to recognize at the outset of this relearning process that while the challenge isn't too hard, it is also not without the need for commitment, practice and application. And with this discipline, you will see great progress.

Physical, emotional and mental flexibility and resilience is required.

There must be flexibility to alter the physical aspects of speaking, including movements of the tongue, the mouth and the throat, as well as the lungs to power the voice, in new ways. The vocal apparatus has to be used differently to articulate pronunciation patterns the American way.

Emotionally, it is necessary to be steadfast until practice results in the creation of new speaking habits. There must also be the willingness and adaptability to articulate words in ways that will initially seem uncomfortable and strange to you. You will gradually become comfortable with your new way of speaking.

Mentally, you need to be observant as you hear words being spoken by model native speakers of American English, and to become sensitive to your own way of articulating English by comparison.

Chapter 7:
How Much Change is Possible, and,
How Long does Change Take?

This Course provides comprehensive materials that consist of both high level guidelines that have broad impact across the language, and also very narrowly focused descriptions that are applicable to very specific vocal sounds and sequences. These tell you as much as you need to know for your Accent to merge with the American Accent.

Reaching this level depends on your completing the different stages of the program and applying them to the way you speak. As you go through the different stages, your Accent increasingly merges with the American way of speaking. Greater change happens more rapidly in larger steps at initial stages, while change is slower and more incremental at later stages.

By following this Course, I expect the progression of your Accent toward the American Accent to be in the shape of an inverted 'L' curve: You can see from the steep, abruptly rise of the curve from the very start that most of the learning takes place early in the process. Then, as you get closer to the American Accent, progress levels off with more gradual improvement, until your Accent merges with the American Accent.

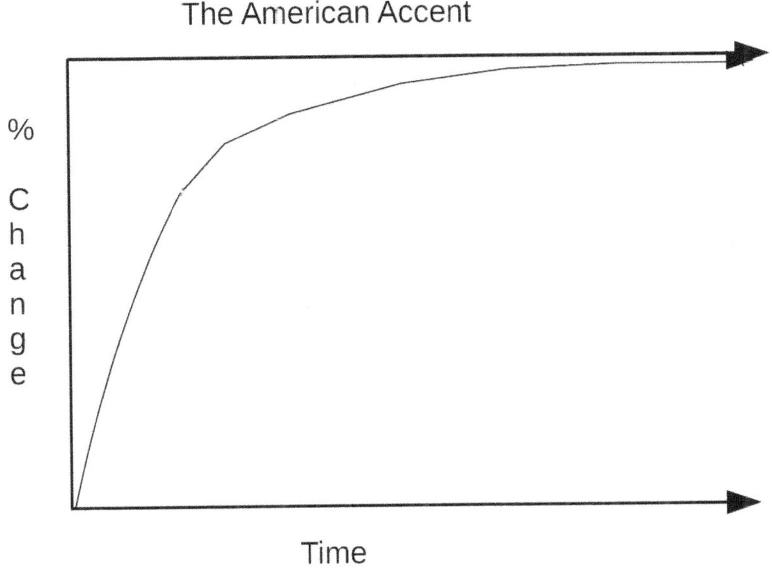

> Note: The curve above is the consequence of first, a proper foundation to impart correct understanding and good basic form initially, and second, effective means to continue improvement. This Course provides these. Without such guidance, there would be no reason for the curve to rise or to show progression. It would likely be erratic.

The Course begins with the Four Lane Route that addresses the four factors or "Lanes" that underlie the American Accent, namely Syllabication, Tempo, Voice and Articulation. On a self-learning basis, in favorable circumstances, the typical person may be expected to read and understand this in a period varying between one month to three months. Though this part of the program really tells you all you need to understand, I believe, at this point you would have covered only about 50 percent of your journey. This is because, time is needed to improve in actual performance.

Training could condense this time to under a week or less, depending upon specific objectives.

The Course enables further development beyond this point via Vocal Pattern Tables. Vocal Pattern Tables provide detailed guidance on recurring vocal sequences, called Vocal Patterns. With the specific information they contain, they also serve to provide feedback on how effectively you are applying the understanding achieved from the Four Lane Route.

Viewed from the perspective above, the Course consists of two big learning steps:

> First, of achieving understanding and translating it to action. Completing this step happens quickly with learning the Four Lane Route. This is like trying to perform an act of skill for the first time after being provided guidance. For example, like trying to drive after being told how. Instruction and a few practice drives are clearly not enough, though it gets you out onto the road. At this point you would therefore only be about half way though your learning journey.
>
> Second, you look to see what needs to be improved. This is enabled by the Course through the Vocal Pattern Tables (and corresponding Word List tables that provide more examples). Going through the Vocal Pattern Tables is an incremental process which consolidates and improves the understanding you gained through the first step. It tells you how well you are applying your new understanding. It provides you feedback on how words containing specific Vocal Patterns are vocalized, enabling self correction and further improvement. It is a process that leads to higher level performance.

There are three Vocal Pattern Tables. Each contains Vocal Patterns categorized according to the level of their impact on the American Accent. The Vocal Pattern Bridge Table contains those with Great impact. The Vocal Pattern Inland Table contains those with Substantial impact. The Vocal Pattern Summit Table contains those with Significant impact.

Using the Vocal Pattern Tables, you can select and focus on learning those Vocal Patterns that you vocalize differently than Americans. You will have completed about three-fourths of your journey when you know how to vocalize the Vocal Patterns in the Vocal Pattern Bridge Table. About nine-tenths of your journey will be complete when you know the Vocal Patterns in the Vocal Pattern Inland Table. Your Accent will closely merge with the American Accent, when you also know the Vocal Patterns in the Vocal Pattern Summit Table.

Note: The first Coursebook, "The American Accent Learnway – Cross the Bridge, Over the Divide", contains the Vocal Pattern Bridge Table with just over 100 of the most Distinctive Vocal Patterns. The second Coursebook, "The American Accent Learnway – Together, On the Road Inland", contains the Vocal Pattern Inland Table with 200 very Distinctive Vocal Patterns. The third Coursebook, "The American Accent Learnway – As One, On the Summit", contains the Vocal Pattern Summit Table with just over 300 clearly Distinctive Vocal Patterns.

Although the Vocal Pattern Tables contain a considerable number of Vocal Patterns, selecting the Vocal Patterns you need to change is a relatively brief exercise, like a yes or no test. For each Vocal Pattern Table, it will take a few hours. It can comfortably be spread over a few days. The outcome of selection is a reduced number of Vocal Patterns to learn – i.e. your own personal Accent development plan. Other than flagging Vocal Patterns that contrast with your own vocalization, this selection exercise also produces development gains. Explanation provided in the Four Lane Route, relating to Syllabication, Tempo, Accentuation and Modulations will be reinforced in your mind as you it see it manifest in Vocal Pattern after Vocal Pattern, with few exceptions.

More thorough review of the Vocal Patterns you select, from the three Vocal Pattern Tables, will take several months. This is not unlike the development of any other complex skill – conceptual understanding is achieved much faster than skill development. This investment leads to true gains as your Accent merges with the American Accent across close to all Distinctive Vocal Patterns that span English, spoken the American way.

Assuming an individual has selected two-third of listed Vocal Patterns, and is committed to a schedule of learning 15 Vocal Patterns a week on average, it would take about 5 weeks to learn the Vocal Pattern Bridge Table, about 9 weeks to learn the Vocal Pattern Inland Table, and about 14 weeks to learn the Vocal Pattern Summit Table. Altogether, this is approximately seven months. This is at a comfortable learning rate. A substantially faster learning rate is possible.

For many people, more important than the speed of change is continual even if gradual improvement. As a self learning Course, each individual has the flexibility to proceed at whatever pace they want.

Sustaining Accent Change and preventing slippage back to old vocalizations can be prevented by periodically returning to the Vocal Pattern Tables. They help to keep change on the right track.

The Vocal Pattern Tables also offer the following advantages to expedite learning:

-Vocal Patterns with greater impact on Accent are presented before Vocal Patterns with lower impact so that you learn what matters more, sooner.
-With all three Tables at your disposal, a specific Vocal Pattern found in certain words can be looked up, to see how it is vocalized.

PART 2:
THE WAY AMERICAN ENGLISH IS SPOKEN.

Chapter 8:
The Four Lane Route –
Factors Underlying the American Accent.

Four underlying factors contribute to speaking American English in contrast with British English. These are Syllabication, Tempo, the American Voice, and Articulation. Like the lanes of a highway, each of these enable progress, as you pass from one to the next, continuing back and forth between them to reach your destination: Speaking the American way, with the global American Accent. This is why each of these is referred to as a "Lane". The highway, constituting learning material for these Four Lanes is called the Four Lane Route.

Lane 1: Syllabication.

This is about the system of vocalizing the Syllables within words – the manner in which each Syllable is emphasized in relation to the others in the word. There is a clear distinction between the American and British ways of doing this. Learning this difference and making the shift is a fundamental requirement in transitioning from the British to the American way of speaking. It is essential for speaking the American way. This shift will produce a dramatic and pronounced impact on the way you speak.

Lane 2: Tempo.

This is about how tempo is regulated in American speech. Americans articulate words the way they are written, rarely leaving any Syllable silent or abbreviating them. Yet, they are able to speak with speed by following a systematic approach to combining Syllables into parts. Understanding the logic of this is another necessary step to speaking the American way.

Lane 3: Voice.

This is about the adoption of the characteristics of the American voice that are essential for speaking with the American Accent. Even if the other factors are applied, without this third Lane, the Accent would retain a pronounced foreign element. These characteristics have to do with the way Americans use their physical speaking apparatus, which is distinctive.

Lane 4: Articulation.

This is about the distinctive way Americans articulate certain Vowel and Consonant Sounds in contrast to the English. These differences reflect in how they pronounce words. Understanding the impact of their articulation on speech adds significant finishing touches to understanding how words are pronounced the American way.

The first three Lanes are essential, while the fourth Lane takes you further in closing Accent gaps by bringing in significant refinement.

Chapter 9:
Lane 1: Syllabication – The System of Articulating Syllables – the American Way.

I begin this chapter on Lane 1 with a point on intent. My effort is to keep things as simple and practical as possible. It would be easy to get stuck on complex definitions of terms used in linguistics. Simple working definitions are given where necessary. The focus is on the what and the how to! So now, moving ahead.

As I analyzed the way Americans speak I was struck by a fundamental insight, all important to crossing the divide between the American and British ways of speaking:

Americans have a tendency to begin Syllables within words with a Consonant (the first Syllable doesn't count – it begins with the first letter whatever it is) and where possible, except in a few contexts, they end them with a Vowel (including the first Syllable). I call this the "American Syllabication Principle". By contrast, in the British way of speaking, Syllables often begin with a Vowel and end with a Consonant, but fairly often the opposite also happens.

> Note: A Pause is any interruption or break in vocalization between the beginning and end of a Word. A Pause separates each Syllable from the next.

> Note: A Syllable is a note or stream of vocalization from a Pause to a Pause forming an integrated, separable vocal unit.
>
> They form the building blocks of words. Each is separated from the next by shorter or longer Pauses between them. A Syllable may even be only a single letter, if separated by a Pause.
>
> Some words consist of only a single Syllable of no more than one letter e.g. "A" or "I".

> Note: There are exceptions to most rules – even physical laws (even gravity doesn't work everywhere). The American Syllabication Principle is no different. Even in Spoken American English, there are some patterns of words where Syllables begin with Vowels. The existence of these alternate patterns does not compromise the general truth of the American Syllabication Principle.

Conversely, Americans rarely begin Syllables with a Vowel if there is an option, while the British often do so.

Transitioning from speaking the British way to the American way therefore requires a change to the pattern of beginning Syllables within words with a Consonant and where possible ending them with a Vowel! There are many words in which the Syllables separate at the same place whether speaking the American way or the British, but there are also many where they are different. It is with these where transition is needed.

The effect of beginning a Syllable with a Consonant is to make it sound more deliberate and defined. The effect of beginning a Syllable with a Vowel has the effect of minimizing and smoothing the gaps between Syllables. Try and observe this when you compare American and British ways of speaking. The smoothing effect of beginning some Syllables with Vowels, frequently seen in the British way of speaking, is sometimes hard for American ears to catch. If you articulate such words the British way, you may sometimes be met with a look of "What was that you said?"

Part of the effect of beginning Syllables with Consonants regularly as do the Americans is that latter Syllable(s) are given stronger emphasis than the first Syllable. By contrast, with English spoken the British way, emphasis is more often placed on a preceding Syllable, often the first.

> Consider the word "Brother", as an example. In this case, the Americans Pause after the Vowel 'O' and begin the last Syllable with the Consonant Sound 'TH' ('th' has the more defined character of a Consonant Sound), breaking the word into the Syllables 'BRO' and 'THER' {Bro-ther}. Observe that the first Syllable ends with a Vowel and the latter begins with a Consonant Sound, as is characteristic of the American way. The effect of this is also to bring the emphasis onto the latter Syllable. The British way, by contrast, Pauses after the 'TH', thus dividing the word differently into the Syllables 'BROTH' and 'ER' {Broth-er}. They end the first with a Consonant and begin the latter with a Vowel. In this example, it may be observed how the American and British ways often contrast, both as regards the American Syllabication Principle and how emphasis is applied to different Syllables within a word.

In this chapter, we examine the American Syllabication Principle at work by comparing American and British ways of pronouncing different types of words. Pronunciation descriptions provided through this Course are based on the Course Vocal Fidelity Phonetic System.

Note: The Vocal Fidelity Phonetic System has enhanced Accent sensitive features. The Phonetic System will be explained at different stages, as needed, as you progress through the Course.

Note: Different dictionaries use their own phonetic systems. Phonetic systems may vary in their ability to pick up different vocal sounds.

Note: Syllable divisions in the word examples highly correlate, if not fully conform, with online voice recordings provided by authoritative dictionaries. You can observe from listening to these that they reflect the American Syllabication Principle. The American Syllabication Principle explains how Syllable division occurs in English spoken the American way and distinguishes it from the British.

Note: For cross-referencing of American pronunciation, I recommend the Merriam-Webster Dictionary, and, for additional cross referencing, I recommend the Cambridge Dictionary which provides both American (USA) and UK (United Kingdom) pronunciations. In case of discrepancy between them as regards American pronunciation, I recommend the Merriam-Webster Dictionary. For cross-referencing of the British Accent, I recommend the Cambridge Dictionary.

Note: The pronunciation of a word or Vocal Pattern was usually determined as follows. I would confirm my knowledge of the pronunciation of particular words or of words with a particular Vocal Pattern from direct observation of: -Everyday conversation with people at work and recreation. -American news and other television channels and radio stations. -Excellent communicators in commercials. -Recordings of spoken American English available on the internet in the public domain. I would then look at the phonetic transcription of the word or words with a particular Vocal Pattern in reputed dictionaries, and listen to their on-line model voice recordings provided. In case of any inconsistency, I would finally base my transcription on the model voice recording.

This could involve adding or otherwise adjusting phonetic elements not included in the dictionary provided phonetic transcription.

Sometimes, when a particular pronunciation is pervasive, I would include this as a pronunciation option, usually in addition to the pronunciation based on the voice model recording.

Note:
Using voice model recordings as an object for direct observation is ideal for the development of knowledge concerning the spoken language because it provides speech samples of the way the language is vocalized by those who speak it well. It is particularly appropriate for the development of a Course that is focused on the spoken language.

Note:
Great care has been taken during the development process to eliminate error. Other than the fact that different phonetic systems produce outcomes with some variation of little significance, the reason for differences between pronunciation shown in dictionaries and this Course. is most likely because:

-Additional phonetic information is included, (consistent with the Accent sensitive features of the Vocal Fidelity Phonetic System).
-A different popular pronunciation has been accepted.

The American Syllabication Principle as stated above will help you figure out how a word is likely to be split into Syllables if it is unfamiliar to you when said the American way. You can use it as a direction finder and verify the pronunciation from your own observation of how American speakers articulate the word. This is a good enough general guideline to get you started on splitting words into Syllables the American way.

Tables with different kinds of word examples illustrate the American Syllabication Principle. It is good to be aware of how the American Syllabication Principle may work with different kinds of words.

Observe the application of the American Syllabication Principle in the following types of words in the tables which follow:

Course Note: Symbols used for Pauses.

Dashes, '-', are used to identify relatively longer or Major Pauses. Dots, '.', are used to identify relatively shorter or Minor Pauses.

-In Mono-Syllabic words there are no Pauses. Neither dashes nor dots are needed.
-In Di-Syllabic words, only dashes are used to show the single Pause in such words.
-In Multi-Syllabic words, dashes (for Major Pauses) and dots (for Minor Pauses) are used when contrasts are distinguishable.

Remember: A Pause is any interruption or break in vocalization between the beginning and end of a Word. A Pause separates each Syllable from the next.

-Split of Syllables in Di-Syllabic words with a single mid-word Consonant.
-Certain Di-Syllabic words with a single mid-word Consonant articulated as if repeated.
-Split of Syllables in Di-Syllabic words with two different adjacent mid-word Consonants.

-Split of Syllables in Di-Syllabic words with two similar adjacent mid-word Consonants.
-Split of Syllables in Multi-Syllabic words of more than six letters.

In this chapter, the term "Mid-Word Consonant" is used to describe a Consonant that is in the middle of a word. Later in the Course, the term "Middle Consonant" is specifically defined to refer to a Consonant that is in the middle of a Syllable.

Based on the American Syllabication Principle, Americans regularly Pause to separate Syllables in Di-Syllabic words after the Vowel preceding the Mid-Word Consonant. By contrast, the British very often Pause after the Mid-Word Consonant, though they also Pause for a fairly large number of specific words after the Vowel before the Middle Consonant, as the Americans do pervasively.

Note: In this chapter, the term "Mid-Word Consonant" is used to describe a Consonant that is in the middle of a word. Later in the Course, the term "Middle Consonant" is specifically defined to refer to a Consonant that is in the middle of a Syllable.

Table:
Pauses In Di-Syllabic Five-Letter Word Examples

The Word	The American Way	The British Way
Baker	Ba-ker	Ba-ker or Bak-er
Baton	Ba-ton	Bat-on
Begin	Be-gin	Beg-in
Canal	Ca-nal	Ca-nal
Caper	Ca-per	Cap-er
Delay	De-lay	Del-ay
Feral	Fe-ral	Fer-al
Fever	Fe-ver	Fe-ver
Final	Fi-nal	Fin-al
Irate	I-rate	I-rate
Joker	Jo-ker	Jok-er
Haven	Ha-ven	Hav-en
Later	La-ter	Lat-er
Major	Ma-jor	Ma-jor
Minor	Mi-nor	Min-or
Miser	Mi-ser	Mis-er
Motel	Mo-tel	Mo-tel
Motor	Mo-tor	Mo-tor
Olive	O-live	Ol-ive
Penal	Pe-nal	Pen-al
Paper	Pa-per	Pa-per
Polar	Po-lar	Pol-ar
Ruler	Ru-ler	Ru-ler

Sonar	So-nar	So-nar or Son-ar
Super	Su-per	Sup-er
Tiger	Ti-ger	Tig-er
Ti.tan	Ti-tan	Ti-tan
Note: Observe that in the British way, Syllables may be begun or ended on either Vowel or Consonant, whereas in the American way, the pattern is largely consistent in following the American Syllabication Principle.		

Table:
Pauses In Di-Syllabic Six-Letter Word Examples

The Word	The American Way	The British Way
Bridal	Bri-dal	Brid-al
Crater	Cra-ter	Cra-ter
Figure	Fi-gure	Fig-ure
Future	Fu-ture	Fu-ture
Flavor	Fla-vor	*Fla-vour
Leader	Lea-der	Lea-der
Private#	Pri-vate	Priv-ate
Heater	Hea-ter	Hea-ter
Mutual	Mu-tual	Mut-ual
Mature	Ma-ture	Mat-ure
Revere	Re-vere	Rev-ere
Super	Su-per	Su-per
Tailor	Tai-lor	Tai-lor
Trader	Tra-der	Tra-der
Note: Observe, the British way, Syllables may be begun or ended on either Vowel or Consonant, whereas, the American way, the pattern is largely consistent in following the American Syllabication Principle.		

*British spelling.
#With the silent letters in these words, they are like six-letter words.

> Note: The British way often matches the American way by ending the first Syllable after a Vowel and beginning the next with a Consonant when the Vowel preceding the Consonant is of the "Hard" form, as articulated in words like: "Fade" {FAde}, "Meet" {MEet}, "Tide" {TIde}, "Mole" {MOle}, and "Fume" {FUme}). More is said on the form of Vowels in a separate chapter.

Certain Di-Syllabic words with a single Mid-Word Consonant articulated as if repeated

In the American way of speaking, a certain type of word with a single Mid-Word Consonant is pronounced as if there were two similar Mid-Word Consonants with each articulated separately, one ending the first Syllable and the second beginning the latter. These words do not end the former Syllable after a Vowel sound – inconsistent with the American Syllabication Principle, but the latter Syllable still begins with a Consonant – consistent with the American Syllabication Principle. This is one of the contexts in which a Syllable may not end with a Vowel Sound. Examples are in the table below. You can see by comparing the words below that the form of the Vowel preceding the Consonant are most often the "Soft" Vowel Sound, as articulated in words like: "Bat" {Bat}, "Met" {Met}, "Fit" {Fit}, "Dot" {Dot}, and "Pull" {Pull}), but sometimes the "Short" Vowel Sound as in words like "Dove" {Do1ve} or "Gum" {Gu1m}, regardless of the specific Vowel. Also, the Vowel following the Mid-Word Consonant usually is a "Short" Vowel Sound, but there are exceptions, as in "Rapid" {Rapid} or "Mango" {MangO}. (The Short Vowel Sound, has the same abbreviated Vowel Sound regardless of the specific Vowel that is used in the spelling). More is said on the form of Vowel Sounds in a later chapter.

Note: The Vocal Fidelity Phonetic System has enhanced Accent sensitive features. The Phonetic System will be explained at different stages, as needed, as you progress through the Course.

Table:
Pauses In Di-Syllabic Five-Letter Word Examples
With A Single Mid-Word Consonant Sound Which Is Repeated

The Word	The American Way	The British Way
Camel	Ca-mel or Ca(m)-mel	Cam-el
Color	Co-lor or Co(l)-lor	Col-or
Cover	Co-ver or Co(v)-ver	Cov-er
Felon	Fe-lon or Fe(l)-lon	Fel-on
Gavel	Ga-vel or Ga(v)-vel	Gav-el
Given	Gi-ven or Gi(v)-ven	Giv-en
Lemon	Le-mon or Le(m-m)on	Lem-on
Lover	Lo-ver or Lo(v)-ver	Lov-er
Liver	Li-ver or Li(v)-ver	Liv-er
Manor	Man-or or Ma(n)-nor	Man-or
Metal	Me-tal or Me(t)-tal	Met-al
Merit	Me-rit or Me(r)-rit	Mer-it
Never	Ne-ver or Ne(v)-ver	Nev-er
Revel	Re-vel or Re(v)-vel	Rev-el
Rapid	Ra-pid or Ra(p)-pid	Rap-id
River	Ri-ver or Ri(v)-ver	Riv-er
Seven	Se-ven or Se(v)-ven	Sev-en
Sever	Se-ver or Se(v)-ver	Se-ver
Tepid	Te-pid or Te(p)-pid	Tep-id
Towel	To-wel or To(w)-wel	Tow.el
Tower	To-wer or To(w)-wer	Tow.er
Valor	Va-lor or Va(l)-lor	*Val-our
Vowel	Vo-wel or Vo(w)-wel	Vow.el
Angus	An(g)-gus	Ang-us
Angry	An(g)-gry	Ang-ry
Mango	Ma(ng)-go	Mang-o

Note: Observe, in the British way, Syllables may be begun or ended on either Vowel or Consonant, whereas, the American way, the pattern is largely consistent - following the American Syllabication Principle.

*British spelling.

Note: A Consonant, shown in parentheses above, identifies a Consonant Sound not included in the actual spelling of the word but often heard when articulated.

Note: A particular point to register is that even when an 'R' comes in the middle or the end of a Syllable, it is clearly emphasized as Americans always clearly articulate the 'R'. By contrast, the British way, the 'R' sound in the middle or at the end of a Syllable has the effect only of extending the sound of the previous Vowel while not otherwise being audible as an 'R' sound'. This has the effect of lowering its emphasis. For example, the word "Charm", a single Syllable word, said the British way, rhymes with the word "Calm". You can see that there is no 'R' sound but it is as if the preceding 'A' has been extended.

Note: It should not be surprising that the British have not been immune to American influence on their way of speaking. You may have noticed that there have been British rock stars adopting American pronunciation for their songs. (For example, Mick Jagger sounds very American in the Rolling Stones song "Angie"). A general shift toward the American way of speaking should not be surprising. There are undoubtedly words that were previously pronounced differently by the British now spoken just as Americans.

Table:
Pauses In Di-Syllabic Six-Letter Word Examples
With A Single Mid-Word Consonant Sound Which Is Repeated

The Word	The American Way	The British Way
Boring	Bo-ring or Bo(r)-ring	Bor-ing
Celery	Ce-le.ry or Ce(l)-le.ry	Cel-e-ry
Clever	Cle-ver or Cle(v)-ver	Clev-er
Dragon	Dra-gon or Dra(g)-gon	Drag-on
Driven	Dri-ven or Dri(v)-ven	Driv-en
Eleven	E-le-ven or E(l)-le(v)-ven	El-ev-en
Finish	Fi-nish or Fi(n)-nish	Fin-ish
Forage	For-age or For-(r)age	For-age
Foreign#	For-eign or For-(r)eign	For-eign
Forest	For-est or For-(r)est	For-est
Frigid	Fri-gid or Fri(g)-gid	Frig-id
Granite	Gra-nite or Gra(n)-nite	Gran-ite
Gravel	Gra-vel or Gra(v)-vel	Grav-el

Manage	Ma-nage or Ma(n)-nage	Man-age
Melody	Me-lo-dy or Me(l)-lo-dy	Mel-od-y
Parent	Pa-rent or Par-(r)ent	Par-ent
Relish	Re-lish or Re(l)-lish	Rel-ish
Salary	Sa-la-ry or Sa(l)-la-ry	Sal-ar-y
Shiver	Shi-ver or Shi(v)-ver	Shiv-er
Status	Sta-tus or Sta(t)-tus	Sta-tus
Talent	Ta-lent or Ta(l)-lent	Tal-ent
Travel	Tra-vel or Tra(v)-vel	Trav-el
Vision	Vi-sion or Vi(s)-sion	Vis-ion
Note: Observe, the British way, Syllables may be begun or ended on either Vowel or Consonant, whereas, the American way, the pattern is largely consistent in following the American Syllabication Principle.		

#With the silent letters in these words, they are like six-letter words.

Split of Syllables in Di-Syllabic words with two different adjacent middle Consonants.

In Di-Syllabic words with two different adjacent middle Consonants, the American pattern of ending the first Syllable with a Vowel is sometimes not an option. In these instances, the first Syllable ends with the first Middle Consonant and the second Syllable begins with with the second Middle Consonant. In this manner, Americans still begin the latter Syllable with a Consonant. The American Syllabication Principle, as stated, allows for words ending a Syllable with a Consonant when ending with a Vowel is not possible. The British may either break these words into Syllables the same way as the Americans, or, absorb both Consonants into the first Syllable and begin the latter with a Vowel, as is often the British way.

Table:
Pauses In Di-Syllabic Five-Letter Word Examples
With Two Different Adjacent Mid-Word Consonants

The Word	The American Way	The British Way
Anvil	An-vil	An-vil
Arbor	Ar-bor	*Arb-our
Ardor	Ar-dor	*Ard-our
Ascot	As-cot	As-cot
Ember	Em-ber	Em-ber
Enter	En-ter	Ent-er
Igloo	Ig-loo	Ig-loo
Imply	Im-ply	Imp-ly
Under	Un-der	Und-er
Zebra	Ze-bra	Zeb-ra
Note: Observe, the British way, Syllables may be begun or ended on either Vowel or Consonant, whereas, the American way, the pattern is largely consistent in following the American Syllabication Principle.		

*British spelling.

A type of five-letter word with two different Mid-Word Consonants follows the form of the American Syllabication Principle except that it begins the second Syllable with the Consonant Sound that is the merger of two Consonants. In these words, the two Mid-Word Consonants combine into a single Consonant Sound. Some examples are: “Ashen”{A-shen}, “Ether”{E-ther}, “Other”{O-ther} and “Usher”{U-sher}. The first Syllable for these words ends with a Vowel – the beginning letter, and the second with the merged Consonant Sound. Words like “Aster”{As-ter} or “Igloo”{Ig-loo} are not the same. While they may be divided into two Syllables after the beginning Vowel, the separation may occur between the two Consonants with the first Consonant ending the former Syllable and the second beginning the latter.

Note: In this chapter, the term “Mid-Word Consonant” is used to describe a Consonant that is in the middle of a word. Later in the Course, the term “Middle Consonant” is specifically defined to refer to a Consonant that is in the middle of a Syllable.

Table:
Pauses In Di-Syllabic Six-Letter Word Examples
With Two Different Adjacent Mid-Word Consonants

The Word	The American Way	The British Way
Antler	Ant-ler	Ant-ler
Brother	Bro-ther	Broth-er
Canvas	Can-vas	Can-vas
Cascade	Cas-cade	Cas-cade
Fabric	Fa-bric or Fab-ric	Fab-ric
Father	Fa-ther	Fath-er
Fender	Fen-der	Fen-der
Master	Mas-ter	Mas-ter or Mast-er
Mentor	Men-tor	Men-tor or Ment-or
Postal	Po-stal or Pos-tal	Pos-tal or Post-al
Rental	Ren-tal	Rent-al
Roster	Ros-ter	Ros-ter
Tender	Ten-der	Ten-der
Vendor	Ven-dor	Vend-or
Yonder	Yon-der	Yond-er
Note: Observe, the British way, Syllables may be begun or ended on either Vowel or Consonant, whereas, the American way, the pattern is largely consistent in following the American Syllabication Principle.		

Note: The division of six-letter words, having two different adjacent Mid-Word Consonants, into Syllables, depends on the type of combination of Mid-Word Consonants.

If they can combine seamlessly at the beginning of a Syllable many Americans choose to end the first Syllable on the preceding Vowel and begin the second with the first of the Mid-Word Consonants, as in “Fabric”{Fa-bric}. This way, the two middle Consonants combine into a

Linked Consonant Sequence sound 'BR'. An alternative for Americans in this context is to say {Fab-ric}, dividing the word between the two middle Consonants. The British way, with this kind of word, is typically to divide the word between the Consonants to say {Fab-ric}, as mentioned, the Americans may also do.

If the Miid-Word Consonants do not combine seamlessly at the beginning of a Syllable, Americans will divide the word between the Consonants, as in “Canvas” {Can-vas} or “Mentor”{Men-tor}. Neither 'NV' or 'NT' Consonant Sequences combine seamlessly at the beginning of a Syllable, which is why the words cannot be articulated: {Ca-nvas}, or {Me-ntor}.

Consonant combinations which can be combined seamlessly at the end of a Syllable may be articulated differently the British way. They may be included at the end of the first Syllable, beginning the next with a Vowel. Note that while the Consonant Sequence 'NT' discussed above cannot be seamlessly combined at the beginning of a Syllable, it can at the end of one. So, while some speaking the British way may say “Men-tor”, others may say “Ment-or”. Americans do not begin Syllables with a Vowel if there is an option, and therefore are unlikely to take the latter approach. Similarly, the British may may say “Can-vas” splitting the word like Americans, or they may say “Canv-as”, which the Americans would be unlikely to do.

There are some Consonant Sequences like 'ST' which can seamlessly combine at the beginning or end of a Syllable. In this situation, the alternatives of splitting the word between the Consonants, or pausing either before or after the Consonants, are all open options. For example, consider the word “Master”. “Mas-ter” would be acceptable both to Americans and British ways, but Americans may also say “Ma-ster”, according to the American Syllabication Principle, whereas the British may say “Mast-er”.

Some Consonant Sequences like 'TH' as in “Mother”, or 'SH' as in “Bishop” are Merged Consonant Sequence sounds. Such words are split into Syllables as if they are five-letter words. Americans would typically say “Mo-ther” or “Bi-shop” whereas the British may say either “Moth-er” or “Bish-op”, though they may also say it as do the Americans. No one says, “Mot-her” or “Bis-hop”.

Note: In this chapter, the term “Mid-Word Consonant” is used to describe a Consonant that is in the middle of a word. Later in the Course, the term “Middle Consonant” is specifically defined to refer to a Consonant that is in the middle of a Syllable.

Split of Syllables in Di-Syllabic words with two similar adjacent Mid-Word Consonants.

Where there are two similar middle Consonants in a five letter word as in the table below, Americans pronounce these in either of two ways. The first is to end the first Syllable before the two central Consonants with a Vowel and begin the second with the Consonant Sound (treating the two similar Consonants as if they were only one). The other way is to end the first Syllable after the first Consonant and begin the second Syllable with the second similar Consonant. In the British way, the latter pattern used by some Americans may be followed, or, unlike most Americans they may absorb both Consonants (as if they were one) into the first Syllable, beginning the second Syllable with a Vowel.

Table:
Pauses In Di-Syllabic Five-Letter Word Examples
With Two Similar Adjacent Mid-Word Consonants

The Word	The American Way	The British Way
Anna	A-nna or An-na	An-na or Ann-a
Apple	A-pple or Ap-ple	Ap-ple or App-le
Asset	A-sset or As-set	As-set or Ass-et
Error	E-rror or Er-ror	Err-or
Ellen	E-llen or El-len	El-len or Ell-en
Inner	I-nner or In-ner	In-ner or Inn-er
Issue	I-ssue	Is-sue or Iss-ue
Offer	O-ffer or Of.fer	Of-fer or Off-er
Utter	U-tter or Ut-ter	Ut-ter or Utt-er
Note: In the British way, Syllables may be begun or ended on either Vowel or Consonant, whereas, the American way, the pattern is largely consistent in following the American Syllabication Principle.		

Note: In this chapter, the term "Mid-Word Consonant" is used to describe a Consonant that is in the middle of a word. Later in the Course, the term "Middle Consonant" is specifically defined to refer to a Consonant that is in the middle of a Syllable.

Table: Pauses In Di-Syllabic Six-Letter Word Examples
With Two Similar Adjacent Mid-Word Consonants

Six-Letter words with Two Similar Adjacent Mid-Word Consonants		
The Word	The American Way	The British Way
Butter	Bu-tter or But-ter	But-ter or Butt-er
Dinner	Di-nner or Din-ner	Din-ner or Dinn-er
Fritter	Fri-tter or Frit-ter	Frit-ter or Fritt-er
Missing	Mi-ssing or Mis-sing	Mis-sing or Miss-ing
Mutter	Mu-tter or Mut-ter	Mut-ter or Mutt-er
Supper	Su-pper or Sup-per	Sup-per or Supp-er
Tanner	Ta-nner or Tan-ner	Tan-ner or Tann-er
Note: Observe, the British way, Syllables may be begun or ended on either Vowel or Consonant, whereas, the American way, the pattern is largely consistent in following the American Syllabication Principle.		

Looking at Multi-Syllabic words, you can see that there is a difference between the Americans and the British, in the way almost all these words are pronounced. The dots separating the Syllables follow the Syllabication Principle the American way of speaking, i.e. ending Syllables with a Vowel and beginning new Syllables with a Consonant. The result is a stronger emphasis on the latter Syllables in contrast to the British way where the former Syllables have greater emphasis.

Table: Pauses In Multi-Syllabic Words Of More Than Six Letters

The Word	Syllables – The American Way	Syllables – The British Way
Audacity	Au-da-ci.ty	Aud-ac-it.y
Adventure	Ad-ven-ture	Ad.ven-ture
Calendar	Ca-len-dar	Cal-end-ar
Discover	Dis-co.ver	Disc-ov.er
Extempore	Ex-tem-po.re	Ext.emp-ore or Ex.temp.or.e
Galvanize	Gal-va-nize	Galv-an.ize
Financial	Fi-nan-cial	Fin.an-cial
Individual	In.di-vi-du.al	In.div-idu.al
Magnify	Mag-ni-fy	Mag-nif-y
Mountainous	Moun-tai-nous	Moun-tain-ous
Particle	Par-ti-cle	Part-ic.le
Elephant	E-le-phant	El.eph-ant
Precipitation	Pre-ci.pi-ta-tion	Prec.ipi-ta-tion
Reverence	Re.ve-rence	*Rev-rence
Refrigerator	Re-fri.ge.ra-tor	Ref.rig.er-at.or
Severity	Se-ve-ri.ty	Sev-er-it.y
Spectacular	Spec-ta-cu.lar	Spec-tac-u-lar
Tremendous	Tre-men-dous	Trem-en-dous
Vehicle	*Ve-i.cle or Ve.hic.le	*Ve-ic.le
Note: Observe, the British way, Syllables may be begun or ended on either Vowel or Consonant, whereas, the American way, the pattern is largely consistent in following the American Syllabication Principle.		

*These words omit letters in the spelling that are not articulated.

Note: In this chapter, the term "Mid-Word Consonant" is used to describe a Consonant that is in the middle of a word. Later in the Course, the term "Middle Consonant" is specifically defined to refer to a Consonant that is in the middle of a Syllable.

It is interesting to observe the American Syllabication Principle at work in the American Accent in these longer words. Consider the word "Elephant" in the table above as an example. The first letter "E.." forms the first Syllable in the American Accent, "..le..", the second, and "..phant", the third. Just as with two syllable words, Multi-Syllabic words quite consistently end the first Syllable with a Vowel, begin the second with a Consonant and end it with a Vowel (except where there is no alternative), following this pattern for the remaining Syllables, except for the last which ends with the final letter of the word (no matter Consonant or Vowel). By contrast, in the British Accent, "El.." forms the first Syllable, "..eph..", the second, and "..ant", the third. Here, Consonants often end Syllables and Vowels begin Syllables, but there is greater variation. The examples in the table above show some exceptions to the Principle in the American Accent, and variations that occur in the British Accent.

Section:
Applying the American Syllabication Principle

Understanding and applying the American Syllabication Principle is an essential component of speaking the American way. This is the focus of Lane 1. Try this initially with five and six letter words at first, and then with longer words. It really isn't complicated and is positively simple once you get into the practice of it. Remember, when you encounter a word of any length, to say it the American way, end the first Syllable with a Vowel, and begin successive Syllables with Consonants, when possible. This generally applicable principle in a simple way shows how spoken American English fundamentally differs from British English. It sets the proper foundation for an easier transition.

An Important Tip on How to Articulate Syllables the American Way.

I have found that to speak the American way, the tongue needs to be held shorter relative to when speaking the British way. This provides the necessary additional vigor and control to articulate Syllables characteristic of the American way of speaking, i.e. usually starting Syllables with a Consonant and ending them with a Vowel, i.e. the Syllabication Principal. Try it – if you articulate Syllables the British way, it should work for you too.

Why? A few things work together to make this so:

First, by their nature, Consonant Sounds are more rigid, more abrupt and tend to be shorter (with less momentum) than Vowel Sounds. By contrast, Vowels are more flexible, smoother and tend to be longer (with more momentum) than Consonant Sounds.

As a result, Consonant Sounds often require more energy to "start" than Vowel Sounds, and Vowel Sounds require more energy to "stop" than Consonant Sounds.

If there was a graph depicting effort expended at different moments of articulation, Consonant Sounds would emerge as peaks (representing more energy used) and Vowels would emerge as dips (less energy used).

Therefore, when speaking the American way (according to the American Syllabication Principle), more start-up energy is used to begin a Syllable with a Consonant, and, also more energy is used to break the momentum of the following Vowel to create a Pause. A shortened tongue helps achieve this.

It is the opposite when speaking the British way where Syllables often begin with a Vowel and end with a Consonant. The Vowel requires less start-up energy and its momentum carries forward to power the articulation of the Consonant. The Pause that follows after the Consonant then comes at a time when momentum has been expended and so happens more naturally without having to force a stop. As a result, less effort and regulation is needed. Therefore, when speaking the British way, the tongue can be more relaxed and left naturally elongated.

A parallel from a different activity:

Like the more compact form of a polo pony helps it manage the sudden stops and starts seen in the game of polo, the more compact tongue helps to negotiate the different stops and starts of English spoken the American way.

By contrast, like the more elongated languid form of a race horse is better suited to an uninterrupted run, a more relaxed, elongated tongue is better suited to the British way of speaking.

An overlooked and major reason that the American Accent is generally perceived as louder or more forceful than other English speakers is because of the contrasting way in which they articulate Syllables – with their more energetic Syllable starts and stops!

Section:
Exceptions to the American Syllabication Principle

The relationship of Vowel Sequences and Syllables.

Note: Vowel Sequences refer to Vowels that follow one after another in succession, in the spelling of words.

Words with Vowel Sequences often do not conform with the American Syllabication Principle when speaking the American way.

Remember: The American Syllabication Principle states that Syllables are usually formed in a way that they begin with Consonants and end with Vowels.

When there are Vowel Sequences in a word, – whether two or more – there may or may not be Pauses between them. If there is a Pause, i.e. a Syllable break between them, a Vowel will end one Syllable and another will begin the next Syllable. If there isn't a Syllable break between them, the adjacent Vowels might end, begin or fall in the middle of a word or part of a word.

Just as the American Syllabication Principle is essential to recognize the regular format of Syllable construction the American way, the occurrence of non-conforming types of Syllable construction should be recognized as well.

Below, exceptions to the American Syllabication Principle with examples to illustrate are shown.

A Vowel Sequence at the end of a Syllable followed by a "regular" Syllable.

Consider the word "Coalesce". Pronounced the American way, the first Syllable ends with the first 'A', not with the first 'O', thus the Vowel Sequence of 'OA' ends the first Syllable. The 'OA' Vowel Sequence Links together a form of 'O' and a form of 'A' at the end of the first Syllable. The next Syllable is regular in that it begins with a Consonant, 'L', in conformity with the American Syllabication Principle. Such a word, with the first Syllable ending with a Vowel and the next beginning with a Consonant, is in full conformity with the Syllabication Principal.

The different Vowel forms are explained in Chapter 12: Lane 4 – The Way Americans Articulate Vowel and Consonant Sounds.

An uncoupled Vowel Sequence.

Consider now the word "Chaos". The Vowel combination 'AO' is split by Syllabication between the two Vowels. So, the first Syllable ends with a Vowel, 'A', and the next Syllable begins again with a Vowel, 'O'. A form of 'A' is followed after a Pause to a form of 'O'. When there is a split between the Vowels by a Pause, the Vowels though adjacent are integrated more closely with the Consonants in their respective Syllables than to each other. This is an Uncoupled Vowel Sequence.

Compare the sound of "Chaos" word with words like "Taos", a city in New Mexico, or "Laos", a country in Asia. Both "Taos" and "Laos" words are pronounced by Americans without a

Syllable division. They are therefore not "uncoupled". Both these words exhibit a Vowel Sequence Linking the 'A' Long to the 'O' Soft.

The different Vowel forms are explained in Chapter 12: Lane 4 – The Way Americans Articulate Vowel and Consonant Sounds.

An integrated Vowel Sequence in the middle of a word.

Many words have an integrated Vowel Sequence in the middle, i.e. they are unbroken by a Pause. Common examples are "Rail", "Caught", "Staunch", "Seat", "Toast", "Boil", "Choir", "Root", "Cloud", "Quality", "Quick". As you can see, many of these have single straightforward Vowel Sounds like a form of 'A' (as in 'Rail"), a form of 'E' (as in "Seat"), and a form of 'O' (as in "Toast") or a form of 'I' (as in "Quick"), or a form of the Vowel 'O', (as in "Root"). But there are also others where there is a transition from one form of a Vowel to another Vowel of a particular form as in "Boil" with the 'O' Linking with the 'I', or as in "Cloud", where the 'O' Links with a 'U'.

A Vowel Sequence at the end of a Syllable followed by an "irregular" Syllable.

Now consider a word like "Acquiesce". The uncoupled Vowel Sequence of 'UIE' is split after the 'I' resulting in the second Syllable beginning with a Vowel, a form of 'E', in non-conformity with the American Syllabication Principle i.e. it begins with a Vowel – not a Consonant.

A Vowel at the end of a Syllable followed by a "semi-regular" Syllable.

There are also words with uncoupled Vowel Sequences like "January" or "Estuary", where the latter Syllable apparently begins with a Vowel but when pronounced, it is as if a Consonant 'W' is inserted before the 'A' Vowel so that the Syllable effectively begins with a Consonant, even if it not in the actual spelling of the word. In the American way both "January" and "Estuary", the latter Syllable ending in "...ary" is articulated as if it were {-wa.ry} just like the word {Wa.ry}.

Note: The Consonants 'W' and 'Y' have forms which are like Vowels, and more emphatic forms where they function like Consonants. More about this in Lane 4 on Articulation.

An integrated Vowel Sequence at the beginning of a word.

There are many words in English which begin with a Vowel Sequence, such as "Aid", "Aisle", "Eastern", "Either", "Eon", "Eugene", "Ion", "Oats", "Oar", "Oil" and "Out" are examples. Some of these examples exhibit a single Vowel Sound, as in the example word, "Aid", while others exhibit a transitioning sound from the first Vowel to the one that follows, as in the example word, "Oil".

Exercise.

1. Use word lists in this chapter to Pause at the end of each Syllable. Practice each word the American way in a deliberate manner, until you get it right.

2. Note: After you have covered the Chapter on Tempo, you will learn to combine Syllables in Multi-Syllabic words with a Pause between word parts.

Chapter 10:
Lane 2: Tempo when Speaking the American Way.

Americans speak with a distinctive tempo, an essential facet of speaking the American way.

Though Americans articulate Syllables more completely than the British, they also are able to speak quickly by combining Syllables in multi- Syllable words into “Parts”.

By identifying the Parts, in addition to the Syllables within a word, you will have the key to pronouncing words with the American Tempo.

A “Part” is a section of a word separated from other sections by a long or Major Pause. It may consist of one or more Syllables.

> Course Note: Remember Symbols used for Pauses.
>
> Dashes, '-', are used to identify relatively longer or Major Pauses. Dots, '.', are used to identify relatively shorter or Minor Pauses.
>
> -In single Syllable words there are no Pauses. Neither dashes nor dots are needed.
> -In Di-Syllabic words, only dashes are used to show the single Pause in such words.
> -In Multi-Syllabic words, dashes (for Major Pauses) and dots (for Minor Pauses) are used when contrasts are distinguishable.

> Remember: A Pause is any interruption or break in vocalization between the beginning and end of a Word. A Pause separates each Syllable from the next.

Showing Tempo with dots and dashes in Multi-Syllable words.

In this course to show the tempo in articulating words, Major Pauses separating Parts are shown by a dash and Minor Pauses separating Syllables within a Part are shown by a dot. With single Syllable words, which have no Pause, neither dots or dashes are needed. In two Syllable words, where the Pause between the Syllables is a definite break, it is represented by a dash '-' as used to denote a Major Pause. Tempo in words of three or more Syllables may contain both Major and Minor Pauses, for which both dashes and dots may be needed to show the separate Parts and Syllables.

Multi-Syllable words can have two or more Parts. All words of two Syllables or more may be divided into a “First Part” a “Last Part” and one or more “Mid Parts”. Mid Parts are Parts which are separate from the First and Last Parts – and from other Mid Parts if there is more than one. The First Part, covers the preliminary Syllables – often only the first, whereas the Last Part, comprises an accelerated string of the remaining Syllables in a single stream of connected Syllables.

There is no shortage of words with central Mid Parts. Examples are provided in a table further below.

> Some rare words have over 25 letters. If you google them under “Long English Words”, they can make for some difficult tongue twisters, but they will get attention if you use one of them in conversation! A word with many parts that has struck my imagination is “Concatenated” {Con-ca.te-na.ted}.

We will look again below at some of the long word examples provided in earlier chapters. The Parts and Syllables identified by dots and dashes show how a word is articulated giving it shape.

> Though we are speaking of sounds, it is accurate to describe the form of a word as a shape, as it is theoretically and technically possible to graphically capture the shape of a stream of sound by tracking frequency and volume from the beginning to the end period of its articulation.

When speaking with the right tempo, the Syllables within each Part are combined almost seamlessly. The First Part, consisting most often of a single Syllable but possibly more, is followed by a Major Pause, symbolically shown by a dash, separating it from latter Parts. In Mid and Last parts, Syllables are often combined by accelerated articulation into a single stream of sound with or without Minor Pauses.

Let's now apply the concepts of tempo, i.e. "Parts" and "Syllables" and "Pauses" to pronouncing words the American way.

> Americans, in contrast to the British, always articulate the Last Part of a word strongly, whereas the British, by different convention pronounce the former Syllables relative to the latter in a more audible way.
>
> Consider the word "Perfect". The Americans will pronounce the first Syllable {Per} completely with the American 'R' which is very audible, and the Last Part of the word {fect} as clearly as or more strongly, in a way that the 'E' sounds clearly like an 'E'. By contrast, the British "Per.." has the smooth British 'R', sometimes hard for some American ears to make out, and the 'E' in "..fect" sounds more like an 'I', making the latter Syllable shorter and softer.
>
> For longer Syllable words consider "Certificate", 'Distributor" and Performance". The long Pause in each of these words comes after their second Consonant, dividing the words into two parts. The second and Last Part in each of these words consist of two or more Syllables, but they are almost seamlessly woven together, in a way that speeds up their articulation.

Dashes and dots for Major and Minor Pauses are used in the table below. Looking at the first example in the table, in "Audacity" {Au-da.city}, the "Au-" is the First Part, and "da.city" the Last Part. "Au", the First Part is clearly separable from the rest of the word by a Major Pause. The Syllables "da" and "city" making up the Last Part and are strung together into a single stream forming "da.city", with a Minor Pause between them enabling almost seamless transition between these Syllables. See the other examples in the table below. Their sounds are similarly constructed with a First Part and a Last Part.

Table:
Showing Pauses: Parts and Syllables – The American Way

Note: In this table a dash denotes a Major Pause and a dot a Minor Pause.		
Multi-Syllabic Word Examples	Showing major Pauses between "Parts" only – The American Way	Parts and Syllables – The American Way
Audacity	Au-da-city	Au-da-ci.ty
Adventure	Ad-ven-ture	Ad-ven-ture
Calendar	Ca-len-dar	Ca-len-dar
Certificate	Cer-tificate	Cer-ti.fi.cate
Contribute	Con-tribute	Con-tri.bute
Creativity	Crea-tivity	Cre-a-ti.vi.ty

Distributor	Dis-tri-butor	Dis-tri-bu.tor
Discover	Dis-cover	Dis-co.ver
Galvanize	Gal-va-nize	Gal-va-nize
Humidity	Hu-mi-dity	Hu-mi-di.ty
Magnify	Mag-ni-fy	Mag-ni-fy
Minimalist	Mini-ma-list	Mi.ni-ma-list
Particle	Par-ticle	Par-ti.cle
Performance	Per-for-mance	Per-for-mance
Elephant	Ele-phant	E.le-phant
Severity	Se-ve-rity	Se-ve-ri.ty
Spectacular	Spec-ta-cular	Spec-ta-cu.lar
Vehicle	Ve-hicle	Ve-hi.cle

The American way is to emphasize the Last Part more strongly or at least as strongly as the First Part, whereas the British emphasize the first Syllable(s) more strongly than the ending Syllable(s). Bear in mind, Americans primarily emphasize with volume whereas the British to a greater extent place emphasis using pitch or frequency. And, even though Americans combine Syllables into parts in characteristic American tempo – into a single continuous vocalization – they rarely abbreviate or leave elements of words silent as do the British. They remain committed to the nuances of Syllables within each part. For example, the word "general" is pronounced {ge-ne.ral} the American way, whereas in customary British form, the word is pronounced {Gen-ral}, with the sound of middle 'e' silent or largely silent.

> Note: Some English Accents are known to have been described as having "crystal or cut glass clarity", and "clipped". Even so, observe that the Americans articulate words more legibly than the English, or stated otherwise say them as they are written:
>
> The British leave certain sections of words silent. Consider the word "General". The Americans say {Ge-ne-ral} or {Ge-ne.ral} (clearly articulating the Mid Part). By contrast, the English say {Gen.ral} with a Minor or {Gen-ral} with a Major Pause, omitting the middle part altogether, i.e. without the articulation of the "e". The word "Boisterous" is a similar example.

In the table below are examples of words which have Mid Parts, i.e. an in-between vocalization requiring separation from the First and Last Parts:

Table: Word Examples With Mid Parts

Note: In this table a dot denotes a Minor Pause and a dash a Major Pause.		
Word	Showing Parts – The American Way	Showing Parts – The British Way
Attorney	A-ttor-ney	Attor-ney
Aggressive	A-ggre-ssive	Agg-ress.ive
Boisterous	Boi-ste-rous	Boist-rous

Corporate	Cor-po.rate	Corp-orate
Concatenate	Con-cat.enate	Conc-aten-ate
Calendar	Ca-len.dar	Cal.en-dar
December	De-cem.ber	Dec-em.ber
Extempore	Ex-tem-pore	Ext-em-pore
Interesting	In.te-re.sting	Int-resting
Financial	Fi-nan.cial	Fin-anc.ial
General	Ge-ne-ral	Gen-eral
Individual	Indi-vi.du.al	In.div-idu.al
Mesothelioma	Me.so-the-li.oma	Mes-othel-ioma
Mountainous	Moun-tai.nous	Mount-ain.ous
Precipitation	Pre-ci.pi.ta.tion	Prec-ipit-at.ion
Premier	Pre-mi-er	Prem-ier
Reindeer	Rein-de.er	Rein-deer
Rebellion	Re-be.lli.on	Reb-ell.ion
Reverence	Re-ve.rence	Rev-erence
Refrigerator	Re-fri.ge.rator	Ref-rig.er-at.or
Tabulate	Ta-bu-late	Tab-u.late
Tremendous	Tre-men.dous	Trem-en.dous

Tempo in Single Syllable words.

We have considered tempo for longer words, but what about single Syllable words? The key here is to be clear in the articulation of the last letter.

> From the way I once articulated the word "Bit", I was told that it sounded foreign. I realized that I was not emphasizing the last letter clearly as would American raised speakers. They would Extend the 'I' and Repeat it, as they ramp up to articulating the final 'T' in a manner that seems to wrap around the letter.

There are a large number of frequently occurring single Syllable words. It is necessary to become aware of these, articulating their last letters, with the same level of Accentuation given to the latter Syllables in Multi-Syllabic words. The last letter is clearly articulated whether it is a Vowel or a Consonant.

Table:
Single Syllable Words Which Occur Frequently

Note: The sound of the last letter is clearly articulated always.		
Am	For	No
And	Go	Not
Are	Had	Now
Be	Him	Our
Big	Her	She
Bring	He	So

But	Hi	To
Can	How	You
Did	I	Who
Far	My	

Table:
Other Common Single Syllable Words

Note: The sound of the last letter is clearly articulated always.	
Bill	Part
Bit	Ran
Car	Sit
Find	Plant
Her	Sport
Him	Stand
Jill	Start
Jim	Ten
John	Thanks
Lamp	Them
Land	Tim
Man	Word

The inner balance of words.

This chapter has discussed how parts within words effect the tempo with which words are spoken giving them an American character and shape. A final point on this subject concerns a tendency toward a temporal balance between the constituent parts within a word:

> It is as if the component parts must tend toward closer matching of the amount of time taken to articulate each one, to find an overall inner temporal balance within the word.

As an example, take the often used word, “Adventure”. This may may be said in two ways. One, with three parts, the other with two:

> In the first way, there is a Major Pause between each of the Syllables, i.e {Ad-ven-ture}. Though the Syllable lengths are all different, they each take about the same amount of time to vocalize, as in this case each Syllable is also a Part.

Note: A Syllable is nothing other than a note or stream of vocalization from a Pause to a Pause forming an integrated, separable vocal unit.

Remember: A Pause is any interruption or break in vocalization between the beginning and end of a Word. A Pause separates each Syllable from the next.

Note: As the discussion here is about the components of single words, the focus here is on very

small intervals of time. The thrust here is not to measure the interval of each unit but just of how they hang together in relation to each other on a time dimension.

In the other way, there is a Major Pause between, “Ad”, and “venture”, separating the word into two Parts, with a Minor Pause between “ven” and “ture” to create a two Syllable second Part. Here, the vocalization of “venture” {ven.ture} is accelerated to catch-up with the shorter time taken to articulate the First Part, “Ad”, for better temporal balance.

The idea of balance helps further in finding the tempo characteristic of the American way of speaking.

Exercise.

1. Use word lists of Multi-Syllabic words provided in this course and others you come across to Pause between parts, weaving through the nuance of the Syllables combined within each part. Impart power to the Syllable-Beginning Consonant of mid and last parts with your breath.

2. Become conscious of the commonly used single Syllable words, by reviewing the examples given noting that they require distinctive pronunciation.

3.After studying the pronunciation of the specific letter combinations in the Chapter “Word List Tables”, you will know how these should be pronounced. Come back to the Table: Single Syllable Words Which Occur Frequently, and practice repeating each word one after another and use them in sentences.

Chapter 11:
Lane 3: Characteristics of the American Voice.

The American Accent is Low and Even.

The American Accent is characterized by a lower tone with less variation than the British Accent.

In general, the American speaking voice is low and deep; even toned – with lower variation between the lowest and highest notes; and is heard from further away. When Americans use their voice to emphasize a point, they use volume – i.e. they emphasize points by speaking louder or softer – rather than using frequency – to speak higher or lower. One may even encounter American voices that are so low in tone that the speech rasps, a bit like static on an AM radio frequency. In terms of tone, some voices can be perceived as monotonous. This is true for both men's and women's voices.

The British by contrast, speak at a higher tone and utilize a broader range of frequencies from the highest to lowest notes. For emphasis, rather than volume, they rely on changes in frequency, often raising the tone to a higher pitch. Unlike Americans, it is not unusual for the British to use the upper regions of the throat constricting the air passage to enable the higher notes that are more frequently used. Characteristically, the British use a heightened note to indicate curiosity or a question.

One may visualize differences between American and British ways of speaking with a graph of sound frequencies as speech is recorded. Typically, spoken American English exhibits fewer distinctive peaks and these are of lower height than in British English. This reflects their lower reliance on frequency for emphasis, and the more level tone from beginning to end of words, and, through the course of a sentence. When hearing the British way of speaking, I visualize many spiky peaks, whereas for Americans I see the peaks flattened out and the frequency graph more even across the recorded band.

The American Accent has additional Modulations.

The American Accent brings in interesting variation into vocalization i.e. Modulation, in their treatment of Vowel and Consonant sounds. This is in contrast to tone, in respect of which as noted above, the American Accent is very uniform.

The following points are an overlap of Lanes 3 on Voice and Lane 4 on Articulation. They are briefly touched upon here and covered in detail in Lane 4.

Essentially American Character of Certain Consonant and Vowel Sounds.

The specific Consonant Attributes explained below apply to the American Accent. The points below flag important contrasting voice characteristics in relation to these Consonant sounds. (As there is an overlap of Lane 3 on Voice and Lane 4 on Articulation concerning these points, they are touched upon here but dealt with in more detail in Lane 4.)

-The 'R' toward the end and at the end of Syllables is articulated with a low Rasp, as in the word "Car" or "Farm". The 'R' is clearly heard in these latter Syllable positions where in the British Accent it is muted. To produce this sound the tongue is cupped and curled upward toward the roof of the palate. It is necessary to become accustomed to making this sound in places where it was not required in the British Accent. The sound which recurs normally several times across a sentence effectively pegs tone to a low level across the spectrum of vocalization in the American Accent.

-The 'N' toward the end and at the end of Syllables is often Nasal, as in “Man” and “Can't”. This is caused by partially cutting of airflow from the oral to the nasal cavity by movements of the tongue and vocal apparatus. The Nasal sound is often also Extended. Nasality is regularly heard from spoken sentence to sentence. More on other aspects of 'N' later.

-There is a form of the Consonant 'T' which appears to merge with 'D' that is sometimes used in certain words. It is located at the beginning of a Syllable other than the first and Accentuated at a Weak to moderate level. It is heard for example in one way of pronouncing words like “Enter” {En-ter} and “Center” {Cen-ter} (there are at least three different pronunciations for these words in the American Accent – more on this later). It is also heard in the names of places like “Seattle” {Se.a-ttle} and “Minnesota” {Mi.nne-so-ta}.

-You will be introduced later to a Consonant Attribute called “Lilting”. It is associated with the Consonant Sounds 'L', 'M' and 'N' when these occur toward the Syllable end as in “Belt”, “Lamp” and “Can't” or at the end of a Syllable or word, as in “Bell”, “Ram” and “Man”. The sound of the Consonant seems to almost circle or wrap around itself, with a curve or bend that occurs over the course of its articulation. The tongue also curls or twists to achieve this sound. Lilting is a Consonant Attribute about which more will be said later. It is characteristic of the American Accent and will need to be recognized and adopted.

-There is a particular Vowel Sound that needs replaced if you are you speak in the British way. This is the 'O' Soft-Tall. It is heard in the way the British pronounce words like “Board”, “Door”, “Employer”, “Join”, “Morning”, “Score”, “Sport”, “Thought” and “Toy”. Americans use the 'O' Soft-Round where the British use the 'O' Soft-Tall. The point to note here is that the 'O' Soft-Tall is a British Vowel sound which is replaced with the 'O' Soft-Round in the American Accent. More on this in Lane 4.

Using the Vocal Apparatus differently for the American Accent.

Physically, people sound different because of the way they use the body’s vocal apparatus. The distinctive American voice is therefore also the result of a difference in the manner of their utilization of this apparatus. The deeper voice, relative to the British – is the result of:

-Powering the vocal chords with more air from the lungs, making it stronger and carry further.
-Keeping the voice passage more open with the effect of lowering tone.
-Speaking from further down in the throat, chest and the diaphragm, making the voice deeper or full bodied.

To develop the characteristics of the American voice:

-Become conscious of tone variations in your way of speech.

-Keep the tone relatively even from the beginning through to the last sound of the sentence.

-Fill your lungs to generate plenty of air to strongly resonate the vocal chords This is needed to Accentuate latter Syllables and Consonant sounds at the end of Syllables and words.

-Speak from low in the chest and with an open throat. This will add body and lower tone as in the American Accent.

-Learn to work your tongue differently to produce sounds distinctive to the American way. (See Lane 4).

-Adapt the movements of your Vocal Apparatus to American Syllabication (See Lane 1), Tempo (See Lane 2) and additional Modulation in Syllables. The Basic Sound Elements in such Modulation are included in Scripting to describe vocalization. (See Lane 4).

-Recognize and include distinct Consonant Attributes which require different kinds of movement of the vocal apparatus in your vocalization.

Transitioning to the above will seem odd, and may be uncomfortable or even difficult to begin with, but with practice over time will become your new way.

Exercise.

The following basic exercises will help you tune your American Voice. Keep practicing just as musicians work on scales.

1. Become voice aware: Intone or chant in a low note for the duration of a full breath.

2. Read sentences and paragraphs from anywhere aloud, expanding your your throat cavity as you do so and see the effect. It has the effect of lowering tone. Practice reading aloud in this low tone.

3. Read sentences with minimal fluctuation in tone. Keep the tone low and even. Make sure that the pitch does not change much over the course of pronouncing any word or over the course of a sentence.

4. Starting each word with air filled lungs, practice Syllabication and Tempo using the example words in Tables in Lanes 1 and 2, which show Pauses. Filling your lungs leads to stronger Accentuation. Pausing at the places indicated, leads to increased Accentuation at the end of Syllables, as in the American Accent.

5. See if you can identify where your voice seems to begin. Try and have your voice begin not from high in the throat but from as low as the chest and stomach. The torso can become like a boom box to deepen and amplify your voice, if you allow it to resonate. Read anything as practice – billboards, magazine titles, news headlines, commercial slogans. Even, repeat words in TV commercials.

6. Practice vocalizing "Tempo" with Multi-Syllabic words, where a number of Syllables are cascaded together into separate Parts, as in "Humidity" {Hu-mi.di.ty}, "Incendiary", {In-cen-di.ary}, "Certificate" {Cer-ti.fi.cate}, "Distributor" {Dis-tri.bu.tor}, "Interesting" {In.te-res-ting or I.ne-res-ting}. Identify and build a list of such words to practice.

7. Practice vocalizing Multi-Syllabic words that contain Modulations to produce the variation of certain Vowel sounds as heard in the American Accent. For some examples, in Lane 4, see the Table: Single Vowel Modulations In Multi-Syllabic Word Examples. Identify and build a list of such words to practice.

8. Become aware of words with 'R' at the end or toward the end of a Syllable, like "Car", "Farm", "Girl" and "World" and practice forming a cup with your tongue (where it curls up from the edges all around) in the way that elicits a rasping sound.

9. Become aware of words with 'N' at the end or toward the end of a Syllable, as in "Can", "Band", "Man", "Ten" and "Spent", and practice articulating them with Nasality, blocking free access of air through the Nasal cavity, as if you have a cold.

10. After reading about the forms of the 'O' Vowel in Lane 4 on Articulation:

If you use the 'O' Soft-Tall in words where it is used in the British Accent, practice applying the 'O' Soft-Round instead. And practice using the 'O' Soft-Flat, Extended in words where Americans use it, in most words where the British use the 'O' Soft-Round.

Chapter 12:
Lane 4: The Way Americans Articulate Vowel and Consonant Sounds.

With the first three Lanes spanned, more than half of your journey is achieved. This Fourth Lane, adds vital finessing. You've taken care of the foundation and built the house, but without painting, molding and polish it is not complete yet. It is in a way the most detailed part of the transition and will require persistence. This is what happens here: We get into how to vocalize the most fundamental elements of speech, i.e. alphabetic sounds.

For this, a Phonetic System is an indispensable tool. This chapter introduces a Phonetic System which adds Script to words to read pronunciation at a level of detail that can detect subtle distinctions between different English Accents. It has been developed for easy learning and use. This is:

“The Vocal Fidelity Phonetic System”.

It adds Script to words as they are actually spelled, following a precise protocol, making them phonetic, i.e. revealing their true pronunciation. It can be used to describe any English Accent. This is ideally what a phonetic system should be intended for and be able to do. The Vocal Fidelity Phonetic System is used in this Course to describe the American Accent and also to compare it with the British, for contrast. It is also useful to describe your current Accent to see how it diverges from the American way in the articulation of specific words.

The System also includes descriptions that distinguish American ways of articulating Vowels and Consonants.

Now, plunging ahead...

This chapter serves two functions:

1. Provides insight into the effect Vowel and Consonant vocalization has on pronunciation.

    For example, the word “Man”, said the American way, has a nasal sound because the 'N' at the end of a word or Syllable is articulated with a nasal effect. The 'A' in “Man”, while articulated similarly in both American and British ways, is differently treated by the two traditions. It is “Extended” and “Repeated” (more explanation on this later in the chapter) the American way.

2. Shows how to transcribe Vowels and Consonants in the way they should be vocalized.

> The Vocal Fidelity Phonetic System of this course adds Scripting to the proper spelling of a word, indicating how the letters should be transcribed, for their correct articulation.
>
> Scripting uses simple Symbols to make written English phonetic, by:
>
> -Showing Pauses,
> -Silencing sounds,
> -Inserting sounds, and,
> -Modifying sounds.
>
> The Symbols for different Vowel and Consonant Sounds are explained below in Scripting Conventions. (See Appendices I. A, I. B, and I. C.)

> The term Scripting refers to the transcribing of regular text into phonetic Symbols, according to this Course's Vocal Fidelity Phonetic System Conventions, to enable correct deciphering and

reproduction of pronunciation. And, the word Script is sometimes used to refer specifically to the Scripting Symbols used.

The Vocal Fidelity Phonetic System Scripts with Symbols that are simple and familiar using only English letters, numbers and punctuation marks.

The Vocal Fidelity Phonetic System has important differences from other phonetic systems you might encounter elsewhere:

A. By learning a relatively small number of Scripting Conventions, you gain the ability to understand a wide range of Scripting Symbols. You only need to remember the conventions, not the numerous Symbols. You can then interpret or transcribe the pronunciation of any word. It is easy to learn and practical to use.

B. The original spelling of the word is retained intact, but symbolically adjusted, to make it phonetic, using Scripting Conventions. The proper phonetic treatment of each letter in the word's actual spelling can then be interpreted for proper pronunciation. Other Phonetic Systems separate the original word spelling from its phonetic transcription rather than integrating them. This system helps you overcome the confusion caused by the all too common gap between how words are spelled and pronounced.

C. The Phonetic System uses very few simple key-board keys to Script Symbols. These are limited to:

-Regular or italic form, or, lower or upper case,
-A tag: The number '1' or '2', an asterisk mark or an apostrophe,
-Parentheses and brackets, and,
-A dash or a dot.

It does not use strange Symbols like the characters of another language which are hard to relate with.

D. Different words with the same pronunciation are transcribed differently, for example "Tale" or "Tail", (because the original spelling is always retained but symbolically adjusted) yet both transcriptions produce the intended similar vocalization.

The Vocal Fidelity Phonetic System includes Symbols that are representative of specific sounds as well as Symbols that are instructional on how a Symbol is to be vocalized.

The Vocal Fidelity Phonetic System eliminates the ambiguity inherent in the way English is written by adding elements to make it phonetic and Accent sensitive for people who have lived in different language and Accent milieus.

Note: No two phonetic systems produce identical results. They produce equivalent results which converge. It's like saying almost the same thing in different ways:

> As using the Imperial or the Metric number systems to specify a weight or a distance – they may be close but not quite identical. Converting from Pounds to Kilos or from Inches to Centimeters can sometimes result in minor differences.

Likewise, no two Phonetic Systems are identical, but, they produce results that are similar.

The Vocal Fidelity Phonetic System is flexible, nuanced and sound sensitive. For example:

It can show inserted sounds, Modulations and different levels of Accentuation for each Consonant, sometimes not shown in other phonetic systems:

For example:
-In "Peal", a Modulation of the central Vowels is heard that may not be shown in the phonetic system of some dictionaries.
-In one way of articulating "So", there is an inserted Vowel Sound, that is regularly heard, that is not shown in some dictionaries.
-In words like "Gig", "Did" or "Pop", in some dictionaries no distinction is made in the Accentuation of the first and last Consonant Sounds, though these are not identical.

Note: There is a Short Alternative of the Vocal Fidelity Phonetic System, not used for this Course. This omits from Scripting silent Vowels and Consonants but includes inserted Vowel and Consonant Sounds heard in the pronunciation that are not in the spelling of the word. This shortens the phonetic transcription of words by taking out the silent letters, the asterisk Symbol used to silence them, and the enclosing parentheses that identify inserts. The Short Alternative has the convenience of greater brevity but sacrifices the advantage of being explicit on the treatment of each letter in the spelling of words which clarifies discrepancies between word spelling and pronunciation. The Vocal Fidelity Phonetic System serves this purpose.

A General Distinction Between American and British Ways of Speaking.

Americans, in general, articulate Syllables and even single letter sounds more completely than the British. Compared with Americans, the British more often leave many written parts of words silent, or in some way abbreviate them, or use non-phonetic variations of certain letter combinations.

Note:

For example, consider the way the British say "Birmingham". They end the word with a condensed "..hm" almost as if there were no Vowel between the 'H' and the 'M', or "..um" as if there were no 'H' and the 'A' is almost a 'U'. The Americans by contrast, very clearly say "..ham" at the end, just like the word "Ham". This is just one example of the American preference for pronouncing words the way the words are spelled. But, one needs to be aware of exceptions to this generalization. Look at the word "Wyndham" which ends like Birmingham. The Americans pronounce the word just like the British, articulating it the way the British end the last Syllable of "Birmingham", as I described above. While American English has distinguished itself from British English, in certain ways and instances, it exhibits such similarities with its traditional British heritage.

Another example is "Schedule". Americans begin it with the 'S', 'C' and 'H' sounds all clearly articulated (pronounced as it is spelled), in contrast with the British way in which the word begins with a 'SH' sound. Another example: In "Preposterous", the 'E' between the 'T' and 'R' is clearly articulated by the Americans but is silent when said the British way.

Though spoken American English tends to articulate words as they are written, there remain many words which are pronounced in way that is inconsistent with or not apparent from their spelling.

Contrast the pronunciation of the words "Message" and "Massage". While very similar, the ends of both words have very different pronunciations.

Section:
An Overview of the Vocal Fidelity Phonetic System

The Vocal Fidelity Phonetic System captures the Basic Vocal Elements that are associated with vocal sounds – including individual Vowel Sounds, Consonants Sounds and sequences of Vowels and Consonants.

The differences between Accents are found in the Basic Vocal Elements. The Vocal Fidelity Phonetic System will enable you detect the Basic Vocal Elements that distinguish between different Accents. It will enable you to identify the elements unique to the American way that you need to pick up, and those that are foreign.

Basic Vocal Elements include:

-Presence, absence and position of Pauses – Major and Minor.
-Different Vowel forms.
-Vowel Modulations.
-Different Consonant Versions.
-Level of Consonant Accentuation.
-Extension of Consonants.
-Consonant Attributes.

The Basic Vocal Elements are explained in the Sections below.

The Vocal Fidelity Phonetic System comprises:

-Symbols for Pauses.

-Separate Tables for:
- -Scripting Conventions for Vowels.
- -Phonetic Symbols for Vowels.
- -Scripting Conventions for Consonants.
- -Phonetic Symbols for Consonants.

Symbols are a function of the Scripting Conventions. The Scripting Conventions enable you to understand and read the Symbols.

How are the Symbols Scripted? In essence, the particular sound characteristics are represented using:

-Dots or dashes.
-Upper or lower case.
-Italic or regular text.
-A number following a letter.
-A Symbol following a letter.
-Parentheses enclosing certain letters.
-Square brackets enclosing certain adjacent Consonants.

More explanation on interpreting the Script follows further down in this chapter.

Section:
Vocal Fidelity Phonetic System
– Pauses

Pauses have been explained earlier in the Course, but are presented again below, as a reminder:

> Reminder Note: A Syllable is nothing other than a note or stream of vocalization from a Pause to a Pause forming an integrated, separable vocal unit.
>
> They form the building blocks of words. Each is separated from other such units by shorter or longer Pauses between them. A Syllable may even be only a single letter, if separated by a Pause.
>
> Some words consist of only a single Syllable of no more than one letter e.g. "A" or "I".

> Reminder Note: Symbols used for Pauses.
>
> Dashes, '-', are used to identify relatively longer or Major Pauses. Dots, '.', are used to identify relatively shorter or Minor Pauses.
>
> -In single Syllable words there are no Pauses. Neither dashes nor dots are needed.
> -In Di-Syllabic words, only dashes are used to show the single Pause in such words.
> -In Multi-Syllabic words, dashes (for Major Pauses) and dots (for Minor Pauses) are used when contrasts are distinguishable.

> Remember: A Pause is any interruption or break in vocalization between the beginning and end of a Word. A Pause separates each Syllable from the next.

> Course Note:
> Authoritative on-line dictionaries with audio recordings of word pronunciations have been extensively used to cross-reference observation of American and British ways of pronunciation.

Section:
Introducing Vowels and Consonants

What are Vowels and Consonants? How should we understand them – without being too technical!

> Think of Consonants as those letters which form the structure or hard bones of a word and the Vowels as the soft connective tissue. The Consonants are harder edged sounds and the Vowels are the softer shaped sounds between them. Vowels provide padding and connections between Consonants, just as bones need the support of soft tissue. That's a sufficient foundation to work with!

The Vowels are: 'A', 'E', 'I', 'O' and 'U'. These Vowels have different forms, e.g. 'A' in "Cat" or 'A' in "Gate".

The Consonants are: 'B', 'C', 'D', 'F', 'G', 'H', 'J', 'K', 'L','M', 'N', 'P', 'Q', 'R, 'S', 'T', 'V', 'X', 'Y'*, 'Z'. Some Consonants have more than one Version, e.g. 'S' in "Sit" or 'S' in "Has". Other Consonant Sounds are produced with pairs of Consonants. E.g. 'SH' in "Ship" or 'TH' in "Three".

Note: The 'W' and the 'Y' in some of their forms are like a Consonant and in other ways they are like a Vowel Sound. E.g., the W' is similar in some of its forms to an 'O' (as in the 'O' Hard sound in "Flow" or the 'U' Soft sound in "Clown"), and the 'Y' is similar to certain "forms" of the Vowel 'I' (as in the 'I' Soft in "Syrup" and the 'I' Hard in "Psycho").

Note: See Appendix I. B for the Vocal Fidelity Phonetic System Table: "Scripting Conventions for Vowel Sounds".

Section:
Vowel Forms and Symbols

Before proceeding to the underlying Scripting Conventions for Vowels it is necessary to first understand their different forms.

Each Vowel has several different articulations or forms, with some more common and better recognized, and, others less known. The different forms of Vowels are named, described and given a phonetic Symbol in the table below. (The names given here are specific to the Vocal Fidelity Phonetic System in this Course.)

By cross referencing pronunciations of the word examples for a particular Vowel Sound (said the American way), you will be able to understand how each form is pronounced.

Table:
Vocal Fidelity Phonetic System
Vowel Forms And Symbols

1. When examples of words are given, the writing convention used in this table is that only the Vowel(s) under discussion in a word example are Scripted phonetically. Also, word examples are written starting with a capital as part of the writing convention, not as a phonetically Scripted Symbol, unless the Vowel under discussion is the first letter, in which case, the first letter is Scripted to show how it is articulated.
2. Vowel Sounds tend to flow from a start (or a linking point from a preceding letter) to a finish (or a connecting point with the next letter). Yet, some Vowel Sounds are shorter and some longer with their distinctive nuances as explained in this Table. And, they may also be Modulated. Modulations are explained later.
3. Speaking the American way, Vowel Sounds are kept at the same low frequency as the rest of the word – in British English the frequency is often raised marginally within a word for many Vowel Sounds.
4. There is a Short Vowel Sound which has a common Vowel Sound regardless of the specific written Vowel used to elicit it. For example in the words – "Festival" {Festiv*al*}, "Principal" {Princip*al*}; "Rivet" {Riv*et*}, "Mystery" {Myst*ery*}; "Penitent" {Pen*i*tent}, "Destined" {Dest*i*ned}; "contain" {C*o*ntain}, "Contribute" {C*o*ntribute}; "Campus" {Camp*u*s} – the italicized Vowels all sound the same though they are different Vowels in the word spellings. This will be represented with the specific lower case Vowel used in the word followed by a "1", e.g. {Fes-tiv.a1}. As you can see from the above examples, the Short Vowel Sound is always a short sound. It is also often used at the end of words and names like "Beta" {Beta1}, "Data" {Data1}, "Cola" {Cola1}, "Soda" {Soda1}, "Sofa" {Sofa1}, "Stamina" {Stamina1}, "Terra" {Terra1}, "Linda" {Linda1} and "Tina" {Tina1}. The phonetic Symbol used to phonetically Script the sound is the lower case of 'A' with

the number '1' i.e. {a1} – the Symbol for 'A' Short – as this is the specific letter used in the examples. It represents the same Short Vowel Sound. The same Symbol is used to describe the same Short Vowel Sound at the beginning of words beginning with 'A' as in "Astonish" {a1stonish}, "Attention" {a1ttention}, "Attend" {a1ttend} and "Acrylic" {a1crylic}.

The Short Vowel Sound is also the sound that is usually heard in words with a middle 'U' Vowel such as in words like "But" {Bu1t}, "Fun" {Fu1n} and "Run" {Ru1n} (just as it sounds in "Come" {Co1me}).

5. This concerns the Single Vowel Sound Modulation. Certain forms of Vowels may exhibit the Single Vowel Sound Modulation. (The different Vowels in their various forms are shown in this Table, below.) A Single Vowel Sound Modulation occurs when a single Vowel Sound is Extended or is Extended and Repeated.

The Extension of a Vowel Sound is produced by lengthening it from an instant to more than one instant. The Repetition of a Vowel Sound is produced by "echoing" it. The echo or Repetition is heard after the first articulation of the Vowel fades, but does not break. Note that there is no intervening Pause between the first articulation and the Repetition.

Soft Vowel Sounds of all the Vowels may be Extended, but only the Soft Vowel Sounds of 'A', E' and 'I' may be both Extended and Repeated. Hard forms may be only Extended. (The different forms of all Vowels – 'A', 'E', 'I', 'O' or 'U' – are explained in the table below.)

How are these Modulations phonetically represented?

The Vowel itself is depicted by Scripting it per the Conventions in the Table below to show whether it is Soft or Hard or whatever its particular form in a word. If it is a Soft Vowel, it will be in lower case and without a number following it. If it is to be Extended, the lower case letter is further Scripted with a single apostrophe (') to show that it is Extended. If in addition to being Extended, it is also to be Repeated, this is shown with a second apostrophe. A Soft Vowel with both Extension and Repetition is therefore followed by two apostrophes ("). The first denotes Extension and the second, Repetition.

For example, the word "Dad", exhibits the Soft form of the 'A' Vowel with both Extension and Repetition. Writing the Vowel in lower case shows that it is the Soft form of 'A'. Extension is then shown by following the Vowel with an apostrophe. Repetition is then shown by following it with a second apostrophe. The Vowel Sound in this word is therefore shown as follows: "Dad" {Da"d}.

Extension and Repetition occurs with the Soft form of the Vowels 'A', 'E' and 'I' but not with the Soft 'O' or 'U' which might only be Extended. Take the Soft form of 'E' as an example with another Vowel: The word "Bed" is represented, {Be"d}, as the Vowel is in the Soft form and is both Extended and Repeated in this word.

> The Extension and Repetition Modulations of a Soft Vowel may also be explained as a volume and tone dip after the initial extended articulation of the Vowel which is then followed by a rise to the original volume and tone. These are often encountered in three letter single Syllable words with a middle Soft Vowel. Common examples are "Dad" {Da"d}, "Bed" {Be"d} and "Win" {Wi"n}.

For an example where the Vowel is Extended but not Repeated, take the word "Flag". The Vowel 'A' in this word is phonetically represented: {Fla'g} (-a'-). The lower case shows that it is the Soft form of the Vowel. The single apostrophe shows Extension. Absence of a second apostrophe indicates that the Extension is not followed by Repetition.

Hard form of Vowels may exhibit Extension but are not Repeated as may occur with the Soft form. The Hard form of a Vowel is shown in upper case, e.g. {-A-}. If it is Extended, it will be followed by a single apostrophe, as in {-A'-}. An example of a word with the Hard form of the Vowel 'A' where it exhibits Extension is "Brave" (BrA've). (More on Modulation in Lane 4.)

6. This concerns a Dual Vowel Sound Modulation. Sometimes a Vowel included in the spelling of a word (i.e. the Internal Vowel) is Linked to another Vowel Sound, which is not included in the spelling of the word (i.e. the External Vowel). This type of Modulation involves two different Vowel Sounds. These Vowel Sounds are a pair from the different Vowel forms in the table below. The Internal and External Vowels are adjacent to each other and may be in any sequence and have a sound that Links from the former to the latter. Such Dual Vowel Modulations are covered in a table in the next section, not in the present one below. The External Vowel Sound is enclosed within parentheses and Scripted to show how it is articulated.

7. Not to be confused with "Extension" of certain Vowel forms, a distinct Vowel form is the Long form, e.g. the 'A' in "Palm", "O" in "Whom" and 'U' in "Rule", which have a different kind of lengthened vocalization. The phonetic Symbol for this kind of Vowel Sound is the given Vowel in lower case followed by the number, '2'. Thus, the Vowel Sounds in the given examples are phonetically Scripted: {Pa2lm}, {Who2m} and {Ru2le}.

Sometimes, the Long form of a Vowel Sound is elicited by two of the same Vowels next to each other as in "Room". To represent such cases phonetically, the first Vowel is marked silent with an asterisk, and the second is Scripted with a 2, as in {Ro*o2m}. The second Vowel covers the sound intended for the two Vowels together.

Two adjacent similar Vowels do not always elicit the sound of a Long form. For example, in the word "Cook", the 'O' sound is like the Soft form of 'U' as in "Put". The Scripting varies to correspond with the vocalization.

While two adjacent 'E' Vowels elicit a lengthened sound, it is not a distinct sound – rather, it the same sound as the 'E' Hard, but Extended. The double 'E' is therefore Scripted with the first Vowel marked silent with an asterisk and the second Scripted like the 'E' Hard but Extended with an apostrophe as in {e*E } as may be seen in the word example, "Feet" {Fe*Et}.

8. Some Vowels have a form where they sound like other Vowels. E.g. the first 'E' in "Fete" sounds like the Hard form of 'A', and the 'I' in "Pique" sounds like the Hard form of 'E'. In such cases, the written Vowel(as spelled in the word) is marked silent by representing it in lower case and following it with an asterisk, and then replacing the silenced Vowel with the Vowel Sound that it actually resembles, by inserting the Scripted replacement Vowel within parentheses as in {Fe*(A)te}, after the silenced Vowel. Vowels that sound like other Vowels are named by associating them with the Vowel they resemble as in: "'E' Like 'A' Hard". Such forms are also included in the table below.

9. Unlike other Consonants which are more strongly Accentuated at the end or toward the end of a Syllable, 'H', 'W' and 'Y' are more weakly Accentuated at the end or toward the end of a Syllable, and resemble other Vowels in these positions. Again, unlike other Consonants which are more weakly Accentuated at the beginning of a Syllable, 'H', 'W' and 'Y' are more strongly Accentuated and possess the character of a Consonant. They may be thought of as being a Consonant in a Syllable-Beginning position, and as a Vowel in a Syllable-End position.

10. Each Vowel Form is not necessarily associated with a distinct Vowel Sound. E.g. 'A' Like 'E' Soft and 'E' Soft have a common Vowel Sound. Each Vowel Form is a name that is associated both with a Vowel Sound and with the distinctive way it is transcribed.

No.	Vowel Form	Description
1	Short Vowel Sound	Symbols: a1, e1, i1, o1, u1. Comment: See Note 4 above for explanation and examples.
2	'A' Soft.	Symbol: a Examples: "Aberration, Absent, Apple, Arrow, Bat, Badger, Calendar, Cafeteria, Candy, Capital, Fantasy, Gavel, Hat, Magical, Manager, Rapid, Tackle." Comment: An apostrophe, as in {a'} Extends the sound, and a second apostrophe, as in {a''} Extends & Repeats the sound. (See Note 5 above). The 'A' Soft is articulated in the traditional way, i.e. in the manner of the British Accent (as in the way they say "Hat" or "Cat"), but, with American Modulation (Extension, or, Extension and Repetition), it may be slightly modified. When the 'A' Soft is Extended it leans toward sounding like an 'E' Soft while still remaining a bit more 'A' than 'E'. The lean toward 'E' Soft element may also be heard in words where the 'A' Soft is Extended and Repeated. It is least evident when there is neither the Extension, or, the Extension and Repetition Modulation, as may often happen when the 'A' Soft is immediately followed by a Pause, as in some of the Examples above {A-be.rra-tion, A-pple, A-rrow, Ba-dger, Ca-len-dar, Ca-fe-te.ria, Ca-pi-tal, Ga-vel, Ma-gi-cal, Ma-na-ger, Ra-pid, Ta-ckle}. Where the 'A' Soft occurs in words between a Syllable-Beginning and Syllable-End Consonant, Extension or Extension and Repetition is more likely with the lean toward an 'E' Soft becoming more noticeable. E.g. in "Branch" {Branch}, "Candy" {Candy}, "Cat" {Cat}, "Fantasy" {Fantasy}, "Flat" {Flat}, "Hat" {Hat}, "Land" {Land}, "Map" {Map}, "Pad" {Pad}, "Sang"{Sang}, "Tank" {Tank}. While this lean toward 'E' Soft is popular, it may not be evident in a substantial proportion of the population. Separately, there are a number of words where an 'A' precedes an 'R' where it clearly becomes like the 'E' Soft. See below the row on: 'A' Like 'E' Soft, Extended.
3	'A' Hard.	Symbol: A Examples: "Bale, Fade, Kate, Sale, Trade." Comment: The 'A' Hard sound may be Extended with an apostrophe to represent a slightly lengthened Hard 'A' as heard in words like "Crane" or "Train".
4	'A' Short.	Symbol: a1 Examples: "Cola, Flora, Laura, Tina, Attend, Astonish." Comment: The Short 'A' is tagged with a '1', so that it shares the same Symbol as the Short Vowel Sound. (See Note 4 above for explanation of "Short Vowel

		Sound".) This is the 'A' at the end of a word or Syllable such as at the end of "Laura", "Tina", "Linda", "Data", or "Cola". This 'A' is also found in the middle of a word e.g. "Adamant" where the second 'A' is the 'A' Short. You also hear this form of 'A' at the beginning of words, as in: "Acrylic", "Alarm" and "Astonish".
5	'A' Long.	Symbol: a2 Examples. "Balm, Blather, Calm, Father, Nevada, Palm, Plaza, Drama, Pasta, Shah." Comment: This form of 'A' has a distinctive lengthened sound very different in sound than the 'A' Soft or Hard, Extended forms.
6	'A' Like 'I' Soft.	Symbol: a*(i) Examples: "Courage, Forage, Message, Postage, Savage (Second 'A')." Comment: The 'A' is replaced with the 'I' Soft Vowel Sound.
7	'A' Like 'E' Soft, Extended.	Symbol: a*(e)' Examples: "Air, Arrow~, Care, Fare, Mary, Parent, Stare." Comment: The 'A' is replaced with the 'E' Soft Extended Vowel Sound. It often precedes an 'R' Consonant Sound. See the Comment under 'A' Soft.
8	'A' Like 'E' Soft.	Symbol: a*(e) Examples: "Caring, Dairy, Mary, Parent, Scary, Sharing, Staring, Wary." Comment: Often precedes an 'R' Consonant Sound. See the Comment under 'A' Soft.
9	'A' Like 'O' Soft-Round	Symbol: a*(o) Examples: "Appalling, Awl, Ball, Bawl, Call, Caught, Fall, Fault, Haul, Launch, Law, Lawn, Mall, Maul, Malt, Paul, Quarter, Stall, Swan, Swarm, Tall, Wall, Wallet, War, Wash, Water". Comment: The symbol for the "A' Like 'O' Soft-Round is the lower case 'A' followed by an asterisk, then, within parentheses – an 'O' in lower case, as in "Ball" {Ba*(o)ll}. An apostrophe may be added in case of Extension, as in "Ball" {Ba*(o)'ll}. (Both vocalizations occur.) The 'A' is replaced with the 'O' Soft-Round Vowel Sound. It has a rounded vocalization, produced by the lips forming an 'O' shape. (See the row on the 'O' Soft-Round.) When the 'O' Soft-Round replaces the 'A' Soft, it may be articulated with or without Extension. Americans often Extend the 'O' Soft-Round. With such words, in the British Accent, the 'A' is replaced with the 'O' Soft-Tall sound. To show vocalization the British way, It is transcribed just like the 'A' Like 'O' Soft-Round {-(a*(o)-} except that the 'O' is in lower case italic {a*(*o*)-}. (See the row on 'O' Soft-Tall.)
10	'A' Silent.	Symbol: a* Examples: Abroad, Boat, Cloak, Goal, Hoard, Load, Roam, Toast. Comment: The preceding Vowel Sound is articulated, whereas the subsequent 'A' is simply not articulated.
11	'E' Soft.	Symbol: e Examples: "Bed, Deck, Left, Met, Ned." Comment: An apostrophe, as in {e'} Extends the sound, and a second

		apostrophe, as in {e"} Extends & Repeats the sound. (See Note 5 above).
12	'E' Hard.	Symbol: E Examples: "Cedar, Pete (First 'E'), Veto, Zero." Comment: The 'E' Hard form can be Extended. Though, just a Modulation of the 'E' Hard, it is shown separately on the row below as an 'E' Long substitute. The Consonant 'E' does not have an 'E' Long with a distinct sound – the 'E' Hard, Extended occupies its place. Many words with a single 'E' Vowel without an adjacent Vowel may be articulated with either an 'E' Hard or with an 'E' Hard, Extended as a matter of emphasis. The 'I' Hard sound as heard in words like "Sardine" or "Iodine" (Second 'I') have the 'E' Hard sound.
13	'E' Hard, Extended.	Symbol: E' (See Note 5 above). Examples: "Fee, Been, Deed, Seek." Also, the first 'E' in words like "Cede", "Pete" and "Swede" have the 'E' Hard, Extended with the 'E' at the end of these latter examples, silent. It is also heard in words such as "Cleat", "Read" and "Seat". Comment: A 'E' Hard, Extended sound is elicited in certain words with a single 'E' and in others with two side-by-side, as in the examples above. This sounds just like the 'E' Hard, but with an Extension. It is phonetically Scripted with the same Symbol as the 'E' Hard, with an apostrophe to signify its Extension. If the sound is elicited in a word with two 'E's side-by-side, the first is in lower case and followed by an asterisk, signifying that it is silent, and the second is Scripted like the 'E' Hard, Extended with an apostrophe. 'E' does not have a distinct Long form other than the 'E' Hard, Extended like the Vowel forms 'A', 'O' and 'U', which have a Long form with a sound that is distinct from their Hard forms Extended. The Long form of 'I' sounds like the 'E' Hard e.g. as in "Sardine". The Long forms of the other Vowels are phonetically Scripted differently, as seen in this Table, by showing in lower case followed by the number, 2: 'a2', 'i2', 'o2' and 'u2'. Not all words with side-by-side 'E's have the long 'E' sound, e.g. the sound breaks too soon in words like "Beer" and "Feel". Many words with a single 'E' Vowel without an adjacent Vowel may be articulated with either an 'E' Hard or with an 'E' Hard, Extended for emphasis.
14	'E' Short.	Symbol: e1 Examples: "Ardent, Calendar, Fern, Honest, Hornet, Mystery, Stern, Torrent." Comment: The Short 'E' is tagged with a '1', so that it shares the same Symbol as the Short Vowel Sound. (See Note 4 above for explanation of "Short Vowel Sound".)
15	'E' Silent.	Symbol: e* Example: "Bale, Came, Name, Sane, Take." Comment: A silent 'E' is often seen at the end of a word. In fact, being Silent, it is not a sound. It must be identified in the Vocal Fidelity Phonetic System for what it is, as it commonly occurs in written English.

16	'E' Like 'A' Hard.	Symbol: e*(A) Examples: “Fete (first 'E'), Beta, Mesa.” Comment: The 'E' is replaced with the 'A' Hard Vowel Sound.
17	'E' Like 'I' Soft.	Symbol: e*(i) Examples: “Because, Begin, Require(First 'E'), Revise (First 'E'), Serious.” Comment: The 'E' is replaced with the 'I' Soft Vowel Sound. This sounds like the Soft form of 'I' without Extension or Repetition. The 'I' is silenced with an asterisk and replaced with the Soft form of 'I' inserted within parentheses.
18	'E' Like 'O' Hard.	Symbol: e*(O) Examples: “Sew, Sewn.” Comment: The 'E' is replaced with the 'O' Hard Vowel Sound. There are not many instances of this. It is likely to occur before a 'W'.
19	'E' Like 'O' Long or 'U' Long.	Symbol: e*(o2), or, e*(u2) Examples: “Lewd~, Renew~, Renewal~, Renewing, Screw, Sinew, Sinews.” Comment: This form or 'E' is like the similar 'O' Long or 'U' Long Vowel forms. There are not many instances of this. (The ~ tag denotes that the tagged words have an alternate pronunciation not shown here.)
20	'I' Soft.	Symbol: i Examples: “Bid, Lid, Kid, Simple, Sit.” Comment: An apostrophe, as in {e'} Extends the sound, and a second apostrophe, as in {e''} Extends & Repeats the sound. (See Note 5 above).
21	'I' Hard.	Symbol: I Examples: “Bide, Flight, Hike, Mine, Ride.” Comment: Note the sound Hard 'I' sound may be Extended with an apostrophe to represent a slightly lengthened Hard 'I' as heard in words like “Cried”, “Climb” and “Isle”.
22	'I' Short.	Symbol: i1 Examples: “Apprentice, Canister, Corridor, Gullible, Reticent.” Comment: The Short 'I' is tagged with a '1', so that it shares the same Symbol as the Short Vowel Sound. (See Note 4 above for explanation of “Short Vowel Sound”.)
23	'I' Long.	Symbol: i2 Examples: “Iodine (2nd 'I'), Fiona, Benzine, Pique, Mystique.” Comment: The 'I' Long sounds Like the 'E' Hard as heard in “Pete” or “Read”. It may be Extended if needed as for example in “Pique” or “Mystique”.
24	'O' Soft-Round.	Symbol: o Examples: “Board, Bored, Bought, Boy, Brought, Chord, Core, Cost~, Cough, Court, Door, Employer, Fore, Forest, For, Foster, Foyer, Join, Joy, Lord, Morning, Port, Score, Song, Short, Store, Storage, Strong, Toy, Thought, Vortex, Wrong, Wrought.” Comment: The symbol for the 'O' Soft-Round is the lower case 'O' – as in [-o-} E.g. “Boy” {Boy}. The 'O' Soft-Round is one of four forms of the 'O' Soft. (the 'O' Soft-Round; the 'O' Soft-Round, Extended; the 'O' Soft-Flat, Extended and the 'O' Soft-Tall). The 'O' Soft-Round form has a characteristic rounded vocalization produced

		with the lips forming an 'O' shape. In the American Accent, the 'O' Soft-Round is heard both with and without Extension in the same words. In fact, Americans often Extend the 'O' Soft-Round. (See the row on the 'O' Soft-Round, Extended.) Few of the words where Americans use the 'O' Soft-Round are articulated the same way in the British Accent. Most are articulated using a different, more lifted 'O' Soft, called the 'O' Soft-Tall. (See the row: 'A' Like 'O' Soft-Tall.) The British use the 'O' Soft-Round in words where Americans use an 'O' Soft-Flat, Extended. (See the row on the 'O' Soft-Flat, Extended.) Similar articulation of the 'O' Soft-Round in both Accents consistently occurs when an 'O' Soft precedes certain Consonant Sequences, as in "Song", "Wrong" and "Loft", and, inconsistently preceding other Consonant sounds in individual words. Also, see how the 'O' Soft-Round form in certain contexts replaces an 'A'. (See the row: 'A' Like 'O' Soft-Round.)
25	'O' Soft-Round, Extended	Symbol: o)' Examples: "Board, Bored, Bought, Boy, Brought, Chord, Core, Cost~, Cough, Court, Door, Employer, Fore, Forest, Fort, Foster, Foyer, Join, Joy, Lord, Morning, Port, Score, Song, Short, Store, Storage, Strong, Toy, Thought, Vortex, Wrong, Wrought." Comment: The symbol for the 'O' Soft-Round, Extended is the lower case 'O' followed by a closing parenthesis and apostrophe – as in {-o)'-}. E.g. "Cost" {Co)'st}, "Sought" {So)'u*ght}. The 'O' Soft-Round, Extended is one of four forms of the 'O' Soft. (the 'O' Soft-Round; the 'O' Soft-Round, Extended; the 'O' Soft-Flat, Extended and the 'O' Soft-Tall). The examples for the 'O' Soft-Round, Extended are the same as those for the 'O' Soft-Round because the same words are heard with and without Extension. Americans often Extend the 'O' Soft-Round. The 'O' Soft-Round, Extended, retains its rounded character. (See the row on 'O' Soft-Round.)
26	'O' Soft-Flat, Extended.	Symbol: o' Examples: "Clock, Cot, Collar, College, Coliseum, Dot, Dollar, Foster~, Log, Hot, Honest, Not, Possible, Scholar, Shop, Stop, Tom." Comment: The symbol for the 'O' Soft-Round, Extended is the lower case 'O' followed by an apostrophe - as in {-o'-}. E.g. "Dot" {Do't}.

		The 'O' Soft-Flat, Extended is one of four forms of the 'O' Soft. (the 'O' Soft-Round; the 'O' Soft-Round, Extended; the 'O' Soft-Flat, Extended and the 'C' Soft-Tall). The 'O' Soft-Flat, Extended has a flat sound – in contrast to the round sound of the 'O' Soft-Round. It is always Extended. The 'O' Soft-Flat, Extended form occurs pervasively in English spoken in the American Accent. The 'O' Soft-Flat, Extended {-o'-} has a flat sound produced with a wider mouth, articulated in a low tone with no variation through the duration of it articulation. The 'O' Soft-Flat, Extended is not as long or as flat as the 'A' Long {-a2-} as heard in the word "Palm" {Pa2lm}, but is flat in contrast with the 'O' Soft-Round {-o-}. The British do not use the 'O' Soft-Flat, Extended. They consistently use the 'O' Soft-Round in words where Americans use the 'O' Soft-Flat, Extended. Contrast the way Americans and British pronounce the words "Dot" or "Stop". Americans articulate them with the 'O' Soft-Flat, Extended form. The British Accent uses the 'O' Soft-Round. The Americans stretch out the 'O' as in: {Do't} and {Sto'p}. The British make it round, as in {Dot} and {Stop}. (See the row on 'O' Soft-Round.)
27	'O' Soft-Tall.	Symbol: *o* Examples: "Boy, Bored, Board, Bought, Brought, Boy, Chord, Core, Court, Door, Employer, Fore, Fort, Foyer, Join, Joy, Lord, Morning, Port, Score, Short, Sought, Sport, Store, Storage, Thought, Toy, Vortex, Wrought." Comment: The 'O' Soft-Tall is one of four forms of the 'O' Soft. (the 'O' Soft-Round; the 'O' Soft-Round, Extended; the 'O' Soft-Flat, Extended; and the 'O' Soft-Tall). The 'O' Soft-Tall is used only in the British Accent and is not exactly replicated in the American. The 'O' Soft-Tall is so called because it seems to lift upward. By contrast, the 'O' Soft-Round, with its rounded articulation does not to rise up as much and is bit more stretched out. The British use the 'O' Soft-Tall in most words where Americans use the 'O' Soft-Round. (See row on 'O' Soft-Round.) The 'O' Tall Vowel sound is the only Vowel Symbol in italic. This is to indicate that this Vowel Sound applies to the British Accent or other Accent in the British tradition but not to the American Accent. The 'O' Soft-Tall is also heard in the British Accent in words where an 'A'

		Vowel is Replaced with the 'O' Soft-Tall, as in "Call" and "Haul". With such words Americans Replace the 'A' with an 'O' Soft-Round. (See the row on 'A' Like 'O' Soft-Round.)
28	'O' Hard.	Symbol: O Examples: "Bone, Foal, Folk, Sole, Host, Toast." Comment: Note the sound Hard 'O' sound may be Extended with an apostrophe to represent a slightly lengthened Hard 'O' as heard in words like "Poll", "Toll" and "Phone".
29	'O' Short.	Symbol: o1 Examples: "Another, Color (First and second 'O'), Mother, Brother, Smother." Comment: The 'O' Short has the same sound as the Short Vowel Sound. It is tagged with a '1' so that they share the same Symbol. (See Note 4 above for explanation of "Short Vowel Sound".)
30	'O' Long.	Symbol: o2 Examples: "Boot, Do, To, Shoe, Tomb, Whom." Comment: The 'O' Long and the 'U' Long share same sound. The 'U' Long is heard in the words "Rude" or "True". It also sounds like the double 'O' in "Too", "Room", "Boot", the 'EW' in "Lewd", the 'UI' in "Suit" and the 'UE' in "Clue". Sometimes, the Long form of a Vowel Sound is elicited by two of the same Vowels next to each other as in "Room". To represent such cases phonetically, the first Vowel is silenced with an asterisk, and the second is Scripted with a 2, as in {Ro*o2m}. As the Scripting of the second Vowel covers the sound intended for the two Vowels together, the first is marked silent. Two adjacent similar Vowels do not always elicit the sound of a Long form. For example, in the word "Cook", the 'O' sound is like the Short form of 'U' as in "Pull". The Scripting varies to correspond with the vocalization. The 'O' Long has the same sound as the 'U' Long.
31	'O' Silent.	Symbol: o* Examples: "Subpoena, Through". Comment: When an 'O' appears in a word, it is rarely Silent, but sometimes when an 'O' is adjacent to another Vowel which can also be Scripted to capture the required Vowel Sound, one of the two is marked Silent while the other is Scripted according to the required Vowel Sound, as in the example "Through". The required Vowel Sound is either an 'O' Long or a 'U' Long, both of which have the same sound. Accordingly, with an 'O' and 'U' next to each other, either one may be marked Silent while the other is Scripted to capture the sound. So, the Vowels in "Through" may be Script ed either showing the 'O' as Silent as in {Thro*u2gh} or the 'U' as Silent as in {Thro2u*gh}.
32	'O' Like 'A' Soft, Extended.	Symbol: o*(a)' Examples: "Bough, Brown, Cow, Loud, How, Howl, Dowel, Shout, Tout, Trowel." Comment: The 'O' is replaced with the 'A' Soft, Extended Vowel Sound. This sounds like the 'A' Soft. The 'O' is silenced with an asterisk and replaced with the 'A' Soft inserted within parentheses. This form of 'O' often precedes a 'U' or 'W' letter and corresponding sound. Extension often accompanies the sound in

		this context which is denoted by the apostrophe. There is never Repetition.
33	'O' Like 'U' Soft.	Symbol: o*(u) Examples: "Foot, Hood, Wood." Comment: The 'O' is replaced with the 'U' Soft Vowel Sound. Usually heard after a double 'O', though not some words with a double 'O where it has a different sound, as in "Food, Root and Tool".
34	'U' Soft.	Symbol: u (See Note 5 above). Examples: "Bull, Bough, Found, Full, Loud, Out, Pulley, Push, Sound, Stout." Comment: Some of the examples above have a single Vowel Sound, the 'U' Soft, as in "Push". Some of the examples, as in "Found" have two adjacent Linked Vowels the 'O' and the 'U', where the sound transitions from an Extended 'O' Like 'A' Soft, to, a 'U' Soft. An apostrophe, as in {u'} Extends the sound, as may be heard for example in "Push" or "Full".
35	'U' Hard.	Symbol: U Examples: "Bermuda, Cute, Cube, Fuse, Mute, Mule." Comment: Note the sound Hard 'U' sound may be Extended with an apostrophe as in {U'} to represent a slightly lengthened Hard 'U' as heard in words like "Accuse" or "Humane".
36	'U' Short	Symbol: u1 Examples: "But, Butter, Cull, Dullard, Hull, Hum, Hummer, Hut, Shutter, Rum." Comment: The 'U' Short is the Short Vowel Sound that is common to all the Short Vowels. It is tagged with a '1' so that they share the same number tag. (See Note 4 above for explanation of "Short Vowel Sound".)
37	'U' Long.	Symbol: u2 Examples "Dune, Dupe, Lube, Studio, Rude, Rule, True, Through." Comment This form of 'U' has a lengthened, distinct sound from other forms of 'U'. However, it sounds like the 'O' Long as heard in "Moon". In the example "Through", where the Vowel Sound is either a 'U' Long or an 'O' Long, one of the two Vowels will have to be marked silent while the other is Scripted to capture the sound. If the 'U' is Scripted 'U' Long {o2} then the 'O' must be marked Silent {o*}.
38	'U' Silent.	Symbol: u* Examples: "Brought", "Caught", "Ghoul", "Through." Comment: The preceding Vowel Sound, whether 'A' or 'O', is articulated in the appropriate form, whereas the subsequent 'U' is simply not articulated. In some of the above examples, ("Ghoul" and "Through"), which have the sound of either a 'U' Long or an 'O' Long, one of the two Vowels will have to be marked silent while the other is Scripted to capture the sound. If the 'O' is Scripted as an 'O' Long {o2} then the 'U' must be marked be marked Silent {u*}.
39	'U' Like 'I' Soft.	Symbol: u*(i) Examples: Busy, Business. Comment: The 'U' is replaced with the 'I' Soft Vowel Sound. Though these examples are heard often, this form of 'U' is encountered in very few words.
40	'U' Like 'W' Soft.	Symbol: u*(w) Examples: Quagmire, Quarry, Quake, Question, Quell, Squeak, Squid, Require,

		Quit, Quite, Quote. Comment: The 'U' is replaced with the 'W' Soft Vowel Sound. While many sounds of the Consonant 'W' can be substituted by certain Vowel forms, as may be seen in the 'W' rows of this Table, one particular 'W' vocalization cannot be substituted by any Vowel form of 'A', 'E', 'I', 'O' or 'U'. This vocalization itself is Vowel like in character, i.e. without edges or sharp definition. This is the 'W' sound that is heard in lieu of 'U' in words that have a Syllable beginning with 'Q', as in the examples above. It is represented by a lower case 'W' {w}, as it has a Soft Vowel Sound. This Symbol is used only to replace the 'U' in words such as in the examples above. It is named: 'W' Soft. Words such as "Count", "Round" and "Fountain", with a 'U', have a similar sound that is well represented by a 'U' Soft but could also be represented by this very similar though not identical 'W' Soft sound. This course represents these words with the 'U' Soft Symbol, though it would also be accurate to represent them using the 'W' Soft Symbol. While the 'W' Soft is vocalized much like the 'W' in "Wire", it contrasts by being relatively weakly Accentuated. The 'W' in words such as "Wire", is considered a Consonant as it is more strongly Accentuated, and as such is featured in separate Tables in this Course that focus on Consonant Sounds.
40	'H' Silent.	Symbol: h* Examples: "Sarah, Farah, Rahm." Comment: See Note 9 above. May be occasionally seen in the spelling of a name.
41	'W' Silent.	Symbol: w* Examples: "Blow, Glow, Grow, Show, Throw, Tomorrow". Comment: See Note 9 above. As the preceding Vowel is the 'O' Hard, Extended, the 'W' in this context is silent.
42	'W' Like 'O' Soft.	Symbol: w*(o) Examples: "Flaw, Law, Maw, Paw." Comment: See Note 9 above. The 'W' is replaced with the 'O' Soft-Round Vowel Sound. As may be seen from the examples, usually if not always, the W Like 'O' Soft-Round follows an 'A' which may either be articulated as an 'A' Long or an 'A' Like 'O' Soft-Round, Extended. When the 'A' is articulated in the former way, the 'W' is articulated like an 'O' Soft-Round. When articulated the latter way, the 'W' is Silent. An apostrophe, as in {w*(o)'} Extends the sound.
43	'W' Like 'O' Hard.	Symbol: w*(O) Examples: "Sew". Comment: See Note 9 above. The 'W' is replaced with the 'O' Hard Vowel Sound. An apostrophe, as in {w*(O)'} Extends the sound. This Symbol is used only if the previous Vowel Sound is different from 'O' Soft as in the example, "Sew".
44	'W' Like 'O' Long.	Symbol: w*(o2) Examples: "Brew, Crew, Drew, Flew, Grew, News." Comment: See Note 9 above. The W' is replaced with the 'O' Long Vowel Sound. An apostrophe, as in {w*(o2)'} further Extends the sound, as may be heard for example in "Crew" or "Stew".
45	'W' Like 'U'	Symbol: w*(u)

	Soft.	Examples: "Cow, Clown, Frown." Comment: See Note 9 above. The 'W' is replaced with the 'U' Soft Vowel Sound. An apostrophe, as in {w*(u)'} further Extends the sound, as in "Frown"
46	'W' Like 'U' Hard.	Symbol: w*(U) Examples: "Few, Mew." Comment: See Note 9 above. The 'W' is replaced with the 'U' Hard Vowel Sound. An apostrophe, as in {w*(U)'} further Extends the sound, as may be heard for example in "Few".
47	'Y' Vowel Like 'E' Hard.	Symbol: y* (E) Examples: "Caddy, Bully, Pulley, Lady, Identity, Mighty, Moody, Mummy, Putty." Comment: See Note 9 above. The 'W' is replaced with the 'E' Hard Vowel Sound.
48	'Y' Vowel Like 'I' Soft.	Symbol: y*(i) Examples: "Coy, Employ, Synonym, Toy, Lyrical, Syrup." Comment: See Note 9 above. The 'Y' is replaced with the 'I' Soft Vowel Sound.
49	'Y' Vowel Like 'I' Hard.	Symbol: y*(I) Examples: "Fly, Try, Why, Psycho, Buy, Bully, Trolley." Comment: See Note 9 above. The 'Y' is replaced with the 'I' Hard Vowel Sound.
50	'Y' Vowel Like Hard 'E'.	Symbol: y*(E) Examples: "Bully, Crazy, Fury, Jury, Sleepy, Wary, Canary, January." Comment: See Note 9 above. The 'Y' is replaced with the 'E' Hard Vowel Sound.

Note: Why have the Hard and Soft forms of all the Vowels been named as they have, as shown in this table, rather than in the opposite way, i.e. the Soft named Hard and the Hard named Soft? This is because the Hard Vowels have more 'force' associated with them than the Soft. The mouth tends to be more pouted when Vowels are articulated in (what has been identified as) the Hard form, and more open when articulated in (what has been identified as) the Soft form. Sound is pushed out with a greater thrust of air with pouting than when the mouth is more open. This can be established by articulating the Vowels both ways, one after another, in front of a ring with a soap film to blow soap bubbles. The soap film is agitated more when articulating the Hard form of a Vowel than the Soft form.

This is to explain why the Hard and Soft forms of Vowels have been so named. What is more important though, is which Vowel form the labels refer to.

Using the 'O' Soft the American Way.

To change to the American Accent, it is important to be aware that Americans use the 'O' Soft-Round in words where the British use 'O' Soft-Tall. Observe the difference and determine whether you are using the 'O' Soft-Tall. Though similar, it lifts higher than the 'O' Soft-Round. The 'O' Soft-Round is also more stretched out. Bring the 'O' Soft-Tall down and round it out in such words. Further, Extend the 'O' Soft-Round, as Americans often do.

Make the change also in words where you have an 'A' Like the 'O' Soft – where the British use 'O' Soft-Tall sound, as in {Ba*(*o*)ll} while Americans use the 'O' Soft-Round sound, as in "Ball" {Ba*(o)ll}.

The British use the 'O' Soft-Round in words where Americans use the 'O' Soft-Flat, Extended. In such words, the 'O' sound would have to be made Flat and Extended.

Clarity about the different 'O' Soft forms is required to make the changes needed for speaking the American way. In the Table: Vowel Forms And Symbols, see the rows on the 'O' Soft-Round; the 'O' Soft-Round, Extended, the 'O' Soft-Flat, Extended; and the 'O' Soft-Tall (used in the British Accent).

Note:
Keeping it simple: Remember,
-Americans use the 'O' Soft-Round where the British use the 'O' Soft-Tall.
-Americans often Extend the 'O' Soft-Round.
-Most of the time, Americans use the 'O' Soft-Flat, Extended where the British use the 'O' Soft-Round. (The British use the 'O' Soft-Round where Americans use the 'O' Soft-Flat, Extended.)

Section:
Vowel Sequence Vocalization

Other than single Vowels, there are numerous adjacent Vowel Sequences which frequently occur in written English. Knowing how these are pronounced the American way is necessary, but it isn't much more to learn. Many of these adjacent Vowel Sequences have the same sound as Single Vowel Sounds, as you will see in this section. There are also Linked Vowel Sounds which involve a transition from the first to the second Vowel.

Note: In this Course, when one Vowel Sound transitions into a second Vowel Sound, the transitioning sound stream is called a Linked Vowel Sound and the two adjacent Vowels are called Linked Vowels. Such a transition occurs, for example, in the word “Foil” where the 'O' morphs into an 'I' sound. Linked Vowels and Sounds are composed of more than one Vowel or Vowel Sound, i.e. more than a Single Vowel Sound.

Note: When an Adjacent Vowel Sequence is interrupted by a Pause, it is not a Linked Vowel Sound but two separate Single Vowel Sounds. E.g. in the word “Chaos” {Cha-os}, a Pause between the 'A' and 'O' causes separation between the two Vowels.

Note: Adjacent Vowels which are not Linked Vowel Sounds are simply different ways Single Vowel Sounds are traditionally represented when writing certain kinds of words. E.g., in the word “Toast”, only the Vowel Sound 'O' (the 'O' Hard form) is heard whereas the Vowel 'A' is silent. An 'OA' Adjacent Vowel Sequence often represents the 'O' Hard form – a Single Vowel Sound, as in “Boat”, “Goat”, “Float” and “Road”.

To represent this phonetically, the 'O' is capitalized to show it is the 'O' Hard and the 'A' is Scripted as silent by showing it in lower case and tagging it with an asterisk.

Sometimes the vocalized Single Vowel Sound is altogether different from the actual adjacent Vowels used to spell the word, e.g., 'EI' in “Weight” is vocalized 'A' Hard, though there is no 'A' in its spelling.

To represent this phonetically, the internal adjacent Vowels are Scripted as Silent by placing an asterisk after each of the two Vowels, then a single External Vowel is inserted within parentheses, as a replacement of the silenced Vowels, as in {We*i*(A)ght}.

Similar Adjacent Vowel Sequences can be pronounced differently in different words, E.g. 'OU' in "Bough" has a different pronunciation in "Trough".

To represent these phonetically, the Silent Vowels are shown as Silent with asterisks and the audible Vowels are Scripted to show the required sound, as in {Bo*(a)ug*h*} and {Tro*u1g*h*(F)'}. Note, in the Scripting of the preceding two word examples, the last Consonants have also been Scripted. Consonant Scripting is explained in a section further below.

Note: To amuse friends by throwing around some linguistic jargon it is good to know that Vowel Sounds which begin with one Vowel Sound and transition into another are called Diphthongs in Linguistics. By contrast, a Vowel Sound which remains constant throughout its articulation are called a Monophthongs.

See Appendix II. B Table: Scripting Conventions Applied: Phonetic Symbols For Vowel Sequences.

Section:
Vocal Fidelity Phonetic System
– Vowel Modulations

Single Vowel Modulations.

Extension and Repetition Single Vowel Modulations.

Let's better understand the terms of Extension and Repetition with regard to certain Vowel Sounds. Extension and Repetition occurs with the Soft form of the Vowels, 'A', E' and 'I'. Consider the word, "Cab", the first word in the table below for single Syllable words. The first Vowel, i.e. 'A' in "Cab", has a Soft Vowel Sound that is Extended and then Repeated without a Pause break, as it Links to the Consonant 'B' which follows, to form 'AB'. The Vowel Sound is Scripted in the lower case to show that it is the Soft form of the Vowel. The first apostrophe following the Vowel indicates that the sound is Extended and the second apostrophe after it indicates that it is then Repeated {Ca"b}. (Here, the Vowel alone is in Script to show how it is articulated, – the preceding 'C' or succeeding 'B' Consonants are not Scripted.) As a result of these Modulations, the word has a longer duration and greater Modulation articulated the American way. By contrast, said the British English, the pronunciation is a short sounding "Cab" with minimal or no Modulation. While in this example, the Vowel is 'A', Extension and Repetition occurs with the Soft forms of the Vowels, 'A' 'E' and 'I'.

The second word of the same table illustrates an example with the Vowel 'E': In the word "Bed" {Be""} the Soft form of the Vowel 'E' is Extended and Repeated. The first apostrophe indicates Extension and the second apostrophe indicates Repetition.

Note: The Extension and Repetition Modulations of a Soft Vowel may be described as an initial extended articulation of the Vowel Sound followed by a volume and tone dip followed then by a rise back to the original volume and tone. These are often encountered in three letter single Syllable words with a middle Soft Vowels. Common examples are "Dad" {Da"d}, "Bed" {Be"d} and "Win" {Wi"n}.

In contrast with 'A', 'E' and 'I', the Vowels 'O' Soft and 'U' Soft are also associated with a possible Extension Modulation but not with a following Repetition Modulation.

Bear in mind that Extension occurs with Soft Vowels, and Repetition may or need not follow, whereas, other Vowel forms may exhibit Extension but are unlikely to Exhibit repetition. For a case to illustrate the point, contrast “Cap” and “Cape”. The first word with the Soft Vowel Sound of 'A' exhibits both Extension and Repetition, but the second with the Hard form of the same Vowel exhibits only Extension but no Repetition.

A number of examples of Repetition and Extension of Vowels in single, dual and Multi-Syllabic words are given in the tables below, with different Vowel and Consonant combinations, to illustrate.

Table:
Single Vowel Modulations
In Single Syllable Word Examples

Example Words	Vowel Extension, or, Extension and Repetition
Note: With some words, both are possible, as shown.	
Cab	Ca"b, Ca'b
Bed	Be"d, Be'd
Man	Ma"n, Ma'n
Deft	De"ft, De'ft.
Leg	Le"g, Le'g
Nib	Ni"b, Ni'b
Fit	Fi"t
Hot	Ho't
Cod	Co'd
Bush	Bu'sh
Jim	Ji"m, Ji'm
Tom	To'm

Table:
Single Vowel Modulations
In Di-Syllabic Word Examples

Example Words	Vowel Extension or Repetition
Note: With some words, both are possible, as shown. Only Vowels are Scripted.	
Salad	Sa"-la1d, Sa'-la1d
Candid	Ca"n-di1d, Ca'n-di1d
Rafter	Ra"f-te1r, Ra'f-te1r
Tinker	Ti'-nke1r
Rigid	Ri′-gid
Hollow	Ho'-llOw
Topic	To'-pic
Pulley	Pu'-llEy
Cushion	Cu'-shi*o1n

Table:
Single Vowel Modulations
In Multi-Syllabic Word Examples

Note:
In Multi-Syllabic Words, i.e. with more than two Syllables, observe that a Vowel
-may exhibit Extension and Repetition of a Vowel in the beginning Syllable, a middle Syllable, in both or neither, but not in the last Syllable,
-Extension is possible in the beginning, middle or end Syllables.
Note that several vocalizations are possible and acceptable. Only Vowels are Scripted.

Example Words	Vowel Extension or Repetition	Vowel Modulations
Beginner	Be*(i).gi.nne1r, Be*(i)'.gi'.nne1r, Be*(i)'.gi.nne1r	The beginning Syllable, 'I', and middle Syllable, 'I', Vowels may or need not exhibit Extension.
Capacity	Ca1-pa'.ci.ty, Ca1-pa".ci.ty	Only the middle Syllable Vowel, 'A', exhibits Extension, or, Extension and Repetition.
Several	Se'-ve1-ra11	Only the beginning Syllable Vowel, 'E', exhibits Extension, or, not.
Computer	Co1m-pU'-te1r, Co1m-pU-te1r	Only the middle Syllable Vowel, 'U', exhibits Extension, or, not.
Fabulous	Fa'-b((Y)u1-lo1u*s, Fa"-b(Y)u1-lo1u*s	Only the beginning Syllable Vowel, 'A', exhibits Extension, or, not.
Chocolate	Cho'.co1-la1te*	Only the beginning Syllable Vowel, 'O', exhibits Extension.
Magazine	Ma"-ga1-zi*(E)'ne, Ma'-ga1-zi*(E)'ne*	The beginning Syllable Vowel, 'A', may exhibit Extension, or, Extension and Repetition. The End Syllable Vowel, 'E', is Extended.
Mechanic	Me*(i)-cha"-nic, Me*(i)-cha'-nic	The middle Syllable Vowel may be Extended, or, Extended and Repeated.
Director	Di1-re'c.to1r, Di1-rec.to1r, DI'-re'c-to1r, DI-rec-to1r, Di'-rec-to1r, Di-re'c-to1r	When pronounced with 'I' Short, only the middle Syllable Vowel, 'E', exhibits Extension, or not. When pronounced with 'I' Hard, the beginning Syllable Vowel 'I' and middle Syllable Vowel 'E' may, or, may not be Extended.
Employer	e*(i)m-plo)-ye1r, e*(i)m-plo)'-ye1r	The middle Syllable Vowel, 'O', exhibits Extension, or, not.
General	Ge'-ne1-ra11, Ge"-ne1-ra11, Ge-ne1-ra11	The beginning Syllable Vowel 'E', may exhibit Extension, or,

		Extension and Repetition, or, not.
Emerald	e'-me1-ra1ld, e''-me1-ra1ld, e-me1-ra1ld	The beginning Syllable Vowel, 'A', may exhibit Extension, or, Extension and Repetition, or, not.
Lavender	La'-ve1n-da1r, La''-ve1n-da1r, La-ve1n.da1r.	The beginning Syllable Vowel, 'A', may exhibit Extension, or, Extension and Repetition, or, not.
Radio	RA'-di*(E)-O', RA'-di*(E)'-O'	The beginning Syllable Vowel, 'A', and end Syllable Vowel, 'O', are Extended. The middle Syllable Vowel Sound 'E', may, or, may not, be Extended.
Revenue	Re-ve1-nu2e*, Re'-ve1-nu2e*, Re-ve1-nu2'e*, Re'-ve1-nu2'e*	The beginning Syllable Vowel, 'E', may or may not exhibit Extension, and the end Syllable Vowel Sound, 'U', may, or, may not, be Extended. The same is true even when 'U' Hard is used instead of 'U' Long.
Lemonade	Le'-mo1-nA'de*, Le-mo1-nA'de*	The beginning Syllable Vowel, 'E', may or may not exhibit Extension. The end Syllable Vowel Sound, 'A', is Extended.
Appetite	a-ppe1-tIte, a'-ppe1-tI'te, a-ppe1-tI'te, a'-ppe1-tIte	The beginning Syllable Vowel, 'A', and the end Syllable Vowel Sound, 'I', may, or, may not, be Extended.

Exercise.

Use the examples in the tables above to practice articulating Extension and Repetition, as indicated by the apostrophes, while also pausing at the points indicated by a dot or dash between Syllables.

Dual Vowel Modulations.

We have discussed Modulation of single Vowel Sounds which involves either only Extension (of Soft and Hard Vowels), or both Extension and Repetition (of Soft Vowels).

Another type of Modulation involves two Vowel Sounds. It is the Dual Vowel Modulation. There are just a few of these. A Dual Vowel Modulation is like a Linked Vowel Sequence (those that involve transition from the first Vowel to the second – remember, not all Vowel Sequences are Linked), except that an External Vowel, not contained in the word spelling, is inserted into the pronunciation of such a word. This Vowel Sound (the External Vowel) is Linked to a Vowel (the Internal Vowel) in the word's spelling. Some of these Modulations are seen in both American and British ways of speaking. Some are distinctive of the American way alone.

How is a Dual Vowel Modulation shown in the Vocal Fidelity Phonetic System?

The External Vowel is inserted into the word in parenthesis either before or just after the Internal Vowel to which it is Linked, depending on its position in the sequence of articulation.

Both Vowels are Scripted according to the Scripting Conventions for Vowels to show how each is articulated as they Link to each other. Within the pronunciation of the word, the first Vowel is articulated as Scripted which then transitions to the second Vowel, articulated as Scripted.

For example in the word "So", a Dual Vowel Modulation is often articulated. The External Vowel is the Short form of 'A' or alternatively the Hard form of 'A', heard preceding the Internal Vowel 'O'. The Vowel Sounds are Scripted as follows: S(a1)O (if articulated with the Short form of 'A') or alternatively S(A)O, (if articulated with the Hard form of 'A'). The former way appears more widely heard in America.

The parentheses shows that the 'A' is an inserted External letter, i.e. not in the spelling of the word. It is Scripted in lower case and followed by the number '1' to show that it is the Short form of 'A'. Or, alternatively, in upper case to show it is the Hard form of 'A'. The 'O' is not in parentheses as it is the Internal Vowel, i.e. a part of the word's spelling. It is in upper case to show that it is the Hard form of 'O'. In this example the External Vowel precedes the Internal Vowel.

For another example, take the word "File", which contains a Dual Vowel Modulation. Here the External Vowel is the Short Vowel Sound heard just after the Internal Vowel 'I', which is in the Hard form. This Dual Vowel Modulation is Scripted: FI(i1)le. The final 'E' is not Scripted as it is not part of the Dual Vowel Modulation, but is silent in this example.

The 'I' in upper case is the Internal Vowel Sound (as it is not enclosed in parentheses) in the Hard form. The Short Vowel Sound is inserted in parentheses to show it is the External Vowel. The number 1 following the lower case of 'I', shows that it is the Short Vowel form. In this example the External Vowel follows the Internal Vowel.

Characteristics of a Dual Vowel Modulation.

The Internal Vowel (in the word's spelling to which the External Vowel is Linked) is typically in the Hard (Scripted: 'A', 'E', 'I', 'O', 'U') or Long Vowel form (Scripted: a2, o2, u2). These are the most strongly articulated Vowel forms.

The External Vowel (inserted into the pronunciation Linked to the Internal Vowel) is often in a Soft (Scripted: 'a', 'e', 'i', 'o', 'u') or Short Vowel (Scripted: 'a1', 'e1', 'i1', 'o1', 'u1') form. These are the most weakly articulated Vowel forms. However, it may also occur in the Hard form and match the strength of the Internal Vowel.

The two Linked Vowel Sounds i.e. the Internal and the External, can occur in any order, depending on the pronunciation of the particular word.

Note:
Remember, per the Scripting Conventions for Vowels:

-When a Vowel within parenthesis is preceded by a Vowel followed by an asterisk, the Vowel in parentheses replaces the preceding Vowel which is silenced.

-When two Vowel Sounds follow one another, with one of the two in parentheses, this is a Dual Vowel Modulation, with the inserted External Vowel shown in parentheses.

Like "the eye sees not itself", many Americans may be surprised that many words with a single Vowel Sound as indicated by its spelling actually involve Modulation requiring a transition from one Vowel form to another.

I remember a discussion with a person in San Francisco. I pointed out that the way she and others said words like "Room" and "Shoot" included an 'I' before the 'O' sound. (Using the Vocal Fidelity Phonetic System to transcribe the Vowel Sounds, they are Scripted: {R(i)o*o2m} and {Sh(i)o*o2t}.) She became aware of the Modulation from our conversation, as we observed the way she said it and compared it with how the words can be articulated without the 'I' sound.

Table:
Widely Prevalent Dual Vowel Modulations
In The American Accent

Note on Dual Vowel Sound Modulation: Sometimes a Vowel included in the spelling of a word (i.e. the Internal Vowel) is Linked to another Vowel Sound, which is not included in the spelling of the word (i.e. the External Vowel). This type of Modulation involves different successive Vowel Sounds. These Vowel Sounds are made up from a pair from the Vowel forms in the table below. The Internal and External Vowels are adjacent to each other and may be in any sequence and have a sound that Links from the former to the latter. Word Ending Dual Vowel Modulations are covered in a table in the next section, not in the present one below. The External Vowel Sound is enclosed within parentheses and Scripted according to its form.

Internal Vowel Form	Dual Vowel Sequence Scripted	Example Word	Example Scripted Note: If pronunciation without Modulation also exists, this is also shown. (Only the Vowels are Scripted)	Comments
'A' Hard	A(a1)	Bale Rail	BA(a1)l RA(a1)i*l	Often before an 'L' sound.
'A' Hard	A(E)	Grade Fame Rain Wave Maze	GrA(E)de* or GrA'de* FA(E)me* or FA'me* RA(E)i*n or RA'i*n WA(E)ve* or WA've* MA(E)ze* or MA'ze*	Before many Consonants. More often heard as a Single Vowel Modulation with an Extended 'A' Hard, Scripted as: -A'-.
'E' Hard	(i)E	Deal Rear Year	DE'a1l, D(i)Ea1l RE'a1r, R(i)Ea1r YE'a1r, Y(i)Ea1r	Often before an 'L' sound. Often before an 'R' sound.
		Feel Deer	FEe1l, F(i)Ee1l DEe1r, D(i)Ee1r	Often before an 'L' sound. Often before an 'R' sound.
		Seat Pete	SEa*t, S(i)Ea*t PEte*, P(i)Ete*	Before many final Consonant Sounds.
'I' Hard.	I(i1)	File Mile Dire	FI'le, FI(i1)le* MI'le, MI(i1)le* DI're, DI(i1)re*	Often before an 'L' sound. Often before an 'R' sound.
'I' Hard.	(a2)I	Bide Fine Line Mine Side	B(a2)Ide*, BI'de* F(a2)In*, FI'ne* L(a2)Ine*, LI'ne* M(a2)I'ne*, MI'ne* S(a2)Ide*, SI'de*	Before many Consonants. More often heard as a Single Vowel Modulation with an Extended 'I' Hard, Scripted as: {-I'-}.

'O' Hard.	(a1)O or (A)O	Cone Road Phone Hole Hello Low	C(a1)O'ne*, C(A)O'ne* R(a1)O'a*d, R(A)O'a*d Ph(a1)O'ne*, Ph(A)O'ne* H(a1)O'le*, H(A)O'le* Hell(a1)O, Hell(A)O' L(a1)O'w, L(A)O'w'	Before many final Consonant Sounds. Also, before a Vowel Sound at the End of word.
U' Hard.	(i)U	Cute Due Fume Mule	C(i)Ute*, CU'te* D(i)Ue*, DU'e*, (or, D(i)u2e*, Du2e*) F(i)Ume*, FU'me* M(i)Ule*, MU'le*	Before many final Consonant Sounds. Also, before a Vowel Sound at the End of word.
'O' Long.	(i)o2	To Food Who Room Soot	To2, T(i)o2 Fo*o2d, F(i)o*o2d Who2, Wh(i)o2 Ro*o2m, R(i)o*o2m So*o2t, S(i)o*o2t	Before many final Consonants. Also, before a Vowel Sound at the End of word.
'U' Long.	(i)u2	Assume Crude Dude Rule Sue	Assu2me*, Ass(i)u2me* Cru2de*, Cr(i)u2de* Du2de*, D(i)u2de* Ru2le*, R(i)u2le* Su2e*, S(i)u2e*	Before many final Consonant Sounds. Also, before a Vowel Sound at the End of word.

Exercise.

Practice articulating the words in the above table articulating the External Vowel Sound.

Section:
Word Ending Vowel Sounds Said the American Way

For words that end with a Vowel, the Vowel finishes the preceding Consonant Sound, by determining how it ends.

For example, the word “Polo” {Po-lO'}, ends with the 'O' Hard Vowel form. It finishes the Consonant 'L' that begins the word ending Syllable.

The main point to note for word ending Vowel Sounds in the American Accent is that they are often, if not always, articulated at a lower tone and are more Extended than in the British Accent. Bear this in mind when you practice such Vowel Sounds and as you review the different word ending Vowel Sounds in the box below.

The following Vowel Sounds, also heard in other Syllable positions, are also word ending Vowel Sounds:

(Note: Pronunciation is shown in the Vocal Fidelity Phonetic System Script within curly brackets for only the Vowel Sounds under discussion for each example given – the rest of the example, where written, is in regular text.)

-The Short Vowel Sound as in the 'A' at the end of "Soda" {Soda1} is very commonly heard. It is also often heard at the end of female names, e.g. "Linda" {Linda1}.
-The Hard Vowel Sounds (just as we say 'A', 'E', 'I', 'O' and 'U', as stand alone Vowel letters), as articulated in words like "Bay" {..A'}, "Candy" {..E} or "Coffee" {..E'}, "Hi" {..I'}, "Polo" or "Tomato" {..O'}, and "Cue" {..U'}. These Hard Vowel forms may or may not be Extended as is indicated by the apostrophe mark that follows for some of the preceding examples.
-The Soft Vowel Sounds, such as:

-'A' Like the 'O' Soft-Round that precedes a 'W' Consonant as in words like "Flaw" {Fla*(o)'w*} or "Saw" {Sa*(o)'w*}.
-The 'I' Soft that replaces a 'Y' after an 'O' Soft-Round as in words like "Boy" {Boy*(i)} or "Employ" {Employ*(i)}.
-The 'U' Soft that replaces a 'W' as in words like "Cow" {Co*(a)w*(u)} and "Now" {No*(a)w*(u)}, or the final 'U' Soft sound heard at the end of words like "Bough" {Bo*(a)ug*h*}.

-The Long Vowel sounds, such as:

-The 'A' Long as in "Ha" {Ha2}, "Pa" {Pa2}, "Ma" {Ma2} or "Media" {Medi*Ea2} (the more common way of ending this last word is with an 'A' Short {..a1}).
-The 'Y' Like 'I' Long {..i2} as in "Seventy" {Seventy*(i2)} is regularly heard at the end of words.
-The 'O' Long {..o2} as in "Who" {W*H(i)o2} or {W*Ho2'}.
-The 'U' Long {..u2} as in "Sue" {S(i)u2e*} or {Su2'e*} or "Due", {D(i)u2e*} or {Du2'e*}.

-The Hard Vowel sounds, such as the 'E' Hard in words like "Coffee" {CoffE'e*} and "Payee" {PayE'e*}, "Radii" {Rade*(E)'I'}, "Hello" {HellO'} also pronounced {Hell(a1)O}, and "Emu" {Em(y)U'}.
-In some cases, a Dual Vowel Modulation is heard with the Hard or Long form of a word ending Vowel Sound, as you can see in some of the examples above – or as in "To" {T(i)o2..}, "Boo" {B(i)o*o2} and "Flue" {Fl(i)u2e*} – ("To", "Boo" and "Flue" are often pronounced like this, though dictionaries may not show this popular vocalization).
-Word Ending Linked Vowel Sounds are also regularly heard. Examples: 'IA' as in "Dahlia" {Dahli2a1}, 'EA' as in "Area" {ArEa1}, 'IO' as in "Radio" {Radi2'O'}, 'OA' as in "Protozoa" {ProtozO'a1}, 'IEU' as in "Adieu", {AdiEu2} and 'UA' as in "Aqua" {Aqu*(W)a1}.
-Many words that end with the Consonants 'W' and 'Y', and a few with 'H', are replaced with Vowel Sounds, e.g. as in "Fly" {Fly*(I)'} which ends in the 'I' Hard, Extended Vowel Sound. Or, they are in words where they are located at the word end position but silent with the preceding Vowel Sound finishing the articulation of the word, e.g. as in "Flew" {Fle*(o2)'w*} (the preceding 'O' Long, Extended prevails} or "Shah" {Sha2'h*} (the preceding 'A' Long, Extended prevails}.

It is interesting that the Soft Vowel form associated with 'A' and 'E', e.g. as in the 'A' in "Bat", {Ba"t} and in the 'E' in "Red" {Re"d}, while often heard in other Syllable positions is never heard in a word end position.

Table:
Word Ending Hard or Long Vowel Sounds

Vowel Ending Word Vocalization	Phonetic Representation	Examples	Comment
'A' Hard.	A'	Bay, Clay, Flay, Gray, Play, Say, Way.	The ending 'Y' is silent, so the preceding 'A' Hard is the final sound and is Extended.
'E' Hard.	E	Karate.	The 'E' Hard may or may not be Extended. This is also the sound of the 'I' Long.
'E' Hard, Extended.	E'	Be, Ca-rrie, He, See, She, We, Me.	The final 'E' Hard Vowel Sound is Extended.
'E' Like 'A' Hard.	e*(A)	Ci-ne, Me-le, Mediae, Re-nee.	The final 'E' is silenced and replaced with the 'A' Hard.
'E' Like 'U' Hard, Extended.	e*(U)'w*	Few, Mew, Review, Stew, Skew.	The final 'E' Vowel is silenced and replaced with a 'U' Hard which is Extended, and the final 'W' is silent.
'E' Like 'U' Long.	e*u2'w*	Blew, Flew, Grew, New, Threw.	The final 'E' Vowel is silenced and replaced with a 'U' Long which is Extended, and the final 'W' is silent.
'I' Hard.	I/ y*(I)/ y*e*(I)/ I'g*h*/ I'e*/ i*(E)I'	Anti~, Foci, Hi, Semi~ By, My, Bye. High, Sigh, Lie, Radii	These different word ending letters all have the 'I' Hard Sound, and each is Scripted differently to the same effect, as shown.
'I' Like Hard 'E'.	i*(E)	Anti~, Chianti, Semi~.	The final 'I' Vowel is silenced and replaced by the 'E' Hard Vowel.
'O' Hard,	O	Go~, No~, Polo~, So~, Solo~.	This is one vocalization of the 'O' Hard Vowel Sound in these examples.
'O' Hard, Extended.	O/ O', (a1)O', (A)O' / O'e* / O'w*	No~, Go~, No~, Polo~, So~, Solo~, Woe, Hoe, Roe, Toe, Blow, Borrow, Follow, Grow, Mellow, Mow, Pillow, Slow, Tow.	Where the word ends with just the 'O' Hard, there are different treatments: 1. No Extension 2. With Extension 3. Extended but also preceded by the External Vowel{-(a1)-} or {-(A)-}. Where the 'O' Hard is followed by an 'E', it is Extended and the 'E' is silent. Words where a 'W' follows the 'O' Hard, the 'O' Hard is Extended and the 'W' is silenced.
'O' Long.	o2, (i)o2	Do, To~, Too, Shoe, Two, Who.	Words which end with the 'O' Long may exhibit an 'I' Soft, an External Vowel, preceding it, in popular speech.
'U' Hard.	U'e*, (i)Ue*	Cue, Due, Issue.	Words ending with a 'U' Hard, Extended sound is usually followed by an 'E' Silent. A Dual Vowel Modulation[1] with a

			preceding External 'I' Soft may be heard in these words.
'U' Long.	u2e*, (i)u2e*	Blue, Clue, Flue, Glue, Rue, Sue.	Words ending with a 'U' Long are usually followed by an 'E' Silent. A Dual Vowel Modulation[1] with a preceding External 'I' Soft may be heard in these words.
Note: Word ending Vowel Sounds with a Dual Vowel Modulation can be distinctive of the American Accent and should therefore be recognized. Some of these commonly heard Modulations are not shown in Dictionary Phonetic Representations, but because they are so prevalent, you could choose to emulate them.			

Table:
More Examples Of Words Ending With The Short Vowel Sound

'A' Short.	a1	Anna, Beta, Cola, Data, Gala, Flotilla, Feta, Flora, Fauna, Media~, Quota, Sofa, Soda, Stamina.	The 'A' Short is articulated at a lower tone than the British way.

Section:
Understanding Consonants and Consonant Sounds

Note: See Appendix I. C for the Vocal Fidelity Phonetic System Table: "Scripting Conventions for Consonant Sounds".

A 'Consonant' is an alphabet or letter (e.g. B, C, D, F, ...) which is not a Vowel (e.g. A, E, ...) with one or more associated Consonant Sounds any of which have more pronounced vocal lines, edges, features and structure than those of Vowels.

Remember: Consonant Sounds form the structure or hard bones of a word and Vowel Sounds the soft connective tissue. Consonants are associated with harder edged sounds and Vowels are associated with the softer shaped sounds between them. Vowel Sounds provide padding and connections between Consonant Sounds, just as bones need the support of soft tissue.

A Consonant should be distinguished from a Consonant Sound. A Consonant Sound is what is heard when a single Consonant (e.g. as 'B' and 'T' in "Bat") or, when a sequence of Consonants merge together (e.g. 'CH' as in "Chip" or 'TH' as in "Think") is articulated, to produce a single moment or instant of sound. When successive Consonants form a single, distinctive Consonant Sound, these are called "Merged" Consonants.

Note: Merged Consonants transform their constituent Consonant Sounds to some degree. E.g. 'PH' as in "Phone", where the successive Consonants Merge together to sound like the 'F' in "Fox". Sometimes successive Consonants may Merge to produce a soundless or Vowel-like effect, e.g. as with 'GH' in "Bough", which ends like the 'W' in "Cow".

When consecutive Consonants connect with each other not by Merging but by transitioning from the first to the next, producing – not a moment or instant, but instead – a short stream of sound without the interruption of a Pause, these are called "Linked" Consonants. Such a stream can be produced by two or more successive Consonants, e.g. 'DR' as in "Drop" or 'STR' as in "Strap". Such a stream consists of separately identifiable, individual Consonant Sounds that can clearly be associated with each of the successive Consonants. Observe the distinctive Consonant Sounds associated with the successive Consonants 'S', 'T' and 'R' in the word "Strap" as they Link and transition from the first Consonant to the next and on to the third.

Note: In this Course, side by side Consonants have been referred to as being "Pairs", "Adjacent", or as "Sequences".

There are in fact far more Consonant Sounds in spoken English than there are Consonants in the English Alphabet. The additional Consonant Sounds are formed as follows:

-As just discussed – successive Consonants sometimes Merge together to make a distinct Consonant Sound, as with 'SH' in "Ship", a Consonant Sound unlike any other Consonant in the Alphabet.
-Some Consonants have more than one Version, e.g. the 'S' in "Sit" has a different Consonant Sound than 'S' in "His".
-Merged Consonant sequences like 'TH' can also have different Versions, e.g. the 'TH' in "Think" is different than the 'TH' in "This".
-Consonants may have different Consonant Sounds when they are in different positions within a Syllable, e.g. 'N' at the end of a Syllable is more Nasal than at the beginning of a Syllable. Compare the words "Man" with the word "Next".

It is important that we recognize varied Consonant Sounds, how they are different, and where they may occur in spoken American English, so they are articulated as required. More on this, ahead.

Section:
The Accentuation of Consonants

The way Americans Accentuate Consonant Sounds is an important underlying determinant of the American Accent, and a fundamental cause of its difference from the British Accent. It is therefore essential to understand how Americans articulate Consonants to speak the American way.

Accentuation is the level of intensification and amplification (volume or loudness) of a Consonant Sound and its properties. Accentuation is the final result of two types of Accentuation: Intrinsic Accentuation, and, Positional Accentuation. What they are and how they interact is explained further below.

Accentuation is quantified on a scale with four levels between Weak to Strong, as follows:
-Weak.
-Weak to moderate.
-Moderate to strong.
-Strong.

As boundaries between each level are on a continuous scale, there can be a degree of blurring or overlap between their boundaries.

What is Intrinsic Accentuation?

Each Consonant Sound can be distinguished in terms of its intrinsic properties, (just as weather can be distinguished in terms of properties such as "Cold", "Windy", "Wet", etc.). The properties of Consonant Sounds are referred to, in this Course – as part of the Vocal Fidelity Phonetic System – as their Inherent Attributes. Intrinsic Accentuation refers to the articulation of the Inherent Attributes that make up a Consonant sound.

In Appendix II. A, the Table "The Consonant Sound Inherent Attribute List", a list of twelve Inherent Attributes are described to distinguish between different Consonant Sounds. Specific Consonant Sounds can be characterized by the Inherent Attributes they possess or don't possess.

A list of twelve distinct Inherent Attributes are identified in the Vocal Fidelity Phonetic System. One or more Inherent Attribute characterizes each Consonant Sound. They are:

-Buzz
-Flat
-Hiss
-Hum
-Knock
-Lilting
-Nasal
-Pop Heavy
-Pop Light
-Rasp
-Sharp
-Vowelish

Some Consonant Sounds possess only one of the listed Inherent Attributes. Others have two or more.

A contrast, in terms of the presence or absence of even a single Inherent Attribute makes it possible to distinguish between any two Consonant Sounds, including different Consonant Sounds associated with the same Consonant. Sometimes the distinctions between closely resembling Consonant Sounds are slight but observable.

Eg. As observed earlier, 'N' at the end of a Syllable as in the word "Man", has the Nasal Attribute, whereas 'N' at the beginning of a Syllable as in the word "Next", does not. Or, 'T' in "Center" said one popular American way is different from the 'T' in "Telephone", because they possess different Inherent Attributes.

Inherent Attributes are associated with specific Consonant Sounds – not Consonants, as each Consonant can refer to a number of different associated Consonant Sounds.

The Inherent Attributes can also be used to identify differences between Accents in the articulation of certain Consonants.

E.g. the Consonant 'R' at the end of a Syllable, e.g. as in the word "Car", said the American way exhibits the Rasp Attribute. By contrast, said the British way, the same Consonant does not exhibit this Attribute when in Syllable-Middle and Syllable-End positions – check how the British say "Car" or "Farm" in contrast with the American Accent.

The same Consonant Sound can vary in terms of the level to which their Inherent Attributes are Accentuated when in different Syllable positions. Simply a difference in the level of Accentuation of a Consonant Sound as a whole does not make it distinctive – just more or less intense or loud. Consonant Sounds become intrinsically distinctive only when they possess a different combination of Inherent Attributes.

E.g. In the American Accent, the Rasp Attribute in the Consonant 'R' is typically stronger at the end of a Syllable than at the beginning. Compare the 'R' in "Car" and in "Read".

Descriptions of the Inherent Attributes are given in the Table "The Consonant Sound Inherent Attribute List" in Appendix II. A. When you recognize the Inherent Attributes of Consonant Sounds, you will become more sensitive to them and it will then become possible for you to adopt them, to speak in an American Accent. Listen carefully to how American speakers articulate the example words provided, to discern the Attributes in a specific Consonant Sound.

> There must be at least one Inherent Attribute for each Consonant Sound. Some Consonant Sounds exhibit several Attributes whereas some are identified by only one.
>
> Each Inherent Attribute is clearly distinguishable from each other. Each is needed to describe an evident Consonant Sound characteristic to guide pronunciation.
>
> The list includes only the required Inherent Attributes needed to clearly distinguish between different Consonant Sounds. A few others were considered but left out as they would have added complexity without sufficient gain.

> Note: See Appendix III. A for the Table: "The Consonant Sound Inherent Attribute List".

> Note: See Appendix III. B for the Table: "Consonant Sounds and their Inherent Attributes".

> Note: For cross-referencing of American pronunciation, I recommend the Merriam-Webster Dictionary, and, for additional cross referencing, I recommend the Cambridge Dictionary which provides both American (USA) and UK (United Kingdom) pronunciations. In case of discrepancy between them as regards American pronunciation, I recommend the Merriam-Webster Dictionary. For cross-referencing of the British Accent, I recommend the Cambridge Dictionary.

> Note: See Appendix V, "The Development of this Course: Knowledge Creation and Quality" for the approach followed for quality and reliability of knowledge content.

Levels of Intrinsic Accentuation.

When a Consonant Sound is articulated in isolation, its Accentuation level derives exclusively from its Inherent Attributes and may be thought of as its "stand-alone" Intrinsic Accentuation level. It is the expected Accentuation level of a Consonant Sound when unaffected by being in the context of a Syllable or word.

> Remember the twelve distinct Inherent Attributes identified in the Vocal Fidelity Phonetic System, one or more of which characterizes each Consonant Sound. They are: Buzz, Flat, Hiss, Hum, Knock, Lilting, Nasal, Pop Heavy, Pop Light, Rasp, Sharp and Vowelish.

Intrinsic Accentuation is quantified on a scale of Low, Medium and High levels. This scale is used to describe the level of intensification and amplification of stand alone Consonant Sounds.

> By contrast, the Accentuation scale describes the level of Accentuation that is the result of the effects of both Intrinsic, and, Positional (to be explained ahead) Accentuation. The Accentuation scale spans the levels: Weak, Weak to moderate, Moderate to strong, and Strong.

Different scales are used to measure Intrinsic Accentuation and Accentuation levels as they refer to different concepts, though they both concern the intensification and loudness of Consonant Sounds – in different ways. When referring to them, the different scales enable us to discuss them separately without confusion.

The levels of the Intrinsic Accentuation scale correspond to those of the Accentuation scale in terms of the intensification and loudness of the respective Consonant Sounds to which they refer, as follows: Low Intrinsic Accentuation corresponds with Weak, and, Weak to moderate Accentuation. Medium Intrinsic Accentuation corresponds with Moderate to strong Accentuation. And, High Intrinsic Accentuation corresponds with Strong Accentuation.

A Consonant Sound can have one or more Inherent Attributes, each of which has its own Intrinsic Accentuation. level. The Intrinsic Accentuation level of the Consonant Sound is equal to the Inherent Attribute with the highest Intrinsic Accentuation level. This level of Intrinsic Accentuation is sufficient to accommodate all the constituent Inherent Attributes of the Consonant Sound each of which is either of lower or equal Intrinsic Accentuation. Depending on its constituent Inherent Attributes, the Intrinsic Accentuation level of a Consonant Sound can be at either a Low, Medium or High level.

The Intrinsic Accentuation of a particular Consonant Sound is qualitatively effected by all of its different Inherent Attributes, but the resulting Intrinsic Accentuation level of that Consonant Sound is equal to that of the Inherent Attribute with the highest Intrinsic Accentuation level.

The Intrinsic Accentuation levels of different Inherent Attributes of Consonant Sounds are as follows:

-Inherent Attributes that exhibit a High level of Intrinsic Accentuation are:
Pop Light, Pop Heavy and Sharp.
-Those that exhibit a Medium level of Intrinsic Accentuation are:
Flat, Hiss, Knock, Rasp and Vowelish.
-Those that exhibit a Low level of Intrinsic Accentuation are:
Buzz, Hum, Lilting and Nasal.

Note: To see the Inherent Attributes associated with different Consonant Sounds, see Appendix III. B for the Table: “Consonant Sounds and their Inherent Attributes”.

Note: As Consonants can refer to a number of different associated Consonant Sounds, Inherent Attributes are associated with each of the different Consonant Sounds, not with Consonants.

What is Positional Accentuation?

Positional Accentuation is a way of speaking that causes an increased or decreased effect on the Intrinsic Accentuation of a Consonant Sound, depending on its position in the Syllable of a word.

Positional Accentuation effects Intrinsic Accentuation and results in the Accentuation of a Consonant Sound as it is heard as part of a particular Syllable of a word.

Consonants can be in Syllable-Beginning, Syllable-Middle or Syllable-End positions.

Accentuation is the consequence of Positional Accentuation acting on Intrinsic Accentuation.

Positional Accentuation should be understood as a way of speaking, or as a linguistic process, dynamic or mechanism.

Positional Accentuation has an Accentuation decreasing effect on the Intrinsic Accentuation of a Consonant Sound when it is in the Syllable-Beginning position, within the limits of the Accentuation scale. And, it has an Accentuation increasing effect on the Intrinsic Accentuation of a Consonant Sound when in the Syllable-End position, within the limits of the Accentuation scale.

Positional Accentuation effects Intrinsic Accentuation in the following circumstances:

A Consonant Sound which has Low Intrinsic Accentuation as a stand alone Consonant Sound, when at the end of a Syllable, tends to exhibit increased Accentuation. E.g., the Consonant Sound 'L', in the word "Sale" (Low Intrinsic Accentuation) exhibits increased Accentuation (Moderate to strong) in the Syllable-End position.

A Consonant Sound which has High Intrinsic Accentuation as a stand alone Consonant Sound, when at the beginning of a Syllable, tends to exhibit decreased Accentuation. E.g., the Consonant Sound 'B', in the word "Bead" (High Intrinsic Accentuation) exhibits decreased Accentuation (Moderate to strong), in the Syllable-Beginning position.

A Consonant Sound which has Medium level Intrinsic Accentuation as a stand alone Consonant Sound, when at the end of a Syllable, tends to exhibit increased Accentuation. E.g., the Consonant Sound 'R', in the word "Car" (Medium Intrinsic Accentuation) exhibits increased Accentuation (Strong) at the end of the Syllable. When in the Syllable-Beginning position, it tends to exhibit decreased Accentuation. E.g., the same Consonant Sound, 'R', in the word "Run" exhibits decreased Accentuation (Weak to moderate), at the beginning of the Syllable.

Positional Accentuation is rigid on the direction of Accentuation level change, i.e. upward or downward, based on the above circumstances. No change is also possible, but not as likely.

Positional Accentuation does not effect Intrinsic Accentuation in the following circumstances:

A Consonant Sound which has Low Intrinsic Accentuation as a stand alone Consonant Sound, when at the beginning of a Syllable, tends to show corresponding Weak Accentuation, i.e no change. E.g. the Consonant 'L', in the word "Lid" (Low Intrinsic Accentuation), exhibits Weak Accentuation at the beginning of the Syllable. Note, in this circumstance, Accentuation is limited to the minimum of the Accentuation scale, therefore Positional Accentuation can effect no further decrease, beyond Weak.

A Consonant Sound which has High Intrinsic Accentuation as a stand alone Consonant Sound, when at the end of a Syllable, tends to show corresponding Strong Accentuation, i.e. no change. E.g. the Consonant 'D', in the word "Lid" (High Intrinsic Accentuation), exhibits Strong Accentuation at the end of the Syllable. In this circumstance, Accentuation is limited to the maximum of the Accentuation scale, therefore Positional Accentuation can effect no further increase, beyond Strong.

The magnitude of Positional Accentuation impact.

Just like the direction of impact – whether of decrease (downward) or increase (upward) in Accentuation – is dependent upon the position of the Consonant Sound in the Syllable and its Intrinsic Accentuation level, so too is the amount of impact dependent on these same factors – with the possibility of some variation in the amount.

The magnitude of Positional Accentuation impact occurs as follows:

> A Consonant of Low Intrinsic Accentuation when at the end of a Syllable may exhibit an increase to Weak to moderate, or, to Moderate to strong Accentuation, i.e., one to two levels higher on the corresponding Accentuation scale. The example provided earlier of the Consonant Sound 'L', in the word "Sale" illustrates such an increase.
>
> A Consonant of High Intrinsic Accentuation when at the beginning of a Syllable may exhibit a decrease to Moderate to strong, or, to Weak to moderate Accentuation, i.e., one to two levels lower on the corresponding Accentuation scale. The example provided earlier of the Consonant Sound 'B', in the word "Bead" illustrates such a decrease.
>
> A Consonant of Medium Intrinsic Accentuation when at the end of a Syllable may exhibit an increase to Strong Accentuation, i.e. one level higher on the corresponding Accentuation scale. The example provided earlier of the Consonant Sound 'R', in the word "Car" illustrates such an increase.
>
> A Consonant of Medium Intrinsic Accentuation when at the beginning of a Syllable may exhibit a decrease to weak to moderate Accentuation, i.e. one level lower on the corresponding Accentuation scale. The example provided earlier of the Consonant Sound 'R', in the word "Run" illustrates such a decrease.

An impact in an opposite direction seems very unlikely.

> Note: It is helpful to remember the Inherent Attributes and their level of Intrinsic Accentuation.
>
> The Intrinsic Accentuation levels of different Inherent Attributes of Consonant Sounds are as follows:
>
> -Inherent Attributes that exhibit a High level of Intrinsic Accentuation are:
> Pop Light, Pop Heavy and Sharp.
>
> -Those that exhibit a Medium level of Intrinsic Accentuation are:
> Flat, Hiss, Knock, Rasp and Vowelish.
>
> -Those that exhibit a Low level of Intrinsic Accentuation are:
> Buzz, Hum, Lilting and Nasal.

> Note: Consonant Sounds with more than one Inherent Attribute exhibit the Intrinsic Accentuation level of the Attribute with the highest Intrinsic Accentuation level. E.g. 'TH' as in "Them" (not as in "Think") and 'V' as in "Volt", both have the Buzz Inherent Attribute which has low level Intrinsic Accentuation, but they also have other Inherent Attributes with higher level Intrinsic Accentuation, causing the Accentuation level of these Consonant Sounds to be higher than Weak.

> Note: Very few Consonant Sounds actually exhibit Weak Accentuation. These are limited almost entirely to Consonant Sounds located in a Syllable-Beginning position that have exclusively Buzz, Hum, Lilting, or Nasal Inherent Attributes unaccompanied by other Inherent Attributes. Examples are: 'Z' as in "Zephyr", 'L' as in "Lane" and 'M' as in "Man". Among the few exceptions are words with the Consonant Sound, 'N', as heard in words like "Ink", "Mango" and "Sing".

> Positional Accentuation sometimes impacts certain Inherent Attributes of a Consonant more than others depending on its position within a Syllable. Here are some examples:

E.g. the Consonant 'N' is more Nasal at the end of a Syllable, but hardly so at all at the beginning of Syllable. Compare the Nasality of 'N' in the words "Fan" and "Name", where it is heard in the first word and not in the second.

E.g. the Consonant 'R' has more Rasp at the end of a Syllable than at the beginning. Compare the Rasp in "Car" and in "Rap". It is stronger in the former and weaker in the latter.

The Vowelish Inherent Attribute of 'W' and 'Y' Sounds is different from the other Inherent Attributes. Other than when at the beginning of a word or Syllable, these sounds often resemble a Vowel rather than a Consonant. They are usually most strongly Accentuated when they begin a Syllable or word.

Note: See Appendix III. A for the Table: "The Consonant Sound Inherent Attribute List".

Note: See Appendix III. B for the Table: "Consonant Sounds and their Inherent Attributes".

What about the effect of Positional Accentuation on Middle Consonants?

First, though, what is meant here by a Middle Consonant: A Middle Consonant is one which is not at the beginning or end of any Syllable in a word and has a Consonant Sound that links but is not merged with either a Syllable-Beginning or Syllable-End Consonant Sound.

Examples of Middle Consonants:

First, a note of caution. The term Middle Consonant used here refers to a Consonant in a Syllable-Middle position. Consonants in the middle of words like "Tenet", "Cater", "Coral" and "Famous" are actually Syllable-Beginning Consonants. You can see this once you insert the Pauses at the required place in the words, as follows: {Te-net}, {Ca-ter}, {Co-ral} and {Fa-mous}. It can be seen that such mid-word Consonants are often Syllable-Beginning Consonants – even in many longer multi-Syllable words e.g. {Ce-re-mo-ny} or {I-te-ra-tion}.

Middle Consonants are often seen in single Syllable words, e.g. "Bleat", "Club", "Wilt", "Kicks", "Pact", often next to a Syllable-Beginning or Syllable-End Consonant.

Middle Consonants are also in words of more than one Syllable with two or more adjacent Consonants within a single Syllable e.g. as in "Inclement" {In-cle-ment}, "Tenant" {Te-nant}, "Ca-nard" {Ca-nard} and "Entrant {En-trant}. The Consonants in the middle of words that are in Syllable-Beginning and Syllable-End positions should not be mistaken for Syllable-Middle Consonants. It is the Consonants adjacent to these in the same Syllable that may be Syllable-Middle Consonants.

It is interesting that long words with many Syllables without any Middle Consonants, e.g "Infinitesimal" {In-fi-ni-te-si-mal} and "Autonomy" {Au-to-no-mous} are not very difficult to identify, which implies their abundance.

Middle Consonants may also be located next to a pair of Consonants in single Syllable words, either toward the Beginning or End of a Syllable e.g. "String" or "World". Multi-Syllable words with three consecutive Linked Consonants may require a bit more effort to identify, but are nevertheless numerous.

In a single Syllable word that begins with a Vowel, a Middle Consonant usually follows, as in “Ant” or “Ink”.

In words like “Bath”, “Hush”, “Fudge”, “Chat” or “Shut”, Consonants in the middle of a Syllable which Merge with an adjacent Syllable-Beginning or Syllable-End Consonant to form a single Merged Consonant Sound are not considered Middle Consonants – as they do not have a separate sound of their own.

Observe that Syllable-Beginning and Syllable-End Consonant can either Merge or Link with an in between Consonant.

-When it is Merged, it forms a single Consonant Sound together with the Syllable-Beginning or Syllable-End Consonant and is Accentuated as a Merged Syllable-Beginning or Syllable-End Consonant Sound. E.g. 'CH' in “Chip” is a Merged Syllable-Beginning Consonant Sound and 'SH' in “Fish” is a Merged Syllable-End Consonant Sound. In such situations, the Inherent Attributes of the Consonant Sound, as in 'CH' or 'SH', will determine their Intrinsic Accentuation. This is then subject to the effect of Positional Accentuation being in the context of a Syllable.

-When it is Linked, it retains its independent identity. In this situation it is a Middle Consonant. It approximates the level of Accentuation of the Syllable-Beginning or Syllable-End Consonant with which it is Linked. This means that it is Accentuated at either the same level or one step away, whether higher or lower than the Syllable-Beginning or Syllable-End Consonant with which it is Linked. The Accentuation level of the Middle Consonant is the product both of it's Intrinsic Accentuation, i.e. its Inherent Attributes, and its position in the Syllable – depending on whether it adjoins the Syllable-Beginning Consonant or the Syllable-End Consonant. It leans toward a weaker level when it adjoins the Syllable-Beginning Consonant and toward a stronger level when it adjoins the Syllable-End Consonant.

E.g. the Consonant 'R' which has the Rasp Inherent Attribute and a Medium level of Intrinsic Accentuation, in the word “Drink”, exhibits Weak to moderate Accentuation after the Accentuation decreasing effect of being located next to the Syllable-Beginning Consonant ('D'). Whereas, in the word “Cart”, it exhibits Moderate to strong Accentuation after the Accentuation increasing effect of being located next to the Syllable-End Consonant ('T').

In addition to the influence of Intrinsic Accentuation, in the manner of the typical Consonant, Middle Consonants tend to be Accentuated at a stronger level when located toward a Syllable-End position and at a weaker level when toward a Syllable-Beginning position.

Examples of how Middle Consonant Accentuation can vary in their Accentuation level:

1. In the word, “Clot”, 'L' is a Middle Consonant which is Accentuated at a Weak to moderate level, a level one step lower than the Syllable-Beginning Consonant 'C', with which it Links.
2. In the word, “Work”, 'R' is a Middle Consonant which is Accentuated at a Moderate to strong level, a level below the Strongly Accentuated Syllable-End Consonant, 'K', with which it Links.
3. In the word, “Girl”, 'R' is a Middle Consonant which is Accentuated at a Strong level

above the Moderate to strong Accentuation of the Syllable-End Consonant 'L', with which it Links.
4. In the word, "Talk", 'L' is a Middle Consonant which is silent. Such exceptions do occur.
5. Observe: In the word, "Chin", 'H' is located in the middle of a Syllable but is not considered a Middle Consonant as it is Merged with the Beginning Consonant 'C' and is articulated as a single Syllable-Beginning Consonant Sound 'CH', Accentuated at a Moderate to strong or Weak to moderate level.

Remember, When the term "Accentuation" is used, without qualification as either Intrinsic or Positional, the reference is to the combined product of both Intrinsic and Positional Accentuation of a Consonant Sound, as heard when it is articulated as part of a Syllable in a word.

Section:
The American Consonant Accentuation Principle

The effects of Intrinsic Accentuation and Positional Accentuation explain how Accentuation is produced in the American Accent in detail. American speakers practice these underlying dynamics unconsciously. They can do so because they have gained tacit knowledge of how to speak the American way from an early age. With understanding and referring back to the Sections on Intrinsic and Positional Accentuation and the referenced Appendices, learners of the American Accent will move from deliberate to unconscious application of this knowledge, as it becomes internalized.

It is not unlike others skills e.g. walking. Even an apparently simple skill like walking involves complex movements such as weight transfer and balance. If it were not learned at an early age, it would have to be understood and practiced, as if one were learning, for example, to dance.

Accentuation can also be described in a more general and simple way, with the American Consonant Accentuation Principle. It observes:

In the American Accent, Syllable-End Consonant Sounds tend to be more Accentuated than Syllable-Beginning Consonant Sounds.

The American Consonant Accentuation Principle: Syllable-End Consonant Sounds tend to be more Accentuated than Syllable-Beginning Consonant Sounds.

The American Consonant Accentuation Principle should be understood as a description of Accentuation as an outcome of Positional Accentuation acting on Intrinsic Accentuation.

To understand how the American Consonant Accentuation Principle is produced, a teeter-totter (called a seesaw in Britain) with a child on each end, can be used as a metaphor for a Syllable with a Consonant at each end. Just as the children on the teeter-totter have certain weights, the Consonants in a Syllable analogously have a certain Accentuation. Like the teeter-totter would be inclined downward toward the heavier child, a Syllable is weighted toward the end with the Consonant which has more Accentuation.

While Accentuation of the Syllable-Beginning and Syllable End Consonants may be stronger (or weaker) at the Syllable-End or at the Syllable-Beginning, or both ends could be balanced, the American Consonant Principle observes that more often than not, the Syllable-End Consonant is Accentuated more than the Syllable-Beginning Consonant.

Though the American Syllabication Principle states that Syllables usually begin with Consonants and End with Vowels (where the spelling of the word allows), a large part of the vocabulary consists of single Syllable, dual and Multi-Syllabic words that contain Syllables that begin and end with Consonant Sounds. Think of single Syllable words like "Cat", "Dog" or "Hat", dual Syllable words like "Win-ter" or "Man-sion", or Multi-Syllabic word like "E-ter-nal" or "Ca-len-dar", which all exhibit Syllables with Consonant Sounds at both ends.

The Consonant Accentuation Principle refers to a difference in certain pronunciation features that fundamentally separates the American Accent from the British. Increased Accentuation of Consonant Sounds – when these occur in Syllable-End positions, and reduced Accentuation of Consonant Sounds in Syllable-Beginning positions, characterize the American Accent. Though such Accentuation is also seen in the British Accent, it is inconsistent compared with its prevalence in the American Accent.

Though the Consonant Accentuation Principle observes that Syllable-End Consonants are Accentuated more than Syllable-Beginning Consonants, it allows for exceptions where Accentuation of Syllable-Beginning and Syllable-End Consonant Sounds are Reversed (with Syllable-Beginning Consonant Sounds Accentuated more than Syllable-End Consonant Sounds) or Suspended (where they are evenly Accentuated) in certain situations. These alternatives occur when the Accentuation level of the Inherent Attributes of the Consonant Sounds in Syllable-Beginning and Syllable-End positions sufficiently counter the effect of Positional Accentuation, as may sometimes occur.

The American Consonant Accentuation Principle is exhibited with a level of prevalence to be a guide to speaking the American way most of the time. Application of the concepts of Intrinsic and Position Accentuation supplement the American Consonant Accentuation Principle by revealing precisely how Accentuation is determined, when and why the Principle is Upheld (where the Syllable-End Consonant Sound is Accentuated more than the Syllable-Beginning Consonant Sound), Reversed (where the Syllable-Beginning Consonant Sound is more likely to be Accentuated more than the Syllable-End Consonant Sound), or Suspended (where Syllable-End and Syllable-Beginning Consonant Sounds are likely to be equally Accentuated).

Recall the metaphor of the teeter-totter for a Syllable. Imagine that you are standing closer to one end as you look at it. From this vantage point, if the teeter-totter were to be tilted downward on the far end because the heavier child is sitting on that end, it would represent the typical Syllable in which the Syllable-End Consonant is more Accentuated. The tilt toward the far end is indicative of conformity with the Consonant Accentuation Principle – i.e., where it is Upheld – as occurs when the Syllable-End Consonant Sound is more Accentuated than the Syllable-Beginning Consonant Sound. The teeter-totter may also hang in balance, without any tilt, as when a child of equal weight is sitting on the two ends. This symbolizes a situation where the Consonant Accentuation Principle is Suspended, as occurs when the Accentuation of the Beginning and End Consonant Sounds are equal. It is also possible that the teeter-totter may be tilted down at the front end as it would if the heavier child were seated closer to you. This symbolizes a situation where the Consonant Accentuation Principle is Reversed, as occurs when the Syllable-Beginning Consonant is more Accentuated than the Syllable-End Consonant. All of these scenarios are possible, but it is because the first scenario is manifested more often than the other two scenarios that the Consonant Accentuation Principle is useful as a guide for those learning the American Accent. It is one of two fundamental Principles that distinguish the American Accent from the British Accent. It explains the way the majority of words are pronounced across the vocabulary.

The Accentuation differential between the Syllable-Beginning and Syllable-End Consonant Sounds leads to the Consonant Accentuation Principle being either "Upheld", "Suspended" or "Reversed".

Words with a Consonant Sound of High level Intrinsic Accentuation in the End-Consonant position with a Consonant Sound of Low level Intrinsic Accentuation in the Beginning Consonant position will likely be vocalized in way that Upholds the Consonant Accentuation Principle. E.g., as in the words, "Lob" and "Moat".

Words with a Consonant Sound of High level Intrinsic Accentuation in the Syllable-Beginning Consonant position and a Consonant Sound of Low level Intrinsic Accentuation in the Syllable-End Consonant Position will likely be vocalized in way that is a Reverse of the Consonant Accentuation Principle. E.g., as in the words, "Ball" or "Dam".

Words with Consonant Sounds of equal Intrinsic Accentuation levels in the Syllable-Beginning and Syllable-End Consonant positions, will again likely be vocalized in a way that Upholds the Consonant Accentuation Principle (though equally Accentuated Syllable-Beginning and Syllable-End Consonants are also a possibility) because of the effect of Positional Accentuation. E.g. as in "Son" and "Ran".

Just as the Consonant Accentuation Principle is described as a difference in certain pronunciation features that fundamentally separates the American Accent from the British, it is worth recalling here the other fundamental differentiating principle of the American Accent – The American Syllabication Principle. Together, these two Principles account for a large proportion of the observable differences in the way words are pronounced when comparing the American Accent with the British Accent.

Remember: The American Syllabication Principle states that Syllables usually begin with Consonants and end with Vowels (when the spelling of the word permits).

How the concepts of Accentuation were developed:

I first conceived of the American Consonant Accentuation Principle after observing that Syllable-End Consonant Sounds tend to be more Accentuated than Syllable-Beginning Consonant Sounds in the American Accent. This is atypical in the British Accent.

As the American Consonant Accentuation Principle applies to a majority of words, but not all, it became necessary to understand when and why it holds up and when and why it does not.

I recognized then that different Consonant Sounds are Accentuated at different levels at least partly because they have different properties (named Inherent Attributes). Some are naturally Accentuated at a higher level than others. This was how the concept of Intrinsic Accentuation was developed.

This too was not sufficient as an explanation, because it was clear that the Accentuation level of Consonant Sounds were different when they were observed stand alone and when in different positions of a Syllable in a word. A force that adjusted Intrinsic Accentuation was obviously at work – one that had an Accentuation increasing effect on Consonant Sounds when in Syllable-End positions and a decreasing effect when in Syllable-Beginning positions.

Before I could finalize these concepts, I tested them in a random sample of words, to see if they worked. I found the effect of Positional Accentuation on the Intrinsic Accentuation of Consonant Sounds in different Syllable positions enabled graded adjustment of Consonant Accentuation in a way that was consistent with the American Accent.

This test also confirmed that the American Consonant Accentuation Principle prevailed in a good majority of the words studied, while also confirming that when Intrinsic Accentuation was sufficiently great to offset Positional Accentuation in a modest minority of the words, it did not. It thereby affirmed the value of the Consonant Accentuation Principle both as a principle that distinguishes the American Accent, and as a general guide for learning it.

The following, in this box, is not required to speak the American way. It provides additional linguistic insight for those interested.

Features of the American Accent that provide traction for the Consonant Accentuation Principle:

More strongly Accentuated Syllable-End Consonants, as stated in the Consonant Accentuation Principle, are supported by certain common, distinctive features of the American Accent:

-Extension of certain Syllable-End Consonants – support the premise of the Consonant Accentuation Principle.

Extensions of Syllable-End Consonant Sounds commonly occur in the American Accent. This seems to bolster Accentuation of the Syllable-End Consonant, in support of the Consonant Accentuation Principle. E.g. The Extended 'F' sound in “Staff”, the 'S' sound in “Class”, the 'TH' in “Both”, the 'N' in “Phone”, the 'N' in “Sun” are examples of words which exhibit an Extension of the End-Consonant Sound. By contrast, the British tend to complete their Syllable-End Consonants more abruptly.

-Certain Vowel Modulations preceding the Syllable-End Consonants – complement the premise of the Consonant Accentuation Principle.

The Extension and Repetition Modulation of the Soft Vowel form that often precedes a Syllable-End Consonant Sound seems to support the Consonant Accentuation Principle, as in the Soft form of 'A' in “Man”, or the Soft form of 'E' in “Bed”. So too does the Extension Modulation, as in the 'A' Long form, in “Garage”, or the 'O' Hard form in “Phone”.

Features of the American Accent that compromise the Consonant Accentuation Principle:

The Consonant Accentuation Principle is Reversed with some regularity, but for a large proportion of words, it prevails.

The main condition that counters manifestation of the Consonant Accentuation Principle occurs when Intrinsic Accentuation of the Syllable-Beginning Consonant significantly exceeds that of the Syllable-End Consonant.

E.g., in the word “Ball”, the Beginning Consonant 'B', with the Pop Light Attribute with High level Intrinsic Accentuation is paired with the End Consonant 'L', with Low level Intrinsic Accentuation, the Consonant Accentuation Principle is reversed.

Table:
Consonant Position Accentuation Norms.

The Table below crystallizes how Accentuation of Consonant Sounds occurs in American Pronunciation when positioned in the context of a Syllable. This is how Consonant Sounds are Accentuated after the impact of Positional Accentuation on a Consonant Sound's Intrinsic Accentuation.

Introductory Notes:
Note 1. The norms in this Table indicate expected Accentuation levels of Consonant Sounds in the American Accent.
Note 2: Consonant Accentuation is the consequence of both Intrinsic Accentuation and Positional Accentuation. Intrinsic Accentuation comes from the Inherent Attributes of a distinct Consonant Sound. Positional Accentuation is an increasing or decreasing effect on Intrinsic Accentuation that depends on a Consonant's position in a Syllable. Separate scales are used to quantify the level of Accentuation and Intrinsic Accentuation. On the Accentuation scale, the different levels are: Weak, Weak to moderate, Moderate to strong and Strong. On the Intrinsic Accentuation scale, the different levels are: Low, Medium & High. The levels of the two scales correspond as follows: Weak and Weak to Moderate Accentuation corresponds with Low Intrinsic Accentuation; Moderate to strong Accentuation with Medium Intrinsic Accentuation, and Strong Accentuation with High Intrinsic Accentuation. Positional Accentuation does not have its own scale but its effect is seen on the Accentuation scale. The increasing or decreasing effect of Positional Accentuation depends on the position of a Consonant Sound in a Syllable. To Accentuate Consonant Sounds the American way: Recognize the Intrinsic Accentuation of the particular Consonant Sound, whether Low, Medium or High. See Appendix III. B for the Table: "Consonant Sounds and their Inherent Attributes". If the Consonant Sound is at the end of the Syllable, or adjacent to the end, the Accentuation level will tend to be greater than its corresponding Intrinsic Accentuation level. If at Syllable beginning, or adjacent to the beginning, it will tend to be less. However, A Consonant Sound of High Intrinsic Accentuation cannot be higher than the maximum of the Accentuation scale, i.e. Strong. A Consonant Sound of Low Intrinsic Accentuation cannot be lower than the minimum of the Accentuation scale, i.e. Weak. The amount of impact is most likely one or two levels though no impact is also possible.
Note 3: The Inherent Attributes that produce: High Intrinsic Accentuation are: Pop Light, Pop Heavy, and Sharp. Medium Intrinsic Accentuation are: Flat, Hiss, Knock, Rasp and Vowelish. Low Intrinsic Accentuation are: Buzz, Hum, Lilting and Nasal.

Position of Consonant in Syllable	Accentuation Norm
Beginning.	The Beginning Consonant tends to exhibit Weak to moderate Accentuation for most Consonant Sounds. However, a Consonant with High Intrinsic Accentuation could exhibit Moderate to strong Accentuation.
End.	The End Consonant tends to exhibit Moderate to strong, or, Strong Accentuation. However, a Consonant with Low Intrinsic Accentuation could exhibit Weak to moderate Accentuation.
Middle. (See Note B below).	When a Middle Consonant is adjacent to an End Consonant, it tends to be Accentuated at either Moderate to strong, or, Strong Accentuation levels. When it is adjacent to a Beginning Consonant, it tends to be Accentuated at either Weak to moderate, or, at Moderate to strong levels.
Exceptions: 'H', 'W' and 'Y'.	Unlike other Consonants, 'H', 'W' and 'Y': -tend to be Accentuated at an increased level (Moderate to strong or Strong) in the Syllable-Beginning position or immediately adjacent to a Consonant in a Syllable-Beginning position. And, -at a decreased level (Weak to moderate, or Weak), when in the Syllable-End position or immediately adjacent to a Consonant in the Syllable-End position.

Supporting Notes:

A. The Consonant Accentuation Principle is bolstered by factors such as:

-preceding Single Vowel Modulations (Extension, or Extension and Repetition), e.g. as in “Mole” {mO'L'e*} (Extension) and “Cab” {c1*(K)(h)a"B} (Extension and Repetition);

-the American tendency to extend many Syllable-End Consonant Sounds, e.g. as in “Staff” {staF'f*}, “Class” {c1laS's*}, “Both” {BO'TH'}, “Phone” {phO'N'} and “Sum” {su1'M'};

-Inherent Attributes of High Intrinsic Accentuation when associated with Syllable-End Consonants, e.g. as in “Map” {ma"P}, “Lab” {la"B} and “Red” {re"D};

-Inherent Attributes of Low Intrinsic Accentuation when associated with Syllable-Beginning Consonants, e.g. as in “Late” {1AT(h)'} and “Man” {ma"N};

-The Hiss sound, {(h)} that often occurs after many Consonant Sounds can elevate their Accentuation, e.g. 'CH' {[ch]}1 which by itself has a Medium Level of Intrinsic Accentuation (with its Flat Inherent Attribute), when coupled with the Hiss, as in “Champ” {[CH]1(h)a'mP}, has Moderate to strong rather than Weak to moderate Accentuation, but in a word such as “Bachelor” {Ba-[ch]1e1-lo1R} where it is not – it exhibits Weak to moderate Accentuation.

It can be offset or reversed when:

-Inherent Attributes of High Intrinsic Accentuation are associated with certain Syllable-Beginning Consonants, e.g. as with 'D' in “Deaf” {De'a*F'}, 'P' in “Pale” {P(h)A'le*} and 'B' in “Bean” {BE'a*n'};

-Inherent Attributes of Low Intrinsic Accentuation associated with certain Syllable-End Consonants, e.g. as in 'L' in “Fall” {fa*oL'l*}, 'M' in “Drum” {dru1m'} and 'S' in “Rose” {rO's'e*}.

B. What is a Middle Consonant? A “Middle Consonant” in this Course refers to a Consonant that is not in a ^Syllable-Beginning or Syllable-End Position and which has a separately distinguishable Consonant Sound.

A Middle Consonant is usually one that is located next to a Syllable-Beginning or Syllable-End Consonant when it contains a separately identifiable sound that #Links to the sound of the preceding or following

Consonant in the same Syllable (e.g. 'T' in the word “Star”, or 'R' in the word “Farm”). But, when a Consonant next to a Syllable-Beginning or Syllable-End Consonant [%]Merges with the preceding or following Consonant, it becomes part of a Syllable-Beginning Consonant Sound or Syllable-End Consonant Sound and is not therefore a Middle Consonant as referred to in this Course (e.g. 'H' in the word “Ship” or in the word “Fish”).

Many Consonants in words with Vowels before and after them seem to be Middle Consonants but are usually Beginning Consonants. In the American Accent, a Pause usually separates a mid-word Consonant Sound from a preceding Vowel Sound which in fact makes it a Syllable-Beginning Consonant Sound. As can be seen in the following examples, none of the mid-word Consonant Sounds are actually Syllable-Middle Consonants: E.g., “Amity” {A-mi.ty}, “Elephant” {E-le-phant}, “Olive” {O-live}, “Idea” {I-dea} and “Union” {U-nion}.

Footnotes:

[^]The word Syllable refers to the way Americans form Syllables. The American Syllabication Principle holds: When possible, Syllables begin with a Consonant and end with a Vowel.

[#]Successive Consonants with separate Consonant Sounds that follow each other without the separation of a Pause, are referred to as Linked Consonants.

[%]Successive Consonants with a unified sound are referred to as Merged Consonants.

C. A few other Specific Exceptions to the Consonant Accentuation Position Norms to recognize:

1. The Consonant 'G' when at the end of a Syllable and coupled with 'N' in words like “Ring”, “Sing” or “Thing”, is Weak to moderately Accentuated. And, in a Syllable-Middle position when preceding an 'N' in the same Syllable, as in “Align”, “Resign” or “Sign”, it is Silent.
2. The Consonant 'N' in a Middle Syllable position, when combined with 'G' or 'K' at the end of a Syllable in words like “Ring”, “Song”, “Ink” or “Think”, is Weakly Accentuated with just the Nasal Inherent Attribute. In popular American English, an 'N' is Accentuated at a Weak to moderate level in a Syllable-End position when it precedes a 'T' beginning the next Syllable, as in certain words like “En-ter”, “Cen-ter” and “Ren-ter”. (These very same type of words are also articulated in a second popular way with the 'N' becoming the first Consonant Sound after the Pause and the 'T' Silent, as in “E-nter”, “Ce-nter” and “Re-nter”. Pronounced this way also, the 'N' is Accentuated at a Weak to moderate level, but as it is in a Syllable-Beginning position here, it is consistent with American Consonant Accentuation Position Norms.)
3. The Consonant 'T' in a Syllable-Middle position may be Weakly Accentuated as in words like “Eats”, “Dates”, “Kites” and “Rights”.
4. There are a number of Consonants which in certain exceptional or very infrequent cases take on a Silent form. These are identified in Note C of the Table: Consonant Sounds and their Inherent Attributes in Appendix III. B.

D. The Norms given above are categorical, yet flexible. They allow for a degree of latitude. Correct pronunciation could span adjacent Accentuation levels without being wrong.

E. Positional Accentuation in the American Accent explains many of the differences between the American and British Accents. There are also basic differences in the Inherent Attributes of several Consonant Sounds between the two Accents which produce differences in articulation.

See Table: Scripting Conventions Applied: Phonetic Symbols For Consonant Sounds & Sequences in Appendix III. C.

Section: Distinctive Consonant Sounds in the American Accent

As many as 53 distinct Consonant Sounds have been identified for spoken English. These correspond with 79 Consonants and Merged Consonant sequences encountered in written English. These Consonant Sounds are associated with certain positions within a Syllable, i.e. Syllable-End, Syllable-Beginning or Syllable-Middle positions – some with only a particular position, some with two particular positions and some with all three positions. Appendix III. B lists the 79 Consonants and Consonant Sequences with their corresponding 53 Consonant Sounds. The word examples provided are indicative of the different Syllable positions in which such Consonant Sounds may be found. Of all the Consonant Sounds listed, some are distinctive of the American Accent.

Consonant Sounds in different Accents vary or are distinctive in terms of the following characteristics:

-their Inherent Attributes,
-their Accentuation levels when in a Syllable, and,
-whether the Consonant Sound exhibits or does not exhibit Extension.

The truly distinctive Consonant Sounds are those that differ in their Inherent Attributes as articulated in the American Accent when compared with the British Accent or an Accent in the British tradition.

> E.g. The 'R' in Syllable-End and Middle positions in the American Accent has the Rasp Inherent Attribute e.g. as in words like “Car” and “Farm”. In the British Accent, the 'R' in the same Syllable positions are silent (the preceding Vowel is an 'A' Long that is extended). In the Australian Accent, the 'R' in these positions exhibits a vibration that is closer to the Buzz Inherent Attribute than the Rasp Inherent Attribute. The Australian way of speaking is in the British Accent tradition, though the Consonant Sound associated with their 'R' may require the specification of an additional Inherent Attribute.

In addition to differences in Inherent Attributes, these distinctive Consonant Sounds may also differ in terms of the other characteristics mentioned above.

Some other Consonant Sounds also identified as different are not truly distinctive of the American Accent as they contrast from the British only in terms of Accentuation level and in terms of the presence or absence of the Extension modulation – not in terms of their Inherent Attributes.

The most distinctive and different Consonant Sounds are separately presented in tables below. Use these Tables to identify the Consonant Sounds that are articulated differently in the American and the British Accent. To speak the American way, compare how you articulate these Consonant sounds in your own Accent and then, make changes to adopt the American characteristics, while dropping those that characterize other Accents.

It is important to first recall how the American and British Accents differ in terms of the two fundamental Principles which separate them, before progressing to the tables ahead.

> Reminder Note:
> The American and British Accents diverge on two fundamental Principles which account for many of the specific differences between them. These are:
>
> -The American Syllabication Principle, and,
> -The Consonant Accentuation Principle.

Note on Positional Accentuation In the British Accent:

In the British Accent, there is often a Positional Accentuation effect that runs counter to Positional Accentuation in the American Accent.

> Relative to the Intrinsic Accentuation level of a Consonant Sound, the British Accent appears to tend toward increased Accentuation of a Consonant Sound at the beginning of a Syllable and decreased Accentuation of a Consonant Sound at the end of a Syllable.
>
> This counter effect in the British Accent may not occur with the same magnitude or consistency that Positional Accentuation exhibits in the American Accent.

Explanatory Note:
Though the American and British Accents pull in different directions with regard to Positional Accentuation, they are not mirror opposites. In addition, Syllabication happens differently in the two Accents as we have seen:

> The American Accent begins Syllables when possible with a Consonant and ends them with a Vowel. The British Accent more often begins Syllables with a Vowel and ends them with a Consonant, but there is greater variation.

So, a Beginning Consonant for the American Accent may be an End Consonant for the British Accent.

> E.g. 'L', in the word “Relate”, is the Syllable-Beginning Consonant of the second Syllable for the American Accent but is the Syllable-End Consonant of the first Syllable in the British Accent.

As Americans tend to decrease Intrinsic Accentuation of a Consonant Sound in Syllable-Beginning positions and the British tend to decrease Accentuation of a Consonant Sound in Syllable-End positions, the 'L' in the example “Relate” above, is decreased in both Accents. Yet, as the 'L' is actually located in different Syllables, the word as a whole is differently pronounced in the two Accents. In the American Accent, despite Weak Accentuation, it may seem as if it is more Accentuated because it follows a Pause. In the British Accent, because it is located at the end of a Syllable, its reduced Accentuation is more obvious.

> The 'R' Consonant in the same word, “Relate”, which begins the first Syllable is Accentuated at a lower level in the American Accent and at a higher level in the British Accent.

Table:
The Most Distinctive American Consonant Sounds

Note: The C. No. is a reference to the number assigned to a Consonant Sound in the Table: “Inherent Attributes of Consonant Sounds” (Appendix III. B.). Both the Consonant Sound and the Syllable position refer to the American Accent. These could be different in the British Accent.

C. No.	Consonant Sound	Position in Syllable	Example Words.	American Accent	British Accent
31	'M' as in “Him”.	End.	Name, Dome,	Moderate to	Weak to moderate.

			Room, Plum, Sam.	strong. Hum, Lilting, Nasal. Extended.	Hum.
31	'M' as in "Lamp".	Middle.	Clamp, Limp, Tramp, Thump, Limp.	Weak to moderate. Hum, Lilting, Nasal.	Weak. Hum.
34	'N' as in "Can" or "Pen".	End.	Fan, Van, Ten, Been, Soon, Tune.	Strong. Nasal, Hum, Knock, Lilting. Extended.	Moderate to strong. Hum, Knock.
35	'N' as in "Can't".	Middle (Toward End).	Land, Bend, Tent, Went, Wind.	Weak to moderate. Nasal, Hum, Lilting.	Moderate to strong. Knock.
36	'N' as in "Plane".	End.	Clean, Main, Phone, Rain, Tone.	Strong. Knock, Hum, Nasal.	Moderate to strong. Knock, Hum.
36	'N' as in "Lunch".	Middle (Toward End).	Bench, Lunge, Crunch, Cringe, Fringe.	Weak to moderate. Knock, Hum, Nasal.	Moderate to strong. Knock, Hum.
50	'R' as in "Car".	End.	Car, Her, Were, O-ver, Stir.	Strong. Rasp.	Silent.
50	'R' as in "Mart".	Middle (Toward End).	Barn, Cart, Farm, Mart, Learn, Stern.	Moderate to strong. Rasp.	Silent.
60	'T' as in "Bits", "Melts" or "Kites".	Middle (Toward End).	Cats, Eats, Lets, Sits, Writes.	Weak to moderate. Knock.	Moderate to strong. Sharp, Knock.
61	'T' as in "Center~" or "Later".	Beginning (Other than first Syllable).	Ca-ter, En-ter, Win-ter, Ren-ter.	Weak to moderate. Knock, Pop Heavy.	Strong. Knock, Sharp. Hiss from Linked 'H' sound.

Note: On Nasality.
While several 'N' associated Consonant Sounds are popularly articulated with the Nasal Inherent Attribute in the American Accent, some Americans also produce nasal sounds even when the 'N' is absent. Some Americans may even articulate words like "Have", "Hospital" and "Ask" with a nasal overtone associated with the first Vowel. This effect does not prevail across most American Accents, and is also not Standard.

Note on 'N'.
The 'N' has six different Consonant Sounds which are distinguished from one another in terms of specific combinations of up to four Inherent Attributes. Of them, one has all four and one has only a single Inherent Attribute. Two of the five Consonant Sounds located in Syllable-End (as in "Can", "Pen" or "When") and Syllable-Middle (as in "Can't", "Bend" or "Lens") positions have the Nasal and Lilting Attributes which are not heard in the British Accent (– these two Consonant Sounds also have other Inherent Attributes).

There is a particular 'N' Consonant Sound at the end of a Syllable, often preceding a 'T' beginning the next Syllable, as in words like "Enter" {En-ter} and "Center" {Cen-ter}, which has only the Hum and Nasal Inherent Attributes. It is Accentuated at a Weak to Moderate level on the Accentuation scale though it is positioned at the end of a Syllable. This 'N' is contrary to Consonant Position Accentuation Norms which has an Accentuation increasing effect for most Consonant Sounds when toward a Syllable-End position. There is another popular option for pronouncing such words. Here, the Pause occurs before the 'N' with the 'T' Silent. Vocalized in a Syllable-Beginning position, it exhibits the Hum and Knock Inherent Attributes, losing the Nasal Inherent Attribute. And, in this Syllable position, it is Accentuated at a Weak to moderate level consistent with Consonant Position Accentuation Norms. (See Table, "Consonant Position Accentuation Norms" in the preceding Section. Also, see the Table, "Consonant Sounds and their Inherent Attributes" (Appendix III. B)).

An 'N' Consonant Sound heard at the beginning of a Syllable always has the Knock Inherent Attribute. The Knock is also often but not always a characteristic of 'N' associated Consonant Sounds in the Syllable-End position. However, the Knock Inherent Attribute is missing from the different 'N' Consonant Sounds associated with Middle Syllable positions. See the Table, "Consonant Sounds and their Inherent Attributes" (Appendix III. B).

Except for the type of 'N' in the paragraph immediately below, the Hum Inherent Attribute is common to all other 'N' associated Consonant Sounds.

Often, when the 'N' precedes the letters, 'C' as in "Rancor" {Ranc-or} or "Uncle" {Unc-le}, 'G' as in "Ring" {Ring} or "Bangle" {Bang-le}, 'G' as in "Binge" {Binge}, 'K' as in "Drink" {Drink} or "Sink-er" {Sink-er}, 'CH' as in "Lunch" {Lunch}, and 'X' as in "Lynx" {Lynx} – where no Pause intervenes between them – it exhibits only the Nasal Attribute with Weak Accentuation, regardless of its position toward the end of the Syllable. This type of 'N' is also contrary to Consonant Position Accentuation Norms which have an Accentuation increasing effect for most Consonant Sounds when toward a Syllable-End position. (See Table, "Consonant Position Accentuation Norms" in the preceding Section. Also, see the Table, "Consonant Sounds and their Inherent Attributes". (Appendix III. B).)

The 'N' Consonant Sound above is not identical to another distinct 'N' Consonant Sound in words like "Dance" {Da*n*ce}, "Romance" {Ro-ma*n*ce}, "Bend" {Be*n*d}, "Lens" {Le*n*s}, "Hand" {Ha*n*d}, "Land" {La*n*d}, "Tent" {Te*n*t} or "Went" {We*n*t}. This 'N' possesses Nasal, Hum and Lilting Inherent Attributes. Though all three of its Inherent Attributes (Nasal, Hum and Lilting) are characterized by a Low level of Intrinsic Accentuation, when paired with a second Consonant as in these examples, they exhibit only a slightly increased Weak to moderate Positional Accentuation relative to their Low Intrinsic Accentuation level, remaining on the lower side of the Positional Accentuation scale. This is so notwithstanding its position towards the end of the Syllable in contradiction to the Consonant Position Accentuation Norms which indicate increased Accentuation for most Consonant Sounds when toward a Syllable-End position. (See Table, "Consonant Position Accentuation Norms" in the preceding Section. Also, see also the Table, "Consonant Sounds and their Inherent Attributes". (Appendix III. B).

Note on 'R'.
According to Historical Linguistics, most English spoken used to be "Rhotic", where the 'R' at the end of words or towards the end of words (or Syllables – my addition) was audible, as in American English. According to this view, a transition began to occur in certain parts of Britain

where the 'R' weakened to the point that it was no longer vocalized, i.e. becoming non-Rhotic. Sometime between circa 1740 and circa 1770 this change was completed in parts of Southern Britain, including around London. Yet, there remained large swathes of Britain where English continued to be Rhotic. America too remained Rhotic almost in its entirety, except for a few enclaves in North Eastern port cities, influenced by the change in Britain. Overtime, these small non Rhotic niches faded away, as British influence decreased and as America's distinct identity continued to develop.
(Wikipedia, Retrieved 2016. *Rhoticity in English.*
https://en.m.wikipedia.org/wiki/Rhoticity_in_english).

Both American and British Accents exhibit some "Rasp" as with the abrasive sound of a file on wood, when articulating the 'R' in certain positions in a Syllable. With the American Accent it is heard more strongly when the 'R' is located at the end of a Syllable or is adjacent to the Syllable-End Consonant, whereas it is minimally articulated when in a Syllable-Beginning position or adjacent to a Syllable-Beginning position. By contrast, in the British Accent, the Rasp is more pronounced when in a Syllable-Beginning position or next to it; whereas, at the end or toward the end of a Syllable, it is either inaudible or nearly so.

Another point to be alert to: Both American and British English Accents do not exhibit a roll in the 'R'. When changing to speaking the American way, try to identify and remove roll if any. Roll is heard in a number of Indo-European languages from French to Hindi and it can be unconsciously imported from those languages to spoken English.

The American 'R' sound has a customary low tone, produced by an opening or widening of the throat, as it is articulated. It is possible that the frequent occurrence of 'R' in words – is a factor in causing a lowering of tone across American speech as a whole. It is as if the tone of other letters are lowered by being pegged to the low tone of the 'R'. This could be a root cause of the lower tone characterizing spoken American English.

Note on 'S'.
Dictionaries show that there are several words with a 'Z' sound, spelled with either an 'S' or a 'Z' in British English that are always spelled with a 'Z' in American English. The word "Realize" is an example. The British spell it either with an 'S' or a 'Z', but always pronounce it with the 'Z' sound. The Americans always spell the word "Realize" with a 'Z', and pronounce it consistently with the 'Z' sound. This is another illustration of how British English tends to be less phonetic than the American. The word "Organization" is another such word.

Note on 'T'. There is a particular 'T' Consonant Sound, that is characteristic of the American Accent, heard at the beginning of a Syllable other than the first, as in words like "Enter" {En-ter} and "Center" {Cen-ter}, with a sound that merges 'T' and 'D' Consonant Sounds. It is one of the few Consonant Sounds that is always Accentuated at the bottom of the Accentuation scale: Weak.

(Only the specific Vowel and Consonant Sounds under discussion are Scripted within the curly brackets in this paragraph.) Other than after an 'N' and a Pause, as in the example of "Enter" above, this Merged 'T' and 'D' sound follows a Soft Vowel form and a Pause, as in e.g. "Saturday" {Sa-t2*([td})ur-day}, "Petal" {Pe-t2*([td])al}, "Little" {Li-t2*([td])t*le} or "Italy" {I-t2*([td])a-ly}, "Cottage" {Co'-t2*([td])t*age} and "Putting" {Pu-t2*([td])t*ing}. It is also similarly often heard after a Hard Vowel form and a Pause, as in e.g. "Cater" {CA-t2*([td])er}, "Meter" {ME-t2*([td])er}, "Mighty" {MI-t2*([td])y}, "Total" {TO-t2*([td])al} and "Reputed"

{Re-pU-t2*([td])ed}. It may also be heard after the 'O' Long form and 'U' Long form as in e.g. "Rooted" {Ro2o*-t2*([td])ed" and "Duty" {Du2-t2*([td])y} and after the Short Vowel form of 'U', as in. "Butter" {Bu1-t2*([td])t*er}. In all these cases, it is always Accentuated at the bottom of the Accentuation scale: Weak.

Though the Inherent Attributes of the Merged 'T' and 'D' Consonant Sound are Pop Heavy (High Intrinsic Accentuation) and Knock (Medium Intrinsic Accentuation), together implying High Intrinsic Accentuation, in a Syllable-Beginning position (see the two paragraphs above) the Accentuation exhibited is at the very bottom of the Accentuation scale, i.e. Weak. While Consonant Position Accentuation Norms do indicate decreased Accentuation in this Syllable position, this is a decrease of larger than expected magnitude.

For explanation of the phonetic Scripting, see Table: Vocal Fidelity Phonetic System: Scripting Conventions for Consonant Sounds (Appendix I.C), and for specific detail on Symbols, see Table: Scripting Conventions Applied: Phonetic Symbols for Consonant Sounds & Sequences (Appendix III. C).

The amount of 'D' heard when the 'T' and 'D' merge, as in the examples above, varies between American Accents and speakers, with the sound most closely resembling the British Accent when the sound of the 'D' is at its lowest or even absent. Typically, some amount of 'D' is heard in words such as those cited above, in the American Accent.

Section:
Less Different American Consonant Sounds

The Consonant Sounds listed in the Table below are different but not distinctive as they are similar in American and British Accents in terms of their Inherent Attributes. The differences are found only in Consonant Accentuation and Modulation. As these Consonant Sounds are associated with Syllable Positions, if you are applying American Consonant Accentuation Norms to the way you articulate them, you will already be articulating them the American way. The additional adjustment may then only be to Extend some of the Consonant Sounds as shown, for the Consonant Sounds in Syllable-End positions.

Asterisks flagging certain Consonant and Consonant sequences below are intended as an alert to a particular Accent within the British tradition i.e. English as spoken in India. A characteristic "Hiss from a Linked 'H' sound", associated with certain Consonant Sounds i.e. 'C', 'K', 'P' and 'T" (when not in a Middle position in a Syllable) present in both the American and the mainstream British Accents, is typically absent in the Indian English Accent. Also, in this Accent, the Buzz Inherent Attribute associated with the Consonant Sound 'TH' as in "Them" (at the beginning of a Syllable) or in "Bathe" (at the end of a Syllable) is also left out. These characteristics would need to be added by those with this Accent to close this divide.

Table:
Less Different American Consonant Sounds

Note. The C. No. Column Title in the first Column is a reference to the number assigned to a Consonant Sound in the Table: "Inherent Attributes of Consonant Sounds". Both the Consonant Sound and the Syllable position refer to the American Accent. These could be different in the British Accent.

C. No.	Consonant Sound	Position in Syllable	Example Words.	American Accent	British Accent
2*	'C' as in "Cat".	Beginning.	Can, Cat, Caper,	Moderate to	Strong. Sharp;

			Cod, Could, Cover.	strong. Sharp; Hiss.	Hiss.
3	'C' as in "Pact" or "Detect".	Beginning. Middle (Toward End).	Fact, Tract, Elect, Collect, Select, Secret, Vacant.	Moderate to strong. Sharp.	Strong. Sharp.
16	'F' as in "Safe".	End.	Half, Leaf, Reef, Relief, Stuff.	Strong. Hiss. Extended.	Moderate to strong. Hiss.
16	'F' as in "Left".	Middle.	Raft, Deft, Shift, Loft.	Strong. Hiss. Extended.	Moderate to strong. Hiss.
26*	'K' as in "Kin".	Beginning.	Kate, Keep, Kitten, Pi-cket.	Moderate to strong. Sharp; Hiss.	Strong. Sharp; Hiss.
28	'L' as in "Lamp" or "Melon".	Beginning.	Lamp, Live, Ca-len-dar, Sai-lor.	Weak. Hum.	Moderate to strong. Hum.
29	'L' as in "Sale", "File" or "Tell".	Middle (Toward End), End.	A-pple, Ball, Belt, Girl, Meal, Milled, Sale.	Moderate to strong. Hum, Lilting. Extended.	Weak to moderate. Hum, Lilting.
45*	'P' as in "Pat".	Beginning.	Pat, Paste, Peg, Pin, Pure, Pull.	Moderate to strong. Pop Light; Hiss.	Strong. Pop Light; Hiss.
52	'S' as in "Case".	End.	Case, Crease, Boss, Class, Lease.	Strong. Hiss. Extended.	Moderate to strong. Hiss.
52	'S' as in "Coast".	Middle (Toward End).	Flask, Mist, Post, Roast, Must, Risk, Wrist.	Moderate to strong. Hiss. Extended.	Moderate to strong. Hiss.
58*	'T' as in "Tom".	Beginning.	Tab, Ten, Tip, Toast, Tug. Knock.	Moderate to strong. Sharp; Knock; Hiss.	Strong. Sharp; Knock; Hiss.
66	'TH' as in "Math".	End.	Both, Growth, North, South, Sloth, Tooth.	Strong. Hiss. Extended.	Moderate to strong. Hiss.
67*	'TH' as in "Them", "Those" or "Leather".	Beginning.	The, Than, This, These, Them, Then, Those, Leather, Brother, Mother, Weather.	Weak to moderate. Buzz; Flat.	Moderate to strong. Buzz; Flat.
68	'TH' as in "Bathe" or 'Loathe".	End.	Clothe, Loath-some.	Strong. Pop Heavy, Flat; Buzz. Extended.	Weak to moderate. Pop Heavy, Flat; Buzz.

Chapter 13:
Plotting your Progress: Traversing the Lanes.

The areas discussed so far, that make the American way of speaking distinctive, are diagrammatically represented below to increase focus on your position with respect to each of them. You can think of each area as a competency in which progress needs to be made as you shift toward speaking the American way. You can estimate your starting position on the scale (line) with a mark and periodically reassess your current position with respect to each area. You can also use this scale later for Vocal Patterns (to be explained ahead).

Lane 1: Articulating Syllables. (The gist: Beginning Syllables with a Consonant and ending them on a Vowel Sound; articulating the latter Syllables as strongly or more strongly than the former; articulating the last letter of each word).

From this end.
(More the British way).

To this End.
(More the American way).

Plot your position periodically on the scale (line) below with the date.

0%--50%--100%

E.g.^
Date:
Estimated Starting Position.

Date:
Estimated Current Position.

Lane 2: Tempo. (The gist: Clubbing Syllable into parts as in the American way).

From this end.
(More the British way).

To this End.
(More the American way).

Plot your position periodically on the scale (line) below with the date.

0%--50%--100%

E.g.^
Date:
Estimated Starting Position.

Date:
Estimated Current Position.

Lane 3: Other Characteristics. (The gist: Using your vocal apparatus to speak at a deeper tone; powering the voice with more airflow; maintaining a low tone within words and across sentences).

From this end.
(More the British way).

To this End.
(More the American way).

Plot your position periodically on the scale (line) below with the date.

0%--50%--100%

E.g.^
Date:
Estimated Starting Position.

Date:
Estimated Current Position.

Lane 4: Alphabetic Sounds. (The gist: Articulating Vowel Sounds with proper Modulation, and Consonant Sounds with proper Modulation, Accentuation and Inherent Attributes).

From this end.
(More the British way).

To this End.
(More the American way).

Plot your position periodically on the scale (line) below with the date.

0%--50%---100%

E.g.^
Date:
Estimated Starting Position.

Date:
Estimated Current Position.

For Later: The Vocal Pattern Bridge, the Inland Table and the Summit Table.

From this end.
(More the British way).

To this End.
(More the American way).

Plot your position periodically on the scale (line) below with the date.

0%--50%---100%

E.g.^
Date:
Estimated Starting Position.

Date:
Estimated Current Position.

PART 3:
VOCAL PATTERNS IN AMERICAN ENGLISH.

Chapter 14:
Vocal Patterns: Recurring Vowel Consonant Sequences.

In addition to individual Vowel and Consonant Sounds which influence an Accent, another phonetic component, i.e. recurring vocal sequences forming integrated units of Vowel and Consonant sounds, contribute significantly to the shaping of an Accent. Any speaker of English will recognize that there are integrated vocal sequences that recur as components of different words, some that occur more often and others less so. These are Vocal Patterns. Recognizing how Distinctive Vocal Patterns are vocalized is essential for comprehensive Accent learning.

Imagine, a net being cast over spoken English, drawing out, (like different fish caught in a net), all the recurring sound sequences in the language. This indeed is what was done as part of the development of this Course resulting in a Vocal Pattern Master Table. It comprises most of the recurring sound sequences in spoken American English. The Vocal Pattern Bridge, extracted from the Vocal Pattern Master Table, consists of the most Distinctive sequences or Vocal Patterns vocalized in the American way. It is organized in a way that will enable you to identify which Vocal Patterns you articulate well and those you don't. Once you have done this diagnosis, you will also have created a personal development plan, tailored to your specific learning gaps.

In this course a Vocal Pattern:

- -Is a readily recognizable recurring sound sequence heard in different words.
- -Comprises of at least one Vowel and Consonant Sound.
- -Begins with a Vowel and ends with a Consonant.
- -Contains additional Basic Vocal Elements (explained in the next section).

While different standards are possible for defining what should constitute a Vocal Pattern, it was important that one particular standard be adopted for a consistent approach. The above criteria were good enough to define a Vocal Pattern and to enable a consistent approach. They set conditions for extraction of Vocal Patterns from words. In particular, they specify that each should begin with a Vowel and end with a Consonant. In defining the beginning and end of a Vocal Pattern, they prevented overlap of segments across different Vocal Patterns causing duplication and confusion. It was only after Vocal Patterns were so defined that they could be extracted, individually observed, described and categorized.

Note: To learn an Accent, all the distinctive sound patterns out of which a language is composed need to be identified, so they can be reviewed. This involves an extraction of all the recurring sound sequences in the language using a consistent method. It is rather like trying to separate all repetitive patterns on a printed sheet by drawing boxes around each one, ensuring each one is covered, without any box overlapping any other. Vocal Patterns are defined in a similar way, to extract the recurring sounds from the spoken language while avoiding overlaps and gaps.

Vocal Patterns form the front face of an Accent and so are very noticeable. Awareness of Vocal Patterns is a critical part of learning how to speak in the American Accent. Of course, many individual Vowel and Consonant Sounds also stand out prominently, as previously discussed.

Remember: The Vocal Fidelity Phonetic System developed for this Course enables accurate

Scripting to show how words should be vocalized. It separately covers both Vowel and Consonant Sounds, in depth.

-Vowel Sounds also include Linked and Modulated Vowels.
-Distinctively articulated Vowels and Consonants said the American way have already been described to show how they influence the sound of spoken American English.
E.g. the distinctively articulated 'O' in "Dot", and 'R' in "Farm", are examples of how words with distinctive Vowel and Consonant Sounds make the American Accent distinctive.

Section: The Basic Vocal Elements in Vocal Patterns

A representation of a Vocal Pattern in Vocal Fidelity Phonetic System Script enables the contrast of Accents because it reveals Basic Vocal Elements. They exhibit the characteristics that are unique to different Accents, e.g. the American in contrast to other English Accents. Accents exhibit contrast when they differ from each other in terms of one or more contrasting Basic Vocal Elements.

The Basic Vocal Elements within Vocal Patterns that may be differently articulated in American and other Accents are the following:

-The presence, absence and position of Pauses – Major and Minor (# See Note in box below).
-Vowel forms (Soft, Hard, etc.).
-Single Vowel Modulations (Extension, and, Extension and Repetition Modulations).
-Dual Vowel Modulations (when an External Vowel Sound is inserted into a word, linking to a separate Vowel Sound associated with a Vowel shown in the spelling of the word).
-Consonant Accentuation (Weak, Weak to moderate, Moderate to strong, and, Strong).
-Consonant Extension.
-Consonant Sounds and their Inherent Attributes (Different Consonant Sounds have been identified in terms of their distinctive Inherent Attributes. See Appendix III. B).

In addition to the basic characteristics of the voice, (i.e. Lane 3, covered in Chapter 11), the source of difference between any two English Accents can be found in the above Basic Vocal Elements within a Vocal Pattern.

Course Note: Remember the Symbols used for Pauses:

Dashes, '-', are used to identify relatively longer or Major Pauses. Dots, '.', are used to identify relatively shorter or Minor Pauses.
-In single Syllable words there are no Pauses. Neither dashes nor dots are needed.
-In Di-Syllabic words, only dashes are used to show the single Pause in such words.
-In Multi-Syllabic words, dashes (for Major Pauses) and dots (for Minor Pauses) are used when contrasts are distinguishable.

Reminder Note:
Syllables separated by a Major Pause group together to form a word Part. A Part may consist of one or more Syllables.

Note:
Basic Vocal Elements describe both a Vocal Pattern and its context, i.e. the word components

that may precede and follow it (the prefix and suffix, if any). These can be revealed using the Vocal Fidelity Phonetic System.

When Vocal Patterns are vocalized in different Accents, they exhibit varying degrees of Distinctiveness, depending on the extent of the contrast between Basic Vocal Elements. Distinctiveness may be Great, Substantial, Significant or Insignificant. More follows about this later. To change the way we speak, it is necessary to relearn how to vocalize Vocal Patterns in words true to their Basic Vocal Elements.

Section: Understanding Vocal Patterns

Note: The concept and working definition of a Vocal Pattern may lead a learner to ask why one particular recurring vocal sequence is treated as a Vocal Pattern whereas not another. Answers are provided here so that the learner understands the logic.

How are Vocal Patterns located within words? Can a Vocal Pattern exist within another Vocal Pattern? Can there be more than one Vocal Pattern in a word? Can one Vocal Pattern link to another Vocal Pattern? How do Vocal Patterns relate with the Syllables within a word? The answers to possible questions that you may ask yourself about Vocal Patterns, are given here with examples.

A Vocal Pattern may occur in the middle, end or beginning of a word. A Vocal Pattern in the middle of a word has some letters preceding it, called a Prefix, and some letters following it, called a Suffix. A Vocal Pattern at the end of a word has a Prefix but no Suffix. A Vocal Pattern at the beginning of a word has a Suffix but no Prefix. (Note: the words Prefix and Suffix are given a different meaning in this Course from their general meaning, as it is relative to a Vocal Pattern.)

Transitioning to the American way of speaking is facilitated by identifying and becoming familiar with Distinctive Vocal Patterns.

E.g. The word “And” has elements with distinctive American characteristics. The Extension and Repetition of the 'A' Soft, the Nasality of the 'N' and the greater Accentuation of the 'D' at the Syllable-End position are all distinctive of speaking in the American Accent. The word “Hand”, “Band” and “Sand”, contain the same Vocal Pattern, i.e. 'AND'. The word, “Can't” also shares a common, smaller Vocal Pattern, i.e. 'AN' with the above examples. They all contain the 'A' Soft with an Extension, Linked to a Nasal 'N'.

E.g. the Vocal Pattern 'OUN', as in the words, “Account”, “Mountain”, “Boundary” and “Round”, have the Prefixes 'ACC', 'M', 'B' and 'R' respectively, and the Suffixes, 'T', 'TAIN', 'DARY' and 'D' respectively.

Remember, a Vocal Pattern as defined in this course begins with a Vowel and ends with a Consonant.

A Vocal Pattern may be without either a Prefix or Suffix, without both, or with both.

E.g. The Vocal Pattern 'OUT' in the word “Trout” has a Prefix but no Suffix. The same Vocal Pattern in the word “Outs” has no Prefix, but has the Suffix, 'S'. And, the word “OUT” is the same as the Vocal Pattern “OUT” with neither Prefix or Suffix. The word “Shouts” has both.

Sometimes, Vocal Patterns may exist within longer Vocal Patterns.

> E.g. the Vocal Pattern 'OUN', as in the words, "Account" and "Mountain", is a shorter Vocal Pattern within the longer Vocal pattern 'OUNT'. Similarly, it is a shorter Vocal Pattern within the longer Vocal Pattern 'OUND' as heard in the words "Boundary" and "Round".

Bear in mind, though, that it is not necessary that a shorter Vocal Pattern always conforms within a longer Vocal Pattern above.

> E.g. the Vocal Pattern 'ED' as in the word "Shed" does not conform with the longer Vocal Pattern 'EDG', as in the word "Hedge". In the shorter Vocal Pattern, 'ED', the 'D' Consonant is articulated whereas in the longer Vocal Pattern, 'EDG', the 'D' is merged with 'G' with its own distinctive articulation, with the 'D' transformed.

More than one Vocal Pattern may exist in a word. The Prefixes and Suffixes differ in relation to the specific Vocal Pattern used.

> E.g. the Vocal Patterns 'OUN', and 'AR' exists in the word, "Boundary". 'OUN' is a Vocal Pattern because it is a recurring sound sequence beginning with a Vowel and ending with a Consonant, heard in multiple words as we have seen (as in "Boundary" and "Mountain"). Similarly, 'AR' is a Vocal Pattern as it also a sound sequence recurring across words (as in "Boundary" and "Quandary").
>
> Note, there are different variations of Vocal Patterns. E.g. 'AR', in the word "Luminary", which seems similar to "Boundary", is differently vocalized. And the 'AR' in the word "Car" is yet another variant. More is said about Vocal Pattern Variants, and how they are counted among Vocal Patterns in a later section below.

Sometimes, two Vocal Patterns connect to each other directly. As a longer unit they may, or may not, also form a Vocal Pattern.

> E.g. the Vocal Patterns 'AN', and 'UAR' exist in the word, "January". 'AN' is a Vocal Pattern because it is a recurring sequence of sounds, heard in many words (as in "Man" and "Fan") containing a Vowel and a Consonant. 'UAR' is a Vocal Pattern because it also recurs in other words (as in "February" and "Sanctuary"). 'AN' and 'UAR' link directly to each other in the example word "January". If as an integrated unit, i.e. 'ANUAR', this sound pattern were to recur in more than one word, it would also qualify as a Vocal Pattern. Clearly though, as a longer unit, it is likely to recur in fewer words. If it is unique to a single word, it would not be a Vocal Pattern.

Observe also that the length of a Vocal Pattern is not related to its level of Distinctiveness. Shorter Vocal Patterns within a word, are included among the most Distinctive along with longer Vocal Patterns.

Also observe, Vocal Patterns, Prefixes and Suffixes are different than Syllables. They may cross-over Syllable boundaries, whether speaking the American or British ways. This can be seen in the following table with words containing the Vocal Pattern, 'IZAT' as an example. The Vocal Pattern 'IZAT' is shown in bold, its Prefix is shown in regular case, and its Suffix in italics, for both American and British ways of articulating these words. You can see that Vocal Patterns can cross over Syllable boundaries. Syllable boundaries are indicated here by both dots and dashes.

Note: Syllable boundaries are Scripted with dots or dashes. Minor Pauses are shown with dots, '.'s, and Major Pauses are shown with dashes, '-'s.		
Words with Vocal Pattern: 'IZAT'	American Way	British Way
Actualization	Ac.tua-**li.za-t** *ion*	Act.ual-**iz-at.***ion*
Organization	Or.ga-n**i.za-t** *ion*	Org.an-**iz-at.***ion*
Optimization	Op.ti-m**i.za-t** *ion*	Opt.im-**iz-at.***ion*
Realization	Rea-**li.za-t** *ion*	Real-**iz-at.***ion*
Hospitalization	Hos.pi.ta-**li.za-t** *ion*	Hos.pit.al-**iz-at.***ion*

The Vocal Pattern, 'IZAT', said in American and British Accents is described in the box below using the Vocal Fidelity Phonetic System.

> The Vocal Pattern: 'IZAT' in the words: "Actualization", "Organization", "Optimization", Hospitalization", and "Realization" is one Vocal Pattern that separates the American and British ways of speaking.
>
> It is articulated i.*z*A-t*(*sh*) the American way, explained as follows:
>
> > Flowing without Pause from the previous Consonant, the Soft form of 'I' is followed by a Minor Pause, with the next Syllable beginning with a Weak to moderately Accentuated 'Z' Linking to the Hard form of 'A', followed then by a Major Pause following which, the last Syllable begins with a Weak to moderate 'SH' sound in place of the 'T'.
>
> And, it is articulated -IZ-At*(SH). the British way, explained as follows:
>
> > A Major Pause precedes the Hard form of 'I' which Links to a Moderate to strongly Accentuated 'Z' followed then by a Major Pause, with the next Syllable beginning with the Hard form of 'A' that links to the Moderate to strong 'SH' sound in place of the 'T'.

Transitioning to an American way of speaking requires learning the Vocal Patterns which stand out as Distinctive. Some of these are frequently heard, whereas others occur only occasionally. Even occasionally heard Vocal Patterns if Distinctive, should be learned, or they stand out as foreign.

> E.g. The word "Docile" contains the Vocal Pattern 'IL', as does the word "Mobile" and "Facile". Said the American way, these words rhyme with "Hassle", "Gravel" and "Fossil". By contrast, said the British way, they rhyme with "File", "Nile" and "Style". Though some of these words are only occasionally used, if articulated the British way in conversation with Americans, they stand out as strange.

Section:
Representing Vocal Patterns

Naming of Vocal Patterns.

Vocal Patterns are named as they are spelled in the words that contain them, in the form of a Vowel-Consonant Sequence, written in capital letters.

> Eg. the Vocal Pattern 'AN' as heard in the words "And", "Can" and "Fan" is named 'AN'.

Vocal Patterns can have the same name if they are written the same way but have different vocalizations. How they are distinguished from each other is explained ahead. Vocal Patterns have different names when they are spelled differently, even if they are similarly vocalized. This section explains the rules followed to understand and represent Vocal Patterns in a systematic way.

Identifying Vocal Patterns.

Vocal Patterns which are differently spelled but have a similar sound, are separately categorized as different Vocal Patterns.

> Eg. the Vocal Pattern 'OUN' as heard in the word "Count" or "Round" has the same sound as the Vocal Pattern 'OWN' as heard in the word "Town" or "Clown" but as they are spelled differently, they are treated as different Vocal Patterns.

Many Vowel Consonant sequences have more than one way of being vocalized in different word sets, each of which qualifies as a separate Vocal Pattern and is referred to as a Vocal Pattern Variant. Remember, Vocal Patterns are named after the Vowel-Consonant Sequence which constitute them. When there are Variants, the name includes a Roman numeral identifier, e.g. 'IN – IV', following the Vowel Consonant Sequence, to identify its specific vocalization.

> E.g. the Vocal Pattern 'IN' in words "Line" and "Fine" is differently pronounced than in words like "Machine" and "Ravine". These are two of four Variants of the Vocal Pattern with the letters 'IN'. Each Variant is identified by a Roman numeral e.g. 'IN – I' and 'IN – II'. In fact, the two example words contain Variants 'III' and 'IV' as shown in the Vocal Pattern Tables.

When a Vowel Consonant Sequence in a particular word is written the same way as a Vocal Pattern in other words but is pronounced uniquely or rarely, it is an irregular vocalization, i.e. it is articulated in a way that does not recur in other words enough to qualify as a Vocal Pattern. These are irregular Vowel Consonant Sequences and are excluded from the list of Vocal Patterns.

> Eg. the Vocal Pattern 'ORT' as heard in "Fort", "Port" and "Sort", is pronounced differently in the word "Effort". The former is the much more common pronunciation. The latter is a non-conforming exception to that form and is therefore not included in the membership of that Vocal Pattern. It is an irregular vocalization.

Vocal Pattern Families: Combining Similar Vocal Patterns.

It is efficient and convenient to combine similar Vocal Patterns that comprise a common beginning Vowel or Vowels and vocalization, but end with a different Consonant, into a Vocal Pattern Family. As the Vocal Patterns in a Vocal Pattern Family have an analogous sound they are better learned together, like they were a single Vocal Pattern, instead of separately.

A Vocal Pattern Family is a set of Vocal Patterns each of which begins with a common Vowel or Vowel Sequence vocalized in the same way and ends with any Consonant that can be coupled with the preceding Vowel(s) without a change in their vocalization (i.e. a vocalization of the preceding Vowel or Vowels).

The ending Consonant is represented by the Symbol '^' which denotes that it is variable, and is referred to as the "Variable Consonant".

Note: A Variable Consonant is any of different Consonants which can be joined to immediately preceding Vowel(s) so long as the preceding Vowel or Vowel Sequence vocalization remains unchanged.

Note: The '^' Symbol represents "Variable Consonant".

Eg. the Vocal Patterns 'OUN' as heard in words such as "Sound" or "Mount" is analogous to the Vocal Pattern 'OUD' as heard for example in words such as "Cloud" or "Proud". Such analogous Vocal Patterns can be represented by a single Vocal Pattern Family by denoting the final Variable Consonant Sound with the Variable Consonant Symbol '^'. In this case, the Vocal Pattern Family is represented, 'OU^', to refer to any Vocal Pattern, beginning with the similarly vocalized Vowel Sound 'OU' and followed by a Variable Consonant Sound. The word "Shout" also belongs to the same Vocal Pattern Family, 'OU^', with 'T' in the place of the Variable Consonant in this example.

Note: By combining analogous Vocal Patterns into a single Vocal Pattern Family, the overall number of Vocal Patterns that occur in the English language can be reduced while describing without compromise these distinctive vocal blocks that make up its phonetic structure.

Note: Sometimes a particular Consonant following a particular Vowel or Vowel Sequence is associated with a particular Vowel form articulation, in contrast with other Consonants following the same Vowel.

> E.g. When the Consonant 'R' couples with an 'A' Vowel in words like "Care", "Dare" and "Fare", it is associated with the 'A' being articulated like the 'E' Soft as articulated in words like "Deck", "Gel" and "Pen". Or, when the 'R' couples with the 'A' Vowel in words like "Bar", "Car" and "Far", it is associated with the 'A' being articulated in its Long form, in contrast with words like "Bat", 'Has", "Map", where the End Consonants are associated with the 'A' articulated in its Soft form.

Such a Vowel Consonant Sequence cannot be clubbed into a Vocal Pattern Family, as it is differently vocalized, but may qualify as a Vocal Pattern or Vocal Pattern Variant if it recurs in a number of words, as in the example above.

On the other hand, sometimes a particular Consonant preceding a particular Vowel or Vowel Sequence is associated with a particular Vowel form articulation:

> E.g. Often, different Consonants coupled with the 'A' Vowel after it follows a 'W', as may be seen in words like "Walk", "Wander", "War", "Wash", and "Water". In such a context, the 'A' often has the sound of an 'O' in a Soft-Round form.

Section:
Why format a Vocal Pattern as done in this Course?

Note: To quickly learn an Accent, all the distinctive sounds out of which a language is composed need to be identified. To do this efficiently, gaps and overlaps must be avoided. This task is made simpler by carving out all the recurring sounds in a consistent way rather than haphazardly. Recurring sounds are Vowel Sounds, Consonant Sounds and recurring sequences of Vowel and Consonant Sounds or Vocal Patterns. The task is analogous to drawing boxes around printed designs on a sheet of paper or cloth, without boxes overlapping or leaving printed units, in whole or part, unboxed. In a similar way, Vocal Patterns are defined to fit next to each other, without overlapping of Vocal Patterns or leaving any, in whole or part, unboxed.

Vocal Patterns that begin with a Vowel and end with a Consonant connect with a wider variety of prefixes (at their front end), and suffixes (at their back end). Defined this way each Vocal Pattern covers more of the language. Defined differently a greater number of Vocal Patterns would be needed to cover the same language. In minimizing the number of Vocal Patterns to learn, the Accent transition task is made easier.

E.g. In the word "County" the Vocal Pattern 'OUN' is found in many more words than would a differently structured Vocal pattern, such as, 'COU' or 'COUN' (if Vocal Patterns were defined to end with a Vowel or begin with a Consonant). If you formed as many words as possible with each of these alternative formats, trying a few different examples, you will find this to be true. I can think of many more words with the Vocal Pattern 'OUN' than with the sequences 'COU' or 'COUN'.

Also, with this structure, they have the necessary minimum length to contain the Basic Vocal Elements that differentiate Accents.

Remember: As already noted, Vocal Patterns need not necessarily be structured as done in this Course, to capture distinguishing Basic Vocal Elements. An alternative format could be adopted, but it appears that more Vocal Patterns would be needed to cover the same vocabulary.

Remember, the format adopted for a Vocal Pattern in this Course, is that each begins with a Vowel and ends with a Consonant.

This approach minimizes the number of Vocal Patterns that must be learned to speak the American way.

The extent of the difference between the American and British Accents may be surprising to some when it is quantified. The comprehensive review of Vocal Patterns, conducted as part of the development of this Course, shows that the American Accent differs from the British Accent in more than 70 percent of the Vocal Patterns identified.

To illustrate differences in how Vocal Patterns in words are vocalized, look at two well known words: "Source" and "Sauce".

The British pronounce "Source" with the Soft-Tall form of 'O' (not heard in the American Accent), a silent 'U', and a silent 'R', followed finally by a Moderate to strongly Accentuated 'S' Consonant Sound, with Hiss. Scripted, this is represented, {*s*1*o*u*r**S*1e*}. The Americans pronounce "Source" with the Hard form of 'O', a silent 'U' and a clearly articulated and Extended 'R', followed finally by a Strongly Accentuated 'S' Consonant Sound, with Hiss. Scripted, this is represented, {*s*1Ou*R'*S*1e*}.

The British say “Sauce” like they say “Source”. The British substitute the 'A' with the 'O' Soft-Tall form (heard in the British Accent but never in the American) form, with the 'U' left silent before a Moderate to strongly Accentuated final Consonant Sound. Scripted, this is represented {s1a*(o)u*c2*(S1)e*}. (Part of the difference in Scripting is because the words are spelled differently and are therefore adjusted differently). By contrast, the Americans vocalize the two words differently. They substitute the 'A' with the 'O' Soft-Round form and the 'U' with a 'W' before the Strongly Accentuated final Consonant Sound in the pronunciation of “Sauce”. Vocalized this way, it is Scripted, {s1a*(o)u*(w)c2*S1}.

Section:
The Advantage of The Vocal Pattern Tables

There are three Vocal Pattern Tables. These are the Vocal Pattern Bridge Table, the Vocal Pattern Inland Table and the Vocal Pattern Summit Table. They all contain Vocal Patterns extracted from a Vocal Pattern Master Table after Vocal Patterns were identified across the vocabulary and individually assessed in terms of their Distinctiveness and Rate of Occurrence.

The Vocal Pattern Bridge Table is provided with Coursebook One, “The American Accent Learnway – Cross the Bridge, Over the Divide”. The Vocal Pattern Inland Table is provided with Coursebook Two, “The American Accent Learnway – Together, On the Road Inland”. The Vocal Pattern Summit Table is provided with Coursebook Three, “The American Accent Learnway – As One, On the Summit”.

In the next section Vocal Pattern Tables are explained but a preliminary introduction here is useful.

The Vocal Pattern Tables are a tool designed to be used in three different ways:

First, in line with the Course organizing principle of presenting learning content in order of learning value, it lays out Vocal Patterns in order of both their level of Distinctiveness and Rate of Occurrence. In such order, it is a path from beginning to end, for learning the Vocal Patterns that make the most impact on the American Accent.

Second, it is a Diagnostic Tool which can be used to identify the specific Vocal Patterns that you vocalize differently than the American way, so that you can focus on only those that require change.

Third, it is a “Look-Up” where a specific Vocal Pattern with Distinctive American pronunciation can be looked up to find out how it is vocalized.

The Vocal Pattern Tables are a language-wide tool that identifies Vocal Patterns across the span of the English language.

By identifying Vocal Patterns in order of American Distinctiveness (relative to the British Accent), it provides the advantage of focusing learning effort on more Distinctive Vocal Patterns before less Distinctive ones. This enables quicker progress.

The Vocal Pattern Tables show the pronunciation for each Vocal Pattern in the Table – in Vocal Fidelity Phonetic System Script, and provide some word examples that contain the specific Vocal Pattern.

By using the Vocal Fidelity Phonetic System, with its enhanced Accent sensitive features, and by observing the word examples, you are enabled to recognize the Basic Vocal Elements in each Vocal Pattern and to vocalize it authentically the American way.

How are the Vocal Pattern Tables to be used as a Look-up?

The Vocal Pattern Tables serve as a Look-up, not so much of words, but of Vocal Patterns.

You might begin with a particular word that you're not sure how to vocalize. Within the word, you identify the Vocal Pattern your not sure about and look it up in the Vocal Pattern Bridge.

> You are likely to find a number of Vocal Pattern Variants with the same Vowel-Consonant Sequence. You would need to look through the example words provided with each Variant to see if one of them has words that match with the word you are uncertain about. It is possible you might even find the word you started with, listed as one of the examples. You can then check how it is vocalized in Vocal Fidelity Phonetic System Script in an adjacent column.
>
> > Words that match would of course consist of the same Vowel-Consonant Sequence. They would have the Pause – if there is one – in the same place. It would have the same Consonants in the same Syllable-End positions Accentuated at the same level. It would also be similar in terms of its Vowel Modulations. These are shown in the Vocal Pattern Vocalization Column, in Vocal Fidelity Phonetic System Script.
>
> The Vocal Pattern is vocalized in the word you are uncertain about just as it is in corresponding example words given for that particular Vocal Pattern.

Distinctive Vocal Patterns in the Great, Substantial or Significant, Distinctiveness categories can be looked up in the Vocal Pattern Tables. Great or the most Distinctive Vocal Patterns are listed in the Vocal Pattern Bridge Table in the first Coursebook, "The American Accent Learnway – Cross the Bridge, Over the Divide". Substantial or very Distinctive Vocal Patterns are listed in the Vocal Pattern Inland Table in the second Coursebook, "The American Accent Learnway – Together, On the Road Inland". Significant or clearly Distinctive Vocal Patterns are listed in the Vocal Pattern Summit Table in the third Coursebook, "The American Accent Learnway – As One, On the Summit".

If a particular Vocal Pattern is not listed, it is most likely of Insignificant Distinctiveness, meaning that the Vocal Pattern was not sufficiently different from the British Accent, to include in the Vocal Pattern Bridge, Inland or Summit Tables.

Vocal Patterns of Insignificant Distinctiveness are only included in the Master Table and not otherwise listed, as there is too small or no difference between how these are vocalized in the American Accent and British Accent.

Different Vocal Patterns of the same Vowel-Consonant Sequence, i.e. Vocal Pattern Variants – categorized at the same level of Distinctiveness and Rate of Occurrence, each with its own particular vocalization, are in consecutive rows, for convenient comparison.

The Vocal Pattern Bridge in the present Coursebook, include the Great or most Distinctive Vocal Patterns. Distinctive Vocal Pattern Variants in other categories could be in either the Vocal Pattern Inland or Vocal Pattern Summit Tables.

Substantially or very Distinctive Vocal Patterns, are in the Vocal Pattern Inland Table as part of Coursebook Two, "The American Accent Learnway – Together, On the Road Inland".

Significantly or clearly Distinctive Vocal Patterns, are in the Vocal Pattern Summit Table as part of Coursebook Three, "The American Accent Learnway – As One, On the Summit".

A separate list of Vowel-Consonant sequences with words that have Irregular vocalization, i.e. those vocalized in a way that is unique or nearly so, is separately covered in Appendix (Appendix IV – Words with Irregular Vowel Consonant Sequences) – as these are not considered Vocal Patterns.

The Vocal Pattern Master Table includes all the Vocal Patterns identified, including those of Insignificant Distinctiveness. It's development was a prerequisite for the Vocal Pattern Bridge Table, the Vocal Pattern Inland Table and the Vocal Pattern Summit Table, all of which are extractions from it.

Section:
The Vocal Pattern Tables

Vocal Pattern Tables show the pronunciation of each Vocal Pattern in Accent sensitive Script using the Vocal Fidelity Phonetic System and provide example words, to enable proper vocalization in the American Accent. They serve more than one purpose. They constitute the path for learning the American Accent with focus on individual Vocal Patterns. By presenting Vocal Patterns in order of their Distinctiveness and Rate of Occurrence levels, the Vocal Pattern Tables prioritize focus on the Vocal Patterns that make the biggest impact on Accent, thus maximizing impact when learned in the given order. They enable individual learners to diagnose the Vocal Patterns which they articulate differently than the American Accent. They also serve as a look-up for specific Vocal Patterns. In serving all these purposes, they serve as a powerful tool for speakers of English with different Accents to cross over to the American Accent.

The Vocal Pattern Bridge in the first Coursebook contains the most Distinctive Vocal Patterns that make the largest impact on Accent change. It may be visualized as a bridge that enables the crossing over of an Accent to the American way. The Vocal Pattern Inland Table in the second Coursebook, covers very Distinctive Vocal Patterns – the level after the most Distinctive covered in the Bridge. It may be visualized as an inland road that takes you deeper into the American Accent as you explore the Accent further. The Vocal Pattern Summit Table in the third Coursebook, covers clearly Distinctive Vocal Patterns. It addresses Vocal Patterns that are not as Distinct as those in the Inland Table, but nevertheless make a noticeable difference to Accent. The fine refinement added here may be visualized as the summit of your journey, as your Accent merges with the American Accent.

The Vocal Pattern Bridge, Inland and Summit Tables are extracts from the Vocal Pattern Master Table which consists of more than 840 Vocal Patterns.

> Vocal Pattern Variants are Vocal Patterns which share a common Vowel-Consonant sequence but are each vocalized differently. Each Vocal Pattern Variant counts as a separate Vocal Pattern.

The Vocal Pattern Bridge consists of the most Distinctive Vocal Patterns – in the Distinctiveness category of Great. These number just over 100 Vocal Patterns.

The Vocal Pattern Inland Table consists of very Distinctive Vocal Patterns – in the Distinctiveness category of Substantial. These number 200 Vocal Patterns.

The Vocal Pattern Summit Table consists of clearly Distinctive Vocal Patterns – in the Distinctiveness category of Significant. These number just over 300 Vocal Patterns.

The Vocal Patterns in each of the Vocal Pattern Tables could be determined only after all the Vocal Patterns in the Vocal Pattern Master Table were defined.

When a word with an unfamiliar Vocal Pattern is encountered, the Vocal Pattern Tables facilitate learning of the American Accent. It enables looking up the pronunciation of the specific Vocal Pattern, reading how it is vocalized in Vocal Fidelity Phonetic System Script, observing its pronunciation in similar example words, then applying the vocalization change to a set of words (with the same Vocal Pattern) in one go to achieve rapid Accent transition.

Note: With each Vocal Pattern learned, you are enabled to make a change of pronunciation in a block of words at one go – from about half a dozen to sometimes over twenty words. Approached this way, the path to Accent change across an entire vocabulary is made more direct, precise and efficient.

Vocal Pattern Learning Priority Categories.

Vocal Patterns do differ in the amount of impact they each make on Accent. Learning an Accent is quicker if those that make a greater impact on Accent are learned with higher priority. The impact of a Vocal Pattern on Accent depends on two factors. Those that exhibit greater distinctiveness in the American Accent when contrasted with the British Accent is a primary factor. Those that occur in the spoken language at a higher rate is a secondary factor. Based on these two factors, Vocal Patterns have been categorized into groups and sub-groups to prioritize learning. The process of categorization of Vocal Patterns is explained below to show that it is objective, sound and dependable. The categories are labeled according to Vocal Pattern level with regard to these two factors. Further explanation is provided below.

Determining Distinctiveness of Vocal Patterns.

A scale named the American Pronunciation Distinctiveness Estimate (APDE) has been used to prioritize Vocal Patterns in terms of their American Distinctiveness relative to the British Accent. Another scale, named the Rate of Occurrence Estimate (RoOE), has been used to prioritize Vocal Patterns in terms of how often they are heard. Both are based on observable criteria to objectively estimate and categorize Vocal Patterns for priority learning, as explained below.

With regard to the American Pronunciation Distinctiveness Estimate (APDE), the criterion evaluated is the amount of overall audible difference of Basic Vocal Elements in the American Accent relative to the British. This is partly a function of the number of different Basic Vocal Elements and the difference in the level of Consonant Accentuation in the two Accents.

The different Basic Vocal Elements are not equal in their contribution to Distinctiveness. Some Basic Vocal Elements make a greater contribution than others. For example:

-the Single Vowel Extension and Repetition Modulation is more noticeable than, say, a one level difference in Consonant Accentuation.

-the differences in the way a particular Consonant, e.g. the 'R', or a Vowel, such as the 'O', is differently articulated in the American Accent are also more noticeable than, say, the Extension of a Consonant or Vowel Sound.

Such differences concerning Basic Vocal Elements individually and together as found in each Vocal Pattern have also been considered in estimating the Distinctiveness level.

Comparisons between the level of Distinctiveness between American and British Accents with regard to the pronunciation of a Vocal Pattern can quite accurately be made when words with the Vocal Pattern are heard one after the other.

> Note: As part of developing the Principles, the Vocal Pattern Master Table, and other tools that form a part of this Course, on-line audio recordings provided by authoritative Dictionaries of different words with each Vocal Pattern were carefully and repeatedly listened to, and compared, to cross-check pronunciations heard by speakers of the two Accents.

The process of making judgments regarding Distinctiveness was first, one of whether the overall audible difference was a lot or not much. If it was judged to be a lot, it was then decided whether it was "Great" or at a level lower, i.e. "Substantial". If it was judged that the difference was not much, it was then to be decided whether the difference was "Significant" or "Insignificant".

There is likely to be fairly high agreement, even between somewhat knowledgeable observers, (and higher agreement between more knowledgeable observers), when assigning Vocal Patterns to one of these four levels of Distinctiveness when the vocalization of Vocal Patterns in example words in American and British Accents are compared. Online audio recordings provided by authoritative Dictionaries made such rigorous comparison possible. Though a degree of variation in judgments is inevitable, such Estimates of American Pronunciation Distinctiveness are more than sufficiently accurate to be a basis for prioritizing Vocal Patterns according to their Distinctiveness level. Distinctiveness levels are described as follows:

Great: The difference in pronunciation is at the maximum level, or most Distinctive.

Substantial: The difference is below maximum but at a high level, or very Distinctive.

Significant: There is a clear and definite difference in pronunciation, at a medium level, or clearly Distinctive.

Insignificant: Differences between the American and British Accents are not easily noticeable, or at the minimum level, or nearly Indistinct.

> Note: The full* list of Vocal Patterns had to be developed before it was possible to categorize Vocal Patterns at different levels. The full list of Vocal Patterns is recorded in a Vocal Pattern Master Table. "The Vocal Pattern Bridge Table" in this Coursebook include the Vocal Patterns categorized as "Great" on the Distinctiveness (APDE) scale. Vocal Patterns identified as "Substantial" on the Distinctiveness (APDE) scale, comprise "The Vocal Pattern Inland Table" in Coursebook Two entitled, "The American Accent Learnway – Together, On the Road Inland". And, Vocal Patterns identified as "Significant" on the Distinctiveness (APDE) scale, comprise "The Vocal Pattern Summit Table" in Coursebook Three entitled, "The American Accent Learnway – As One, On the Summit".
>
> *By "full", is meant a comprehensive identification of Vocal Patterns across the English Language. Longer Vocal Patterns not specifically listed are mostly represented either by shorter Vocal Patterns that are a segment of these longer Vocal Patterns or by a Vocal Pattern Family.

> Note: Like the name, "Cross the Bridge, over the Divide" implies a crossing over of your Accent to American shores, the name "Together, On the Road Inland" implies a deeper foray into the American Accent just as people crossed the land, after arriving here. Similarly, the name "As One, On the Summit" simultaneously implies enjoying the opportunity of America

and fully speaking the American way.

Remember: The Basic Vocal Elements include Pauses, Vowel forms, Vowel Modulations, Consonant Sounds, Consonant Accentuation levels, Consonant Extension and Consonant Inherent Attributes.

Determining the Rate of Occurrence of Vocal Patterns.

The second scale used to prioritize Vocal Patterns is the Rate of Occurrence Estimate (RoOE). The criteria and descriptions used to define the levels of the scale are as follows:

Frequent (Fre): A Vocal Pattern that is encountered at least once every few sentences, A Vocal Pattern would qualify, even if it recurs in as few as two words.
Occasional (Occ): A Vocal Pattern that occurs in a very small handful of diverse (i.e. not grammatical variations of the same word) words, about five or fewer, none of which is heard often or frequently. As these Vocal Patterns are limited to only a few uncommon words, they are categorized, Occasional.
Often (Oft): A Vocal Pattern that is not Frequent in Rate of Occurrence, nor Occasional as defined above, or as Irregular, as defined just below.
Irregular: When a particular vocalization of a Vowel Consonant Sequence is found in a word, and this vocalization seems unique and impossible or nearly so to find in any other word, such a vocalization cannot be considered a Vocal Pattern, or, a Variant of a Vocal Pattern. This is simply called an Irregular Vowel Consonant Sequence vocalization.

Note: The number of word examples alone can be a misleading indicator of Vocal Pattern Rate of Occurrence. What is actually counted is the frequency with which the specific Vocal Pattern occurs. It could occur Frequently in just one word that is used very regularly. E.g., while there are not a great many words with the Vocal Pattern Variant, 'AS' {a"s2*(*Z*), or, a's2*(*Z*)} where the 'S' sounds like 'Z', the words “As” and “Has” with this Vocal Pattern both occur frequently. Thus, this Vocal Pattern Variant 'AS' is estimated to occur Frequently, though the number of different words associated with it are few. This illustrates why Vocal Patterns that are categorized as occurring Often or Frequently are not necessarily accompanied by a Word List Table: there may be very few words containing the Vocal Pattern, but at least one of these words occurs Often or Frequently.

The above criteria for categorizing Vocal Patterns according to their Rate of Occurrence are objective and operationally defined, making them observable and a clear basis for valid categorization.

It should be recognized that when defined as above, most Vocal Patterns fall into the Often category, while the number that fall into the Frequent and Occasional category are relatively few.

Note: The whole purpose of Identifying the level of Distinctiveness of Vocal Patterns as articulated in the American and British Accents, and, their level of Occurrence is to assign each Vocal Pattern a priority order so that your learning effort can focus on the Vocal Patterns that make a higher impact on your Accent.

The Vocal Pattern Bridge is the starting point for each individual to identify the specific Vocal Patterns they articulate in ways that are different than the American way.

Representing Learning Priority and Learning Sequence.

The Table: "Learning Priority and Learning Sequence" below, shows how each Vocal Pattern is assigned a Learning Priority group and a Learning Sequence subgroup number based on their assessed levels on the American Pronunciation Distinctiveness Estimate (APDE) and Rate of Occurrence Estimate (RoOE) scales.

Table:
Learning Priority and Learning Sequence

The full form of the abbreviations used in this Table are as follows: LP: Learning Priority group APDE: American Pronunciation Distinctiveness Estimate. RoOE: Rate of Occurrence Estimate. LS: Learning Sequence subgroup				
Levels of Learning Priority groups: I, II, III and IV.				
Levels of American Pronunciation Distinctiveness Estimate (APDE) categories: Great (A), Substantial (B), Significant (C), and Insignificant (D).				
Rate of Occurrence Estimate (RoOE) Categories: Frequent, Often or Occasional.				
Learning Priority of Vocal Patterns have been categorized according to the levels of Distinctiveness and include all Rate of Occurrence Estimate levels.				
Learning Priority group (LP)	APDE	Recommended Learning Sequence subgroup Based on APDE and RoOE		
		Frequent	Often	Occasional
I	Great (A)	1	2	3
II	Substantial (B)	4	5	6
III	Significant (C)	7	8	9
IV	Insignificant (D)	10	11	12

Note: Each Vocal Pattern in the Vocal Pattern Tables is linked to a Vocal Pattern Word List Table with additional words examples containing the specific Vocal Pattern – when more space is needed for additional example words. These are for creating awareness of the broader set of words with the Vocal Pattern and for practicing its pronunciation.

The Vocal Pattern Bridge, Inland and Summit Tables are extracts from the Vocal Pattern Master Table which consists of more than 840 Vocal Patterns.

Vocal Patterns in each of the Vocal Pattern Tables are presented in order of Distinctiveness and Rate of Occurrence.

The Vocal Pattern Bridge Table consists of the most Distinctive Vocal Patterns – in the Distinctiveness category of Great. This Table includes just over 100 Vocal Patterns. The Table is

provided with this first Coursebook, "The American Accent Learnway – Cross the Bridge, Over the Divide", of this three Coursebook series. The Vocal Pattern Inland Table consists of very Distinctive Vocal Patterns – in the Distinctiveness category of Substantial. These number 200 Vocal Patterns. This Table is provided with the second Coursebook, "The American Accent Learnway – Together on the Road Inland". The Vocal Pattern Summit Table consists of clearly Distinctive Vocal Patterns – in the Distinctiveness category of Significant. These number just over 300 Vocal Patterns. This Table is provided with the third and final Coursebook, "The American Accent Learnway – As One, On the Summit". The Vocal Patterns in each of the Vocal Pattern Tables could only be determined only after all the Vocal Patterns in the Vocal Pattern Master Table were defined.

Table:
The Vocal Pattern Bridge

Note 1: The Notes for this Table apply to all the Vocal Pattern Tables, i.e. the Vocal Pattern Bridge Table, the Vocal Pattern Inland Table and the Vocal Pattern Summit Table. They provide essential explanation, about Vocal Patterns, to understand these Tables. They also explain the contents of the different columns.
Note 2: The "Vocal Pattern" in this Course has been defined as a recurring sound sequence, beginning with a Vowel and ending with a Consonant, heard in different words. Vocal Patterns are identified in the column headed "Vocal Pattern Name" (Column 2).
Note 3: Fundamentally different vocalizations of a particular Vocal Pattern that like all Vocal Patterns recur across words are called Vocal Pattern Variants. When a Vocal Pattern has Variants, each is considered a separate Vocal pattern and is listed in a separate row in the Vocal Pattern Name column with an identifying Roman numeral extension (Column 2). The name of the Vocal Pattern or Vocal Pattern Variant is the Vowel-Consonant Sequence of which it is composed, and the Roman numeral extension, if any. E.g. the Vocal Pattern 'IN' has several different Variants, e.g., as in the words "Grin", and "Line", which are Variants 'I' and 'II' respectively. These Variants are represented 'IN - I' and 'IN - II', in the "Vocal Pattern Name" column. Variants may be in Different Vocal Pattern Tables, i.e. the Vocal Pattern Bridge, Inland or Summit Tables. (Vocal Patterns of Insignificant Distinctiveness are identified only in the Vocal Pattern Master Table.) When a Roman numeral extension is seen as part of a Vocal Pattern name, in the "Vocal Pattern Name" column, it means that other Variants for that Vocal Pattern exist. To check the vocalization of a particular word which contains a Vocal Pattern that has many Variants, look for the Variant with word examples that are similar, in the "Word Example" column (Column 8) in the rows corresponding with the different Vocal Pattern Variants. A word with a Vowel-Consonant Sequence which has a unique or near unique vocalization is considered an Irregular vocalization and is not included as a Vocal Pattern Variant. E.g. the Vocal Pattern letter sequence 'AN' in the word "Orange" is often vocalized {O-ra*(i)*n*ge} with the 'A' Silent and replaced with

an 'I' Soft sound. This is an Irregular example of this Vowel-Consonant Sequence. Except for a similar sound in the plural of the word, i.e. "Oranges", it is hard to find another word where 'AN' is so vocalized. This is therefore considered an Irregular vocalization of 'AN' and is not included as a Variant of 'AN' Vocal Patterns. (It should be noted that "Orange is also often vocalized {O-ra*(i1)*ng*e} with an 'I' Short – instead of the 'I' Soft, which is not an Irregular vocalization.)

Note 4: Vocal Patterns that begin with Vowel(s) in common but end with a different Consonant thus sharing a similar initial Vowel Sound have often been grouped together as a "Vocal Pattern Family". A Vocal Pattern Family can be recognized from the Variable Consonant Symbol '^' substituting the place of a final specific Consonant Sound.

> E.g. the Vocal Pattern 'OUN' as heard in the word "Count", has a similar initial Vowel Sound as the Vocal Pattern 'OUD' as heard in the word "Cloud". These related Vocal Patterns may be shown under one Vocal Pattern Family by joining the common preceding Vowels with the Variable Consonant Symbol '^' as in 'OU^'. This method is used to include 'OUD', 'OUN', 'OUT', etc. in one Vocal Pattern Family.

The Variable Consonant Symbol '^' applies to any Consonant which when Linked with common immediately preceding Vowels, produces a similar Vocal Pattern vocalization differentiated only by the different End Consonant Sound, such as is illustrated by examples in the "Word Example" column.

Vocal Pattern Families may also have Variants, each with a Distinctive vocalization, as with other Vocal Patterns. They are similarly identified by Roman numeral extensions.

Vocal Pattern Families are listed in the Vocal Pattern Name Column (Column 2), like other Vocal Patterns.

Note 5: Vocal Patterns that are differently spelled but have a similar sound are categorized as different Vocal Patterns. E.g. the end of the words "Sale" and "Pail" are vocalized similarly but as these are spelled differently, they are different Vocal Patterns – each named according to its spelling, (the Vocal Pattern names would correspond with 'AL' and 'AIL' – the Vowel-Consonant Sequences extracted from these examples).

Note 6: In the "Vocal Pattern Vocalization" column (Column 3), a Pause is always only indicated with a dash '-'. This may represent either the Major Pause or the Minor Pause.

In the "Word Example" column (Column 8), Pauses in word examples can be identified as a dash '-' which denotes a Major Pause and a dot '.' which denotes a Minor Pause. However, with Di-Syllabic words – which have one Pause – the dash '-' Symbol is always used to represent the single Pause.

Note 7: In the column, "Vocal Pattern Vocalization" (Column 3), the Vocal Pattern's vocalization is Scripted using the Course's Vocal Fidelity Phonetic System. If a Script Symbol is unfamiliar to you, for clarification, refer as needed to:

> -the Scripting Conventions for Vowel Sounds (Appendix I.B),
> -the Scripting Conventions for Consonant Sounds (Appendix I.C),
> -the Phonetic Symbols for Vowel Sounds (Appendix II.A), and
> -the Phonetic Symbols for Consonant Sounds (Appendix III.C).

Note 8: Often, there are words with relatively small differences in the vocalization of a Vocal Pattern or a Vocal Pattern Variant within them, all of which are acceptable. Where this is so, usually up to two vocalization options are given under the "Vocal Pattern Vocalization" column (Column 2). Options are described using Vocal Fidelity Phonetic Scripting, each separated with a comma. The options include popular and standard vocalizations.

> E.g., the words "Room" and "Shoot" are commonly pronounced with either just an 'O' Long {Ro*o2m, Sho*o2t}, but also frequently with an inserted 'I' Soft preceding the 'O' Long Vowel{R(i)o*o2m, Sh(i)o*o2}. Both articulations are shown, separated by a comma.

The differences in vocalization may be a difference caused by the presence or absence of a Basic Vocal Element, such as:

-an Extension of a Vowel or Consonant Sound,
-an Extension and Repetition of a Vowel Sound,
-the occurrence of the Hiss i.e. '*(h)*' following a particular Consonant,
-the insertion of an External Vowel,
-an audible difference in the Inherent Attributes or Accentuation of a particular Consonant Sound.

It is important to note that the Scripted vocalizations shown do not preclude the existence of other acceptable vocalizations.

Note 9. Certain words have more than one commonly used pronunciation. E.g., the word "Vase" is usually pronounced with an 'A' Hard middle Vowel Sound and the Hissing 'S' (as in "Case", i.e. Consonant Version 'S1'), but it is also sometime pronounced with the 'A' Hard Vowel Sound and the Buzzing 'S' (as in "His", i.e. Version 'S2'). Such word examples with different pronunciations are tagged with the mark '~' in the Word Example column (Column 8). The tag mark indicates that the corresponding Vocal Pattern vocalization is one of more than one commonly used pronunciation of the word example. A tagged word example is also indicative that the word example may be shown again on another row, associated with another Vocal Pattern Variant. In the Table below, the example word "Vase" is tagged ("Vase~") and shown with different pronunciations as a word example under Variants X and XI of the Vocal Pattern 'AS'.

Note 10: In the "LP" or Learning Priority column (Column 4), the Learning Priority of each Vocal Pattern is indicated by a Roman numeral, based on its learning impact on Accent change. Learning Priority has been set to correspond with the Vocal Pattern's Distinctiveness category (APDE) (Column 6).

The most Distinctive Vocal Patterns in the Great Distinctiveness category are Learning Priority I (LP I). Learning these Vocal Patterns delivers great impact on Accent change. LP 'I' Vocal Patterns are covered in the Vocal Pattern Bridge Table in the first Coursebook of the series, "The American Accent Learnway – Cross the Bridge, Over the Divide". Very Distinctive Vocal Patterns in the Substantial Distinctiveness category are LP II. Learning these deliver substantial impact on Accent change. These are covered in the Vocal Pattern Inland Table in the second Coursebook, "The American Accent Learnway – Together, On the Road Inland". Clearly Distinctive Vocal Patterns in the Significant Distinctiveness category are LP III. Learning these deliver significant impact on Accent change. These are covered in the Vocal Pattern Summit Table in the third Coursebook, "The American Accent Learnway – As One, On the Summit".

Note 11: Vocal Patterns are grouped into Learning Sequence (LS) subgroups (Column 5), based on an Estimate of their Rate of Occurrence (RoOE) (Column 7), i.e. upon how often they occur, whether Frequent, Often or Occasional. Within each Learning Priority Group (Note 8 above), those that occur more often are sequenced in the Vocal Pattern Tables before those that occur less often.

In the Vocal Pattern Bridge Table, within Priority Group 'I', Vocal Patterns in LS subgroup 1 are those that Occur Frequently and are presented first. Vocal Patterns in LS subgroup 2 are those that Occur Often and are presented next. Vocal Patterns in LS subgroup 3 are those that Occur Occasionally and are presented last. Similarly, in the Vocal Pattern Inland Table, within Priority Group 'II', Vocal Patterns in LS subgroup 4 are those that Occur Frequently and are presented first. Vocal Patterns in LS subgroup 5 are those that Occur Often and are presented next. Vocal Patterns in LS subgroup 6 are those that Occur Occasionally and are presented last. And again, similarly, in the Vocal Pattern Summit Table, within Priority Group 'III', Vocal Patterns in LS subgroup 7 are those that Occur Frequently and are presented first. Vocal Patterns in LS subgroup 8 are those that Often Occur Often and are presented next. Vocal Patterns in LS subgroup 9 are those that Occur Occasionally and are presented last.

Note 12: In the column "APDE" (Column 6), the American Pronunciation Distinctiveness Estimate is shown for each Vocal Pattern.

In the Vocal Pattern Bridge Table, the Vocal Patterns are all graded 'A', i.e. in the Great Distinctiveness category, indicating that they are the most Distinctive Vocal Patterns. In the Vocal Pattern Inland Table, they are all graded 'B', i.e. in the Substantial Distinctiveness category, indicating that they are very Distinctive Vocal Patterns. In the Vocal Pattern Summit Table, they are all graded 'C', i.e. in the Significant Distinctiveness category, indicating that they are clearly Distinctive Vocal Patterns.
Note 13: In the "RoOE" column (Column 7), the Rate of Occurrence Estimate shows how often a Vocal Pattern is estimated to Occur in the Language. Rates of Occurrence may be Frequent (Fre), Often (Oft) or Occasional (Occ).
Note 14. Each Vocal Pattern in the Vocal Pattern Table below may be referenced to a corresponding Word List Table (in a separate Chapter, per the Table of Contents), when there are enough additional word examples containing the Vocal Pattern to require a separate Table. The Word Lists for each Vocal Pattern further enable you to convert your pronunciation of a larger number of words at one time, rather than only one word at a time. Word List Tables are not provided for Vocal Patterns that have an Occasional Rate of Occurrence. Word List Tables can be looked up from information provided with each Vocal Pattern, in the Table below. If a Word List Table has been provided, the "Word List Table Y/N" column (Column 10) will show 'Y', to indicate that, "Yes", a corresponding Word List Table has been provided and may be looked up from referral information on that row. (If no Word List Table has been provided, then the column will show 'N', meaning that, "No", do not look for a corresponding Word List Table as there isn't one). Word List Tables are presented in the same order as in the Vocal Pattern Tables. If a Word List Table for a Vocal Pattern has been provided (as indicated in Column 10), it will be in order of its Learning Priority Number (Column 4), its Learning Sequence Number (Column 5) and according to the alphanumeric order of its name – including the Roman Numeral Extension in the name, if any (Column 2). The first row of each Word List Table shows the Vocal Pattern Priority-Sequence category, which is the Vocal Pattern's Learning Priority number (from Column 4 of the Vocal Pattern Table below) and its Learning Sequence number (from Column 5 of the Vocal Pattern Table below), separated by an oblique, e.g. 'I/3' or 'II/4'. The second row of each Word List Table shows the Vocal Pattern Name (from Column 2) of the Vocal Pattern Table below. Word Lists are grouped within each Priority-Sequence category in alphanumeric order of the Vocal Pattern name. Accordingly, Vocal Pattern Variants 'AN' - I' and 'AN - II, being in the same Priority-Sequence category 'I/1', have Word List Tables following each other consecutively, as in the Vocal Pattern Table. By contrast, though 'IN - I' (Priority-Sequence: I/1) and 'IN - II' (Priority-Sequence:'II/5') follow each other alphanumerically, the corresponding Word List Tables do not follow each other consecutively as they are in separate Priority-Sequence categories. 'IN - I' follows 'IM - I' and 'IN - II' follows 'IM - II' in alphanumeric order in their respective Priority-Sequence categories in different Vocal Pattern Tables.
Note 15. In the second last Column, "Change OK/C", you can identify the Vocal Patterns you do not articulate in the American way. Mark those that you already articulate as do Americans 'OK', for "No Change Needed" and those that you don't as 'C' for "Change Needed". By assessing yourself on each Vocal Pattern in the Table, you will create a custom learning list based on your specific way of speaking, targeting the specific Vocal Patterns that you need to change. You will identify exactly how many and which Vocal Patterns you need to relearn. You can then proceed to change blocks of words that correspond with each Vocal Pattern at one time. A good indication that change for a particular Vocal Pattern is needed is if you find that you vocalize the Vocal Pattern in one or more of the example words in different ways.
Note 16. Distinctive Vocal Patterns in the Great, Substantial or Significant, Distinctiveness categories can be looked up in the Vocal Pattern Tables. The most Distinctive Vocal Patterns are listed in the Vocal Pattern

Bridge Table. Very Distinctive Vocal Patterns are listed in the Vocal Pattern Inland Table. Clearly Distinctive Vocal Patterns are listed in the Vocal Pattern Summit Table. The Bridge Table is provided in Coursebook One, "The American Accent Learnway – Cross the Bridge, Over the Divide" of this three Coursebook series. The Inland Table is provided in Coursebook Two, "The American Accent Learnway – Together, On the Road Inland". The Summit Table is provided in Coursebook Three, "The American Accent Learnway – As One, On the Summit".

If a particular Vocal Pattern is not listed, it is most likely of Insignificant Distinctiveness, meaning that the Vocal Pattern was not sufficiently different to include in the Bridge, Inland or Summit Tables.

Vocal Patterns of Insignificant Distinctiveness are only included in the Master Table and not otherwise listed, as there is too small or no difference between how these are vocalized in the American Accent and British Accent.

If you encounter a word that has an unusual articulation of a Vocal Pattern that does not match any of the Variants in any of the Vocal Pattern Tables, i.e. the Vocal Pattern Bridge, Inland or Summit Tables, it could be that it is an Irregular Vowel-Consonant Sequence. A Table: "Vocalizing Words With Irregular Vowel Consonant Sequences" is included as Appendix IV.

You may sometimes find that a specific Vocal Pattern has been left out of the Vocal Pattern Tables provided in the Coursebooks. This could be because Vocal Patterns that are not Distinctive are only listed in the Vocal Pattern Master Table. Also, it is simply not possible to ensure inclusion of each and every Vocal Pattern.

Columns									
1	2	3	4	5	6	7	8	9	10
Serial	Vocal Pattern Name	Vocal Pattern Vocalization	LP	LS	ApDE	RoOE	Word Example with Vocal Pattern (Pauses shown)	Change OK/C	Word List Table Y/N
1	AD - I	a"*D*, a'*D*	I	1	A	Fre	Add, Bad, Cad, Dad, Fad, Glad, Had, Mad, Pad, Sad, Tad.		Y
2	AM - I	a"M, a'M	I	1	A	Fre	Am, Ram, Ham, Cam, Sham, Tram, Bur-ming-ham.		Y
3	AN - I	a"*N*, a'*N*	I	1	A	Fre	Can, Can't, Fan, Ran, Flan, Se-dan, Than, Van.		Y
4	AN - II	a"*n*, a'*n*	I	1	A	Fre	And, Ad-vance, Canned, Can't, Dance, Land, Plant, Ro-mance.		Y

5	AND - I	a"*nD(h)*, a'*nD(h)*	I	1	A	Fre	And, Band, Brand, Grand, Hand, Land, Sand, Stand.		Y
6	ANK - I	a"[n*K*]*(h)*, a[n*K*]*(h)*	I	1	A	Fre	Bank, Flank, Frank, Prank, Rank, Sank, Spank, Tank, Thank.		Y
7	ANT - I	a"*n*T*(h)*, a*n*T*(h)*	I	1	A	Fre	Can, Can't, Grant, Pant, Plant, Rant, Scant, Slant.		N
8	AR - I	a2*R*	I	1	A	Fre	Bar, Car, Czar, Far, Jar, Mar, Par, Scar, Spar, Star, Sonar, Tar.		N
9	AR - II	a2R	I	1	A	Fre	Arc, Barn, Car, Dart, Far, Farm, Hard, Large, March, Mar-gin, Scarf.		Y
10	AS - I	a"*S*2', a'*S*2'	I	1	A	Fre	As, Has.		N
11	EM - I	e"M, e'M	I	1	A	Fre	Emp-ty, Gems, Hemmed, Stem, Them, Tempt.		Y
12	EN - I	e"*N*, e'*N*	I	1	A	Fre	Ben, Men, Den, Ken Ten, Then, When.		Y
13	EP - I	e"P, e'P	I	1	A	Fre	A-dept, Depth, I-nept, Re-cep-ti-cal, Skep-ti-cal, Stepped, Wept.		Y
14	ER - I	e1*R*	I	1	A	Fre	A-ver, Ba-ker, Be-tter, Err, Her, Law-yer~, Over, Su-mmer, Under, Were.		Y
15	ER - II	E'(e1)*R*, E'(e1)R	I	1	A	Fre	Deer, Here, Mere, Ra-cke-teer, Veered.		Y
16	ES - I	e"*S*1, e'*S*1	I	1	A	Fre	Best, Con-fess, Less, Guest, Mess, Pest, Press, Rest, Wes-tern.		Y
17	ESS - I	e"*S*1s*, e'*S*1s*	I	1	A	Fre	Bess, Cess, Con-fess, Dress, Ex-cess, Less, Mess.		Y

18	IM - I	i"M, i'M	I	1	A	Fre	Limp, Tim, Jim, Him, Rim, Slim.		Y
19	IN - I	i"*N*, i*N*	I	1	A	Fre	In, Bin, Din, Fin, Grin, Spin, Win.		Y
20	IT - I	i"*T(h)*, i"*T(h)*	I	1	A	Fre	Bit, Flit, Hit, Ha-bit, It, Kit, Lit, Ra-bbit, Sit, Skit, Wit.		Y
21	OM - I	o'M	I	1	A	Fre	Com-pli-cate, From, Stomp, Stomped, Tom.		Y
22	OR - I	o)'*R*, o)*R*	I	1	A	Fre	A-dore, Bore, Core, For, Fu-rore, More, Nor, Or, Score, Shore, Tore.		Y
23	OU^ - I	o*(a)'u^, o*(a)'u*(w)^	I	1	A	Fre	A-ccount, Dough-ty, Loud, Moun-tain, Out, Round, Scout, South.		Y
24	OUR - I	o)'u*R, ou*R	I	1	A	Fre	Four, Pour, Your.		N
25	AF - I	A"F, a'F	I	2	A	Oft	Aft, Af-ter, Craft, Craf-ted, Craf-ting, Draf-ted, Draf-ting, Shaft.		Y
26	ANK - II	a"[nK], a[nK]	I	2	A	Oft	Banks, Banked, Blanked, Frank-ly, Pranks, Ranked, Thanks.		Y
27	ANK - III	a[nK]-(*k*)	I	2	A	Oft	Ank-le, Bank-er, Lank-y, Rank-le, Spank-ing, Tank-er, Thank-ing.		Y
28	ANS - I	a"Ns2*(Z), a'Ns2*(Z)	I	2	A	Oft	Cans, Clans, Fans, Man's, Pans, Plans, Spans, Vans, Tans.		Y
29	ANT - II	a"*nt*, a*nt*	I	2	A	Oft	Grants, Pants, Plants, Rants, Recants, Slants.		N
30	ANT - III	a'N-t2*([td]), a"N-t2*([td])	I	2	A	Oft	Ban-ter, Can-ter, Man-tle, Gran-ted, Fan-tasy, Re-can-ted.		N

31	AP - I	a"*P*, a' *P*	I	2	A	Oft	Cap, Clap, Map, Nap, Tap, Rap, Trap, Slap.		Y
32	APH - I	a"[ph]*(*F*)', a[ph]*(*F*)'	I	2	A	Oft	Graph, Litho-graph, Pho-to-graph.		N
33	APH - II	a[ph]*(F), a"[ph]*(F)	I	2	A	Oft	Graphs, Pho-to-graphs, Pho-to-graphed.		N
34	AR - III	a*(e)'*R*'	I	2	A	Oft	Bare, Care, Hare, Mare, Square, Stare, Ware.		Y
35	ARCH - I	a2R[*CH*](*h*)	I	2	A	Oft	Arch, Larch, March, Parched, Starch.		N
36	ARCH - II	a2R[CH]	I	2	A	Oft	Arched, Marched, Parched, Starched.		N
37	ARCH - III	a2R-[*ch*]	I	2	A	Oft	Ar-ches, Ar-chie, Ar-che-ry, Mar-ches, Mar-ching, Star-chy.		N
38	ARCH - IV	a2R-[ch]**k*	I	2	A	Oft	A-nar-chist~, A-nar-chy~, Ar-cha-ic, Ma-tri-ar-chal, Mo-nar-chy~.		Y
39	ARK - I	a2R*K*(*h*)	I	2	A	Oft	Aard-vark, Bark, Dark, Hark, Lark, Mark, Park, Shark, Spark, Stark.		N
40	ARK - II	a2RK	I	2	A	Oft	Barked, Harks, Larked, Marked, Marks, Parked, Parks, Sharks.		Y
41	ARK - III	a2R-*k*	I	2	A	Oft	Bar-king, Lar-king, Mar-ker, Mar-ket, Par-king, Shar-ky, Spar-king.		Y
42	ART - I	a2R*T*(*h*)	I	2	A	Oft	Bart, Cart, Dart, Gokart, Heart, Mart, Part, Smart, Start, Tart.		N
43	ART - II	a2RT	I	2	A	Oft	Carts, Darts, Parts, Starts, Tarts.		N

44	ART - III	a2R-t2*([td]), a2R-t	I	2	A	Oft	Ar-tist, Car-ting, Mar-tin, Par-ted, Par-ty, Smar-ter, Star-ting.		Y
45	AS - II	a"S1', a'S1'	I	2	A	Oft	Bass, Class, Crass, Gas, Ha-rass, Lass, Mass, Pass, Sur-pass.		N
46	AS - III	a"S1', a'S1'	I	2	A	Oft	Asked, As-pen, Bas-king, Cast, Flask, Grasp, Mask, Sar-cas-tic, Task.		Y
47	ASH - I	a"[SH], a'[SH]	I	2	A	Oft	Ash, Cash, Dash, Flash, Mash, Trash.		Y
48	ASS - I	a"S1's*, a'S1's*	I	2	A	Oft	Bass, Class, Crass, Glass, Lass, Pass, Mass.		Y
49	AST - I	a"S1T(h), a'S1T(h)	I	2	A	Oft	Cast, Last, Past, Fast, Mast, Tele-cast.		Y
50	ATH - I	a"[TH], a'[TH]	I	2	A	Oft	Bath, Math, Ho.meo-path, Psy.cho-path, Wrath.		N
51	EA^ - I	E'a1^	I	2	A	Oft	Clear, Deal, Fear, Meal, Near, Tear~, Year, Zeal.		Y
52	EAR - I	E'a1R	I	2	A	Oft	Dear, Ear, Fear, Gear, Li-near, Tear, Year.		Y
53	EAR - II	E'a1R	I	2	A	Oft	Beard, Ears, Clear-ly, Fears, Near-ly, Tears, Years.		Y
54	ED - I	e"D, e'D	I	2	A	Oft	Bed, Bed-lam, Fed, Fled, Red, Shed, Shred, Sled, Wed.		Y
55	EER	Ee1R'	I	2	A	Oft	Beer, Peer, Ra-cke-teer, Seer, Sheer, Veer.		Y
56	EE^ - I	Ee1^	I	2	A	Oft	Beer, Eel, Keel, Peels, Peered, Reels, Reeled, Seer, Steered.		Y

57	EL - I	e"L', eL'	I	2	A	Oft	A-nna-bel, Bell, Belt, Fell, Felt, Gel, Melt, Pro-pel, Spell, Well.		Y
58	EN - II	e"*n, en*	I	2	A	Oft	Attend, Bend, Lent, Rent, Re-lent, Sent, Tent, Went.		Y
59	EP - II	e"*P(h)*	I	2	A	Oft	Crepe, Hep, Pep, Prep, Rep, Step.		N
60	ET - I	e"*T*, e'*T*	I	2	A	Oft	A-nnette, Bet, Get, Jet, Met, Net, Pet, Rou-lette, Set, Wet, Yet.		Y
61	IF - I	i"*F*', i*F*	I	2	A	Oft	Bai-liff, Cliff, Miff, Stiff, Ta-riff, Whiff.		Y
62	IF - II	i"F, iF	I	2	A	Oft	Drift, Gift, Grift, Lift, Rift, Shift, Sift, Swift, Swift-ly, Thrift.		Y
65	IL - I	i1L'	I	2	A	Oft	Do-cile, Fa-cile, Fo-ssil, Ho-stile, Mi-ssile, Mo-bile.		Y
66	INT - I	i"*nT(h)*, i'*nT(h)*	I	2	A	Oft	Dint, Clint, Flint, Lint, Mint, Print, Sprint, Squint, Stint, Tint.		N
67	IP - I	i"*P(h)*, i*P(h)*	I	2	A	Oft	Flip, Grip, Hip, Lip, Rip, Ships, Sip, Skip, Tip, Trip, Whip.		Y
68	IX - I	i"x*(K)(*S*), ix*(K)(*S*)	I	2	A	Oft	Fix, Mix, Nix, Nix-on, Six.		N
69	OB - I	o'*B*, o"*B*	I	2	A	Oft	Bob, Blob, Cob, Job, Fob, Lob, Mob, Nob, Rob, Snob.		Y
70	OB - II	o'B	I	2	A	Oft	Jobs, Ob-ject~, Ob-jec-tive~, Ob-fus-cate, Ob-scure, Lobbed.		Y
71	OB - III	o'-B	I	2	A	Oft	Co-bble, Ho-bbled, Lo-bbies, Ro-bin, Ro-bert, Ro-bbe-ry, So-bbing.		Y

72	ON - I	O-*n*, O'-*n*	I	2	A	Oft	A-cri.mo.ny, Ce.re.mo-ny, Tes-ti.mo-ny, Po-ny.		Y
73	OR - II	o)'R, o)R	I	2	A	Oft	En-dorse, Form, For-ty, Horse, Norm, Spor-ting, Short, Storm, Stored.		Y
74	OR - III	o)'-*r*, o-*r*	I	2	A	Oft	Fo-reign, Ho-rrid, In-ven-to.ry, Lo-rry, Mo-ral, O-range, Sto-rage.		Y
75	ORN - I	o)'R*N*, o*RN*	I	2	A	Oft	Born, Corn, Horn, Morn, Scorn, Shorn, Torn, Thorn, Worn.		N
76	ORN - II	o)'RN, oRN	I	2	A	Oft	Corns, Horned, Horns, Scorned, Thorns.		N
77	ORN - III	o)'R-*n*, oR-*n*	I	2	A	Oft	Cor-ny, Hor-net, Mor-ning, Or-na-ment, Scor-ning, Thor-ny.		N
78	UB - I	u2-B	I	2	A	Oft	Lu-bri,cant, Lu-bri-cate, Ru-by, Tu-bu-lar~, U-ber.		Y
79	UR - I	(y)u1*R*	I	2	A	Oft	Con-fi-gure~, Fai-lure, Fi-gure~, Se-cure~, Te-nure~.		N
80	AF - II	a"*F*, a'*F*	I	3	A	Occ	Gaff, Riffraff, Staff.		N
81	ALF	a"l**F'*, a'l**F*	I	3	A	Occ	Half, Calf.		N
82	AR - IV	a1*R'*	I	3	A	Occ	Co-llar, Mo-lar, Po-lar, Scho-lar, So-lar.		Y
83	ARCH - V	a2R[ch]**K(h)*	I	3	A	Occ	Mo-narch, Ma-tri-arch, Pa-tri-arch.		N
84	ARCH - VI	a2R[ch]*K	I	3	A	Occ	Mo-narchs, Ma-tri-archs.		N

85	ART - IV	a*oR*T*	I	3	A	Occ	Quart, Thwart, Wart.		N
86	ART - V	a*RT	I	3	A	Occ	Quarts, Thwarts, Warts.		N
87	ART - VI	a*oR-t2*([td]), a*oR-t	I	3	A	Occ	Quar-ter, Thwar-ting, Thwar-ted.		N
88	ART - VII	a2R-t*[*sh*]	I	3	A	Occ	Mar-tial, Mar-tian, Par-tial.		N
89	EF - I	e"*F*, e *F*	I	3	A	Occ	Jeff, Steff.		N
90	ER - III	(Y)e1*R*	I	3	A	Occ	Em-plo-yer~, Fo-yer~, Law-yer~, Saw-yer.		N
91	EU^ - I	e*u2^	I	3	A	Occ	Leud, Pseud, Sleuth.		N
92	EU^ - II	e*u2-^	I	3	A	Occ	Neu-tral~, Neu-ter~, Teu-to.nic~, Pseu-do.		N
93	EUR - I	e1'u**R*'	I	3	A	Occ	A-ma-teur, Ma-sseur, Ra-con-teur, Sa-bo-teur.		N
94	IAR - I	i*(E)a*(e)-*r*	I	3	A	Occ	Be.ne-fi.ci.a-ry, Fi.du-ci.a-ry, In.cen-di.a-ry, To-pi.a-ry.		Y
95	IVER	i-ve1*R*	I	3	A	Occ	Gi-ver, Li-ver, Qui-ver, Ri-ver, Shi-ver.		N
96	IZAT	i-*z*A-t*[*sh*]	I	3	A	Occ	Or.ga-ni.za.tion, Mo.der-ni.za.tion, Rea-li.za.tion.		Y
97	OTH - I	o'[*TH*]	I	3	A	Occ	Broth, Cloth, Froth, Goth, Moth, Sloth~.		N

98	UAR - I	u*(W)a*oR	I	3	A	Occ	Quark, Quar-rel, Quar-ry, Quart, Quar-ter.		N
99	UB - II	u2*B*	I	3	A	Occ	Lube, Tube~.		N
100	UI^ - I	u2-i^	I	3	A	Occ	Dru-id, Flu-id, Je-su.it~, Ru-in.		N
101	UI^ - II	u2-i-^	I	3	A	Occ	Flu-i.di.ty, Fru.i-tion, In-ge-nu.i.ty~, In-tu.i.tive, Ru.i-nous, Tu.i-tion.		N
102	UK - I	u2'*K(h)*, (i)u2*K(h)*	I	3	A	Occ	Duke~, Fluke, Luke.		N

Chapter 15:
Recognizing Vocal Patterns – Using Word List Tables.

The Word List Table provided for most Vocal Patterns will enable you to convert your pronunciation of many words at one time, rather than being limited to learning only single words at a time. Each Word List Table gives you a list of words containing a specified Vocal Pattern, enabling you to vocalize them in the American way. By practicing the Vocal Patterns in these Word List Tables you quickly shift to an American way of speaking English!

Word List Tables are provided for Vocal Patterns for which there are enough words to justify a supplementary Word List in addition to the examples already provided with each Vocal Pattern. Word List Tables are not provided for Vocal Patterns that have an Occasional Rate of Occurrence as there are few such words.

Word List Tables are presented in order of Distinctiveness, Rate of Occurrence and in alphanumeric order.

Each Word List Table begins with a "Priority-Sequence" number in the top row. Priority refers to Priority Group based on Distinctiveness and Sequence refers to the Learning Sequence number based on both Distinctiveness and Rate of Occurrence levels.

Remember, Learning Priority Group categories for Vocal Patterns have been set to correspond with their Distinctiveness (APDE) categories:
Learning Priority Group 'I' corresponds with 'A', i.e. "Great" or most Distinctive Vocal Patterns;
Learning Priority Group 'II' corresponds with 'B', i.e. "Substantial" or very Distinctive Vocal Patterns; and
Learning Priority Group 'III' corresponds with 'C', i.e. "Significant" or clearly Distinctive Vocal Patterns.

> Distinctiveness category 'D', i.e. "Insignificant" Distinctiveness Vocal Patterns which are nearly Indistinct, are only listed in the Master Table and have not been included in the Vocal Pattern and Word List Tables.

And, the Learning Sequence categories based on both Distinctiveness and Rate of Occurrence levels for Vocal Patterns, are:

> In the Vocal Pattern Bridge Table, (in Coursebook One), '1' is for "Frequent" and '2' for "Often".
> In the Vocal Pattern Inland Table, (in Coursebook Two), '4' is for "Frequent" and '5' for "Often".
> In the Vocal Pattern Summit Table, (in Coursebook Three), '7' is for "Frequent" and '8" for "Often".
>
> Word List Tables are not provided for Vocal Patterns with a Rate of Occurrence that is "Occasional", i.e. Learning Sequence category numbers '3', '6' and '9'. Learning Sequence categories, '10', '11' and '12' are associated with category 'IV', i.e. Insignificant or nearly Indistinct Vocal Patterns and are not included in the Vocal Pattern or Word List Tables.

See Table: Learning Priority and Learning Sequence preceding the Vocal Pattern Bridge for Learning Priority and Sequence categories.

Within Priority-Sequence groups, they are in alpha-numeric order. To illustrate:

Vocal Pattern, AM - I (Priority-Sequence I/1) precedes Vocal Pattern, AN - I (Priority-Sequence I/1), among the Word List Tables corresponding with the "Vocal Pattern Bridge Table", because the former precedes the latter in alphanumeric order. However, Vocal Pattern, AR - II (Priority-Sequence I/1) precedes Vocal Pattern, ANK - II (Priority-Sequence I/2), though ANK - II precedes the AR - II in alphanumeric order. This is because the Rate of Occurrence for AR - II is in the higher category, i.e. "Frequent", compared with ANK - II which is in the "Often" category, as may be seen from their Priority-Sequence groups. Both 'AR - II' and 'ANK - II' are listed in the Vocal Pattern Bridge Table, which contains Vocal Patterns categorized 'I/1' and 'I/2'.

"The Vocal Pattern Bridge Table" provided in Coursebook One, "The American Accent Learnway – Cross the Bridge, Over the Divide" of this three Coursebook series, contains just over 100 Vocal Patterns. "The Vocal Pattern Inland Table" in Coursebook Two, "The American Accent Learnway – Together, On the Road Inland" contains 200 Vocal Patterns. "The Vocal Pattern Summit Table", provided in Coursebook Three, entitled "The American Accent Learnway – As One, On the Summit", contains just over 300 Vocal Patterns.

Tables:
Word Lists From Priority-Sequence I/1 Vocal Pattern AD - I
Through Priority-Sequence I/3 Vocal Pattern IZAT

The order of presentation is: Down the first column, down the second column, down the third column, to the first column of the next page, and so on.

Priority-Sequence: I/1
Vocal Pattern: AD - I
In Phonetic Script: a"*D*, a'*D*
Example Words:
Add
Bad
Brad
Cad
Clad
Dad
Fad
Glad
Had
Mad
Pad
Sad
Tad
Priority-Sequence: I/1
Vocal Pattern: AM - I
In Phonetic Script: a"M, a'M
Example Words:
Am
Amble
Ampere
Amplify

Burmingham
Cam
Cram
Dam
Flamboyant
Ham
Hamster
Jam
Jamboree
Lamb
Lamp
Ramp
Rambunctious
Sam
Scam
Scramble
Sham
Slam
Tram
Priority-Sequence: I/1
Vocal Pattern: AN - I
In Phonetic Script: a"*N*, a'*N*
Example Words:
Ban
Can
Clan

Dan
Fan
Flan
Japan
Man
Pan
Ran
Stan
Sedan
Tan
Than
Priority-Sequence: I/1
Vocal Pattern: AN - II
In Phonetic Script: a"*n*, a'*n*
Example Words:
Advance
And
Band
Bangle
Bank
Banned
Branch
Can't
Dance
Drank
Fanned

Flange
Frank
Grand
Grant
Hand
Hang
Land
Manned
Panned
Pants
Rant
Romance
Sand
Shank
Strand
Tangle
Thank
Priority-Sequence: I/1
Vocal Pattern: AND - I
In Phonetic Script: a"*nD(h)*, a'*nD(h)*
Example Words:
And
Band
Command
Brand
Contraband
Demand

Grand
Hand
Land
Operand
Rand
Sand
Stand
Strand
Priority-Sequence: I/1
Vocal Pattern: ANK - I
In Phonetic Script: a"[n*K*]*(h)*, a[n*K*]*(h)*
Example Words:
Bank
Crank
Drank
Flank
Frank
Plank
Prank
Rank
Sank
Spank
Swank
Tank
Thank

Priority-Sequence: I/1
Vocal Pattern: AR - II
In Phonetic Script: a2R
Example Words:
Hard
Arm
Bark
Card
Farmer
Large
Largesse
Harmonic
Harmony
Mark
Marvelous
Narcissist
Park
Parley
Part
Sardine
Scarf
Smart
Start
Startling
Spark
Target
Tart
Priority-Sequence: I/1

Vocal Pattern: EM - I
In Phonetic Script: e"M, e'M
Example Words:
Attempt
Attempts
Empty
Gem
Gems
Hem
Hemmed
Hemp
Stem
Stems
Tempest
Tempestuous
Tempt
Temptation
Tempts
Them
Unkempt
Priority-Sequence: I/1
Vocal Pattern: EN - I
Example Words:
Ben
Den
Glen
Gwen
Hen

Ken
Men
Pen
Sten
Ten
Then
When
Wren
Priority-Sequence: I/1
Vocal Pattern: EP - I
In Phonetic Script: e"P, e'P
Example Words:
Adept
Crept
Depth
Inept
Kept
Kleptomaniac
Neptune
Peptic
Prepped
Receptacle
Reptile
Septic
Skeptic
Skeptical
Slept
Steps

Stepped
Wept
Priority-Sequence: I/1
Vocal Pattern: ER - I
In Phonetic Script: e1*R*
Example Words:
Aver
Baker
Beaker
Better
Buyer
Cider
Cover
Deliver
Destroyer
Dinner
Employer
Ever
Fever
Fixer
Foyer
Gambler
Gander
Hunter
Islander
Kipper
Lawyer~
Layer

Litter
Liver
Master
Mister
Naysayer
Never
Over
Player
Prayer
Proper
Quiver
River
Saber
Sawyer~
Shutter
Soothsayer
Teacher
Tiger
Under
Vintner
Voyager
Wager
Were
Winter
Priority-Sequence: I/1
Vocal Pattern: ER - II
In Phonetic Script: E'(e1)*R*, E'(e1)R

Example Words:
Beer
Deer
Here
Jeer
Jeered
Leered
Mere
Merely
Musketeer
Peer
Racketeer
Reindeer
Seer
Veered
Priority-Sequence: I/1
Vocal Pattern: ES - I
In Phonetic Script: e"*S*1, e'*S*1
Example Words:
Arrest
Bess
Best
Bless
Chest
Confess
Crest
Depressed
Dress

Egress
Excess
Guest
Less
Mess
Nest
Pest
Press
Stress
Stressed
Tess
Western
Priority-Sequence: I/1
Vocal Pattern: ESS – I
In Phonetic Script: e"*S*1s*, e'*S*1s*
Example Words:
Bess
Bless
Caress
Confess
Dress
Egress
Excess
Less
Mess
Press
Stress

Tess
Water Cress
Priority-Sequence: I/1
Vocal Pattern: IM - I
In Phonetic Script: i"M, i'M
Example Words:
Akimbo
Brim
Dimple
Flimsy
Grim
Him
Important
Jim
Kim
Kimberly
Limber
Limbo
Limp
Limpet
Rim
Shim
Simple
Simplicity
Skim
Skimpy
Slim
Tim

Trim
Whim
Priority-Sequence: I/1
Vocal Pattern: IN - I
In Phonetic Script: i"*N*, i*N*
Example Words:
Badminton
Brindle
Cinder
Destined
Hinder
Incident
Indent
Indentation
Indigo
Industrial
Infant
Infiltrate
Infrared
Ingest
Kindle
Kindred
Tinder
Window
Winter
Priority-Sequence: I/1

Vocal Pattern: IT - I
In Phonetic Script: i"*T(h)*, i"*T(h)*
Example Words:
Bit
Flit
Grit
Grit
Hit
It
Kit
Knit
Knit
Lit
Nit
Sit
Skit
Slit
Spit
Split
Wit
Zit
Priority-Sequence: I/1
Vocal Pattern: OM - I
In Phonetic Script: o'M
Example Words:
Abercrombie
Combination

Commodore
Complicate
Compost
Comrade
Dot Com
Insomnia
From
Omnivore
Stomp
Stomped
Thrombosis
Tom
Trombone
Priority-Sequence: I/1
Vocal Pattern: OR - I
In Phonetic Script: o)'*R*, o)*R*
Example Words:
Abhor
Adore
Bore
Core
For
Fore
Furore
Igor
Implore
Lore
Mentor

More
Or
Ore
Or
Pore
Restore
Sore
Score
Shore
Snore
Spore
Store
Tore
Priority-Sequence: I/1
Vocal Pattern: OU^ - I
In Phonetic Script: o*(a)'u^, o*(a)'u*(w)^
Example Words:
About
Account
Astound
Bound
Count
Countess
Flour
Found
Fountain
Gouge

Gout
Grout
Hound
Joust
Loud
Mound
Mountain
Mouse
Noun
Out
Proud
Round
Roust
Rout
Scoundrel
Scour
Scout
Shout
Slouch
Sound
South
Stout
Tout
Trout
Priority-Sequence: I/2
Vocal Pattern: AF - I
In Phonetic Script: A"F, a'F
Example Words:

Aft
After
Craft
Crafted
Crafting
Drafted
Drafting
Graft
Grafts
Shaft
Daft
Raft
Rafter
Rafting

Priority-Sequence: I/2
Vocal Pattern: ANK - II
In Phonetic Script: a"[nK], a[nK]
Example Words:
Banked
Banks
Blanks
Blanked
Cranked
Flanks
Flanked
Franked
Frankly

Pranks
Ranked
Tanked
Tanks
Thanks

Priority-Sequence: I/2
Vocal Pattern: ANK - III
In Phonetic Script: a[nK]-(*k*)
Example Words:
Ankle
Anklet
Banker
Banking
Cranking
Flanking
Frankincense
Franking
Lanky
Manky
Ranking
Rankle
Shanking
Spanking
Tanker
Tanking
Thanking

Priority-Sequence: I/2
Vocal Pattern: ANS - I
In Phonetic Script: a"Ns2*(Z), a'Ns2*(Z)
Example Words:
Bans
Cans
Dan's
Fans
Flans
Fran's
Man's
Nan's
Pans
Plans
Spans
Stan's
Tans
Vans

Priority-Sequence: I/2
Vocal Pattern: AP - I
In Phonetic Script: a"*P*, a' *P*
Example Words:
Cap
Clap
Flap
Lap
Map

Nap
Pap
Rap
Slap
Snap
Strap
Tap
Trap
Zap
Priority-Sequence: I/2
Vocal Pattern: AR - III
In Phonetic Script: a*(e)'*R*'
Example Words:
Bare
Blare
Care
Dare
Delaware
Fare
Flare
Glare
Hare
Mare
Pare
Rare
Scare
Share
Silverware

Snare
Spare
Square
Stare
Tare
Ware
Welfare
Priority-Sequence: I/2
Vocal Pattern: ARCH - IV
In Phonetic Script: a2R-[ch]**k*
Example Words:
Anarchist~
Anarchy~
Archaic
Architect
Architecture
Matriarchal
Matriarchy
Monarchist~
Monarchy~
Patriarchal
Patriarchy
Priority-Sequence: I/2
Vocal Pattern: ARK - II
In Phonetic Script: a2RK

Example Words:
Barks
Barked
Harks
Larks
Larked
Marked
Marks
Landmarks
Parks
Parked
Sharks
Sparks
Sparked
Priority-Sequence: I/2
Vocal Pattern: ARK - III
In Phonetic Script: a2R-*k*
Example Words:
Barking
Darken
Darker
Darkest
Larking
Marker
Market
Marking
Parking
Sharky

Sparking
Sparkler
Priority-Sequence: I/2
Vocal Pattern: ART - III
In Phonetic Script: a2R-t2*([td]), a2R-t
Example Words:
Article
Artist
Artistry
Carted
Carting
Carton
Darted
Garter
Hearty
Martin
Parted
Particle
Parting
Party
Smarter
Smartest
Spartan
Starter
Starting

Priority-Sequence: I/2
Vocal Pattern: AS - III
In Phonetic Script: a"S1', a'S1'
Alas
Ask
Asked
Blast
Broadcast
Cast
Castor
Drastic
Ecclesiastical
Elastic
Fantastic
Fast
Flask
Iconoclast
Last
Lasting
Mask
Masking
Masts
Master
Mastery
Masticate
Nasty
Past
Pastor
Plaster

Plastic
Sarcastic
Spastic
Tasks
Telecast
Priority-Sequence: I/2
Vocal Pattern: ASH - I
In Phonetic Script: a"[*SH*], a'[*SH*]
Example Words:
Ash
Bash
Brash
Clash
Crash
Dash
Flash
Hash
Mash
Nashville
Rash
Slash
Smash
Splash
Stash
Thrash
Trash

Priority-Sequence: I/2
Vocal Pattern: ASS - I
In Phonetic Script: a"s*S1', a's*S1'
Example Words:
Amass
Ass
Bass
Brass
Class
Crass
Crevasse
Glass
Grass
Harass
Lass
Mass
Morass
Pass
Sass
Priority-Sequence: I/2
Vocal Pattern: AST - I
In Phonetic Script: a"S1T(h), a'S1T(h)
Example Words:
Aghast
Blast

Broadcast
Cast
Caste
Contrast
Fast
Forecast
Iconoclast
Last
Mast
Past
Telecast
Priority-Sequence: I/2
Vocal Pattern: EA^ - I
In Phonetic Script: E'a1^
Example Words:
Clear
Deal
Dear
Fear
Gear
Heal
Meal
Near
Peal
Real
Seal
Steal
Teal

Tear
Veal
Year
Zeal
Priority Group: I
Vocal Pattern: EAR - I
In Phonetic Script: E'a1R
Example Words:
Clear
Dear
Ear
Fear
Gear
Hear
Linear
Near
Shear
Smear
Spear
Tear~
Year
Priority-Sequence: I/2
Vocal Pattern: EAR - II
In Phonetic Script: E'a1R
Example Words:
Appears

Appeared
Arrears
Beard
Cleared
Clearly
Ears
Feared
Fears
Gears
Hears
Nearly
Reared
Rears
Sheared
Smeared
Spears
Tears
Years
Priority-Sequence: I/2
Vocal Pattern: ED - I
In Phonetic Script: e"*D*, e'*D*
Example Words:
Bed
Bled
Bedlam
Fed
Fled
Fred

Led
Ned
Red
Shed
Shred
Sled
Sped
Ted
Wed
Priority-Sequence: I/2
Vocal Pattern: EER
In Phonetic Script: Ee1*R*'
Example Words:
Beer
Career
Commandeer
Deer
Jeer
Leer
Musketeer
Peer
Queer
Racketeer
Reindeer
Seer
Sheer
Sneer
Steer

Veer
Priority-Sequence: I/1
Vocal Pattern: EL - I
In Phonetic Script: e"L, eL'
Example Words:
Annabel
Bell
Belt
Cell
Celtic
Excelled
Fell
Felt
Gel
Gelled
Held
Hotel
Melt
Pelt
Propel
Quelled
Sell
Seldom
Shell
Smelt
Spell
Swelter
Tell

Weld

Welt

Priority-Sequence: I/2

Vocal Pattern: EN - II

In Phonetic Script: e"*n*, e*n*

Example Words:

Ascent

Attend

Blend

Content

Dissent

Fend

French

Friendship

Intent

Mend

Relent

Rend

Rent

Resent

Send

Sent

Tend

Tent

Wend

Priority-Sequence: I/2

Vocal Pattern: ET - I

In Phonetic Script: e"*T*, e'*T*

Example Words:

Abet

Annette

Asset

Bet

Cadet

Debt

Fret

Get

Gillette

Jet

Met

Net

Pet

Regret

Roulette

Set

Wet

Yet

Priority-Sequence: I/2

Vocal Pattern: IF - I

In Phonetic Script: i"*F*, i*F*

Example Words:

Bailiff

Biff

Cliff

Skiff

Stiff

Miff

Sheriff

Sniff

Tariff

Tiff

Whiff

Priority-Sequence: I/2

Vocal Pattern: IF - II

In Phonetic Script: i"F, iF

Example Words:

Cliffs

Clifton

Drift

Drifted

Drifting

Gift

Gifted

Lift

Lifted

Rift

Shifted

Shifting

Sifted

Swift

Swiftly

Priority-Sequence: I/2
Vocal Pattern: IL - I
In Phonetic Script: i1L'
Example Words:
Anvil
Docile
Facile
Fossil
Fissile
Hostile
Missile
Mobile
Nostril
Tactile
Tonsil
Priority-Sequence: I/2
Vocal Pattern: IP - I
In Phonetic Script: i"*P(h)*
Example Words:
Blip
Drip
Flip
Grip
Hip
Lip
Nip
Rip

Ship
Strip
Tip
Trip
Whip
Priority-Sequence: I/2
Vocal Pattern: OB - I
In Phonetic Script: o'*B*, o"*B*
Example Words:
Blob
Bob
Cob
Fob
Glob
Job
Lob
Mob
Nob
Rob
Slob
Snob
Sob
Throb
Priority-Sequence: I/2
Vocal Pattern: OB - II
In Phonetic Script: o'B

Example Words:
Bobbed
Bobs
Jobs
Mobs
Nobs
Obfuscate
Object~
Objective~
Oblong
Obscure
Obtuse
Robbed
Robs
Slobs
Throbbed
Throbs
Priority-Sequence: I/2
Vocal Pattern: OB - III
In Phonetic Script: o'-B
Example Words:
Bobbing
Cobble
Cobbled
Fobbing
Hobble
Hobbling
Lobbed

Lobbies
Lobbying
Robber
Robbery
Robbing
Robert
Robin
Sobbing
Snobbery
Throbbing
Priority-Sequence: I/2
Vocal Pattern: ON - I
In Phonetic Script: O-*n*, O'-*n*
Example Words:
Abalone
Acrimonious
Acrimony
Alimony
Ceremonial
Ceremony
Colonial
Parsimony
Phony
Pony
Stony
Testimonial
Testimony

Priority-Sequence: I/2
Vocal Pattern: OR - II
In Phonetic Script: o)'R, o)R
Example Words:
Distort
Endorse
Escort
Form
Fort
Forty
Horse
Lord
Morning
Morph
Morphine
Norm
Port
Scorn
Short
Snort
Sort
Sporting
Storm
Torn
Torpedo
Tort
Vortex
Whorl

Priority-Sequence: I/2
Vocal Pattern: OR - III
In Phonetic Script: o)'-*r*, o-*r*
Example Words:
Borrow
Coral
Correspondent
Corridor
Florid
Forage
Foreign
Forest
Glory
Horrible
Horrid
Horror
Inventory
Lavatory
Mandatory
Moral
Observatory
Oral
Orange
Porridge
Predatory
Sorrow
Sorry
Storage
Story
Territory

Tomorrow
Torrid
Transitory
Priority-Sequence: I/2
Vocal Pattern: UB - I
In Phonetic Script: u2-B
Example Words:
Aruba
Guber
Lubricant
Lubricate
Lubrication
Rubescence
Rubicon
Rubicund
Ruby
Scuba
Tubing
Tubular
Uber
Priority-Sequence: I/3
Vocal Pattern: AR - IV
In Phonetic Script: a1R'
Example Words:
Cellar
Collar

Dollar
Molar
Polar
Scholar
Solar
Stellar
Tankard
Priority-Sequence: I/3
Vocal Pattern: IAR - I
In Phonetic Script: i*(E)a*(e)-r
Example Words:
Auxiliary
Beneficiary
Fiduciary
Incendiary
Judiciary
Pecuniary
Topiary
Priority-Sequence: I/3
Vocal Pattern: IZAT
In Phonetic Script: i-zA-t*[sh]
Actualization
Canonization
Demonetization

Canonization
Demonetization
Finalization
Hospitalization
Optimization
Organization
Polarization
Radicalization
Rationalization
Realization
Standardization
Sterilization

PART 4: VOCALIZING VERY COMMON WORDS THE AMERICAN WAY.

Chapter 16:
Vocalizing Common Words the American Way.

Looking through the words below, you may wonder, "Why focus on words which we know so well?" The reason is that more often than not, they are said differently in the American Accent. And, since they are so common, getting them right quickly takes you a long way toward speaking the American way!

A hundred very common words the pronunciation of which should be mastered are included in the List below.

Table:
Very Common Words Vocalized The American Way

Serial No.	Common Word	American Vocalization Description in Vocal Fidelity Phonetic Script	Verbal Description (If more than one option in previous column, only first is described)
1	And	a"*nD(h)*	'A' Soft: Extended and Repeated.'N': Weak to moderate. Nasal; Hum; Lilting. 'D': Strong. Hiss.
2	About	a1-Bo*(a)u*T(h)*, a1-Bo*(a)u*(w)*T(h)*	Short Vowel. Pause. 'B': Moderate to strong. Pop Light. 'O': Replaced with A' Soft. 'U' Soft.
3	Also	a*o*l*-*s*1(a1)O, a*o*l*-*s*1O(w)	'A': Replaced with 'O' Soft. 'L': Weak to moderate. Pause. 'S': Weak to moderate. Short Vowel: Inserted. 'O' Hard.
4	Am	a"*M,* a'*M*	'A' Soft: Extended and Repeated. 'M': Strong. Hum, Nasal, Lilting.
5	Are	a2*R*'e*	'A' Long. 'R': Rasp. Strong. Extended. 'E': Silent.
6	As	a"s*(Z), a's*(Z)	'A' Soft: Extended and Repeated. 'Z': Moderate to strong.
7	Ask	a"S*K(h), a'SK(h)*	'A' Soft: Extended and Repeated. 'S': Moderate to strong. Hiss. 'K': Strong. Sharp. Hiss.
8	Big	Bi'*G(h)*	'B': Moderate to strong. Pop Light. 'I' Soft: Extended. 'G': Strong. Flat, Pop Heavy, Knock. Hiss.
9	But	Bu1*T(h)*	'B': Moderate to strong. Pop Light. 'U' Short. 'T': Strong. Hiss.
10	Call	c1*(K)*(h)a*o)*'L'l*	'C': Replaced with 'K': Moderate to strong. Sharp. Hiss. 'A': Replaced with 'O' Soft-Round, Extended. 'L': Strong. Extended.
11	Can	c1*(K)*(h)*a"*N,* C*(h)*a'*N*	'C': Replaced with 'K. Moderate to strong. Sharp. Hiss. 'A' Soft: Extended and Repeated. 'N': Strong. Knock, Nasal, Hum, Lilting.
12	Can't	c1*(K)*(h)*a"N*T(h),*	'C': Replaced with 'K'. Moderate to strong. Sharp. Hiss.

		c1*(K)*(h)*a"N*T(h)*	'A' Soft: Extended and Repeated. 'N': Weak to moderate. Nasal, Hum, Lilting. 'T': Strong. Hiss.
13	Car	c1*(K)*(h)*a2*R'*	'C': Replaced with 'K'. Moderate to strong. Sharp. Hiss. 'A' Long. 'R': Strong. Rasp. Extended.
14	Clome	c1*(K)*(h)*o1M'e*	'C': Replaced with 'K'. Moderate to strong. Sharp. Hiss. 'O' Short. 'M': Moderate to strong. Hum. 'E': Silent
15	Do	D(i)o2, Do2'	'D': Moderate to strong. Pop Heavy, Knock. 'I' Soft: Inserted. 'O' Long.
16	Doing	D(i)o2i[ng], Do2i[ng]	'D': Moderate to strong. Pop Heavy, Knock. 'I' Soft: Inserted. 'O' Long. 'I' Soft. 'N': Weak. Nasal. 'G': Weak. Flat.
17	Due	D(i)u2e*, Du2'e*	'D': Moderate to strong. Pop Heavy, Knock. 'I' Soft: Inserted. 'U' Long. 'E': Silent.
18	Early	e1R'-*ly**(E)'	'E' Short. 'R': Strong. Rasp. Extension. Pause. 'L' Weak to moderate. 'Y': Replaced with 'E' Hard. Extended.
19	Ever	e-*v*e1*R'*	'E' Soft. Pause. 'V': Weak to moderate. Buzz. 'E' Short. 'R': Strong. Rasp. Extended.
20	Far	*fa*2*R'*	'F': Weak to moderate. Hiss. 'A' Long. 'R': Strong. Rasp. Extended.
21	Fast	*fa*"S*T(h)*	'F': Weak to moderate. Hiss. 'A' Soft. Extended and Repeated. 'S': Moderate to strong. Hiss. 'T': Strong. Sharp, Knock. Hiss.
22	For	*foR'*, *foR*	'F': Weak to moderate. Hiss. 'O' Soft-Round. 'R': Strong. Rasp. Extended.
23	From	*fr*o1M, *fr*o'M, fr*o1M	'F': Weak to moderate. Hiss. 'O' Short. 'M': Moderate to strong. Hum.
24	Go	g(a1)O, GO'	'G1': Weak to moderate. Flat, Pop Heavy, Knock. Short Vowel: Inserted. 'O' Hard.
25	Gone	goN'e*, Go(w)*N*e*	'G1': Weak to moderate. Flat, Pop Heavy, Knock. 'O' Soft-Round. 'N': Strong. Knock, Hum, Nasal. Extended. 'E': Silent.
26	Got	go'*T(h)*, Go'*T(h)*	'G1': Weak to moderate. Flat, Pop Heavy, Knock. 'O' Soft-Flat, Extended. 'T': Strong. Sharp, Knock. Hiss.
27	Had	*Ha*"*D(h)*, *Ha*'*D(h)*	'H': Strong. Hiss. 'A' Soft. Extended and Repeated. 'D': Strong. Pop Heavy, Knock. Hiss.
28	Has	*Ha*"s*(Z), *Ha*'s*(Z)	'H': Strong. Hiss. 'A' Soft. Extended and Repeated. 'S': Replaced with 'Z'. Moderate to strong. Buzz.
29	Hello	He-*l*l*(a1)O, He-*l*l*O'	'H': Strong. Hiss. 'E' Soft. Pause. 'L': Weak to moderate. Short Vowel: Inserted. 'O' Hard.
30	Her	*He*1*R'*	'H': Strong. Hiss. 'E' Short. R: Strong. Rasp. Extended.
31	Here	*H*E'*R*'e*, HE(e1)*R*'e*	'H': Strong. Hiss. 'E' Hard. Extended. R: Strong. Rasp. Extended.
32	Him	*Hi*"M, Hi'M	'H': Strong. Hiss. 'I' Soft. Extended and Repeated.
33	Hot	*Ho*'*T(h)*	'H': Strong. Hiss. 'O' Soft-Flat, Extended. 'T': Strong. Sharp, Knock. Hiss.

34	Hour	h*o*(a)-(W)u1R, h*o*(a)-u1R	'H': Silent. 'O': Replaced with 'A' Soft. Pause. 'W': Inserted. Strong. 'U': Short. R: Strong.
35	How	Ho*(a)'w	'H': Strong. Hiss. 'O': Replaced with 'A' Soft. Extended. 'W': Weak. Vowelish.
36	In	i"N, i'N	'I': Soft. Extended and Repeated. 'N': Strong. Knock, Nasal, Hum, Lilting.
37	Is	i"s2*(Z), i's2*(Z)	'I': Soft. Extended and Repeated. 'S2': Replaced with 'Z'. Moderate to strong. Buzz.
38	It	i"T(h), i'T(h)	'I': Soft. Extended and Repeated. 'T': Strong. Sharp, Knock. Hiss.
39	Lady	lA-Dy*(E)	'L': Weak. Hum. Pause. 'D': Moderate to strong. Pop Heavy, Knock. 'Y': Replaced with 'E' Hard.
40	Law	la*(o)w	'L': Weak. Hum. 'A': Replaced with 'O' Soft-Round. 'W': Weak. Vowelish.
41	Long	lo)'[ng], lo'[ng]	'L': Weak. Hum. 'O' Soft-Round, Extended. 'N': Weak. Nasal. 'G': Weak. Flat.
42	Less	le"S1's*, le'S1's*	'L': Weak. Hum. 'E' Soft: Extended and Repeated. 'S1': Strong. Extended.
43	Man	ma"N, ma'N	'M': Weak. Hum. 'A' Soft: Extended and Repeated. 'N': Strong. Knock, Nasal, Hum, Lilting.
44	Men	me"N, me'N	'M': Weak. Hum. 'E' Soft: Extended and Repeated. 'N': Strong. Knock, Nasal, Hum, Lilting.
45	More	moR'e*	'M': Weak. Hum. 'O' Soft-Round. 'R': Strong. Rasp. Extended. 'E': Silent.
46	Near	nE'a1R	'N': Weak to moderate. Knock, Hum. 'E' Hard. Extended. 'A' Short. 'R': Strong. Rasp.
47	Never	ne-ve1R'	"N': Weak to moderate. Knock, Hum. 'E' Soft. Pause. 'V': Weak to moderate. Buzz. 'E' Short. 'R': Strong. Rasp. Extended.
48	Not	no)'T(h), no'T(h)	'N': Weak to moderate. Knock, Hum. 'O' Soft-Round, Extended. 'T': Strong. Sharp, Knock. Hiss.
49	Now	no*(a)'w	'N': Weak to moderate. Knock, Hum. 'O': Replaced with 'A' Soft. Extended. 'W': Weak. Vowelish.
50	Of	o1f*(V)	'O' Short. 'F': Replaced with 'V'. Moderate to strong. Buzz, Flat.
51	Off	o)'F'f*, o'F'f*	'O' Soft-Round, Extended. 'F': Strong. Hiss. Extended.
52	Often	o'F-Te1N, o'-f't*e1N	'O': Soft-Flat, Extended. 'F': Moderate to strong. Hiss. 'E' Short. 'N': Moderate to strong. Knock, Hum.
53	On	oN', o(w)N'	'O' Soft-Round. 'N': Strong. 'N': Strong. Knock, Nasal, Hum, Lilting. Extended.
54	Or	oR	'O' Soft-Round. 'R': Strong. Rasp. Extended.
55	Our	o*(a)-(W)u1R, o*(a)-u1R	'O': Replaced with 'A' Soft. Pause. 'W': Inserted. Strong. Vowelish. 'U' Short. 'R': Strong.
56	Out	o*(a)'uT(h), o*(a)'u*(w)T(h)	'O': Replaced with 'A' Soft. Extended. 'U' Soft. 'T': Strong. Sharp, Knock. Hiss.

57	Over	O-*v*e1*R*	'O' Hard. Pause. 'V': Weak to moderate. Buzz, Flat. 'E' Short. 'R' Strong. Rasp.
58	Put	*P(h)u'T(h)*	'P': Strong. Hiss. 'U' Soft. Extended. 'T': Strong. Sharp, Knock. Hiss.
59	Room	*r(i)o2o**M, *r*o2o*M	'R': Weak to moderate. Rasp. 'I' Soft: Inserted. 'O' Long. 'M': Moderate to strong.
60	Round	ro*(a)'u*nD(h)*, ro*(a)'u*(w)*nD(h)*	'R': Weak to moderate. 'O': Replaced with 'A' Soft. Extended. 'U' Soft. 'N': Weak to moderate. Knock, Hum, Nasal. 'D': Strong. Pop Heavy, Knock. Hiss.
61	Small	*sma*(o)*'L'l*	'S': Weak to moderate. Hiss. 'M': Weak to moderate. 'A': Replaced with 'O' Soft-Round. Extended. 'L': Moderate to strong. Hum. Extended.
62	So	*s*(a1)O, *s*O', *s*Ow	'S': Weak to moderate. Hiss. Short Vowel: Inserted. 'O' Hard.
65	Still	*Sti*'L'l*, *sti*"L'l*	'S': Weak to moderate. Hiss. 'T': Weak to moderate. Sharp, Knock. 'I' Soft: Extended. 'L': Moderate to strong. Hum. Extended.
66	Store	*sto**R*'e*	'S': Weak to moderate. Hiss. 'T': Weak to moderate. Sharp, Knock. 'R': Rasp. Extended.
67	Tall	T*(h)a*(o)*'L'l*	'T': Moderate to strong. Sharp, Knock, Hiss. 'A': Replaced with 'O' Soft-Round, Extended. 'L': Moderate to strong. Hum. Extended.
68	Than	[*t*(*d*)*h*]2a'N, [*t*(*d*)*h*]2a"N [*t*(*d*)*h*]2a'N	'TH': Merged. 'D' Inserted. Weak to moderate. Flat, Buzz. 'A' Soft. Extended. 'N': Moderate to strong. Knock, Hum, Nasal.
69a	That	[*t*(*d*)*h*]2a"*T(h)*, [*t*(*d*)*h*]2a*T(h)*	'TH': Merged with 'D' Inserted. Weak to moderate. Flat, Buzz. 'A' Soft. Extended and Repeated. 'T': Strong. Sharp, Knock. Hiss.
69b	The – as in "The elephant..." (Following word begins with a Vowel.)	[*t*(*d*)*h*]2e*, [*t*(*d*)*h*]2E'	'TH': Merged with 'D' Inserted. Weak to moderate. Flat, Buzz. 'E' Hard. Extended.
70	The – as in "The man..." (Following word begins with a Consonant.)	[*t*(*d*)*h*]2e*	'TH': Merged with 'D' Inserted. Weak to moderate. Flat, Buzz. 'E' Hard. 'E': Silent.
71	Their	[*t*(*d*)*h*]2e"i**R*, [*t*(*d*)*h*]2e'i**R*	'TH': Merged with 'D' Inserted. Weak to moderate. Flat, Buzz. 'E' Soft: Extended and Repeated. 'I' Silent. 'R': Strong.
72	Them	[*t*(*d*)*h*]2e"M, [*t*(*d*)*h*]2e'M	'TH': Merged with 'D' Inserted. Weak to moderate. Flat, Buzz. 'E' Soft: Extended and Repeated. 'M': Moderate to strong. Hum.

73	Then	[t(d)h]2e"N, [t(d)h]2e'N,	'TH': Merged with 'D' Inserted. Weak to moderate. Flat, Buzz. 'E' Soft: Extended and Repeated. 'N': Moderate to strong. Knock, Nasal, Hum, Lilting.
74	There	[t(d)h]2e"Re*, [t(d)h]2e'R'e*	'TH': Merged with 'D' Inserted. Weak to moderate. Flat, Buzz. 'E' Soft: Extended and Repeated. 'R': Strong. 'E': Silent.
75	These	[t(d)h]2E's*(Z)e*	'TH': Merged with 'D' Inserted. Weak to moderate. Flat, Buzz. 'E' Hard: Extended. 'S': Replaced with 'Z'. Strong. Buzz. 'E': Silent.
76	They	[t(d)h]2e*(A)'y*, [t(d)h]2e*(A)y	'TH': Merged with 'D' Inserted. Weak to moderate. Flat, Buzz. 'E': Replaced with 'A' Hard. Extended. 'Y': Silent.
77	*This (See Footnote)	[t(d)h]2i'S1	'TH': Merged with 'D' Inserted. Weak to moderate. Flat, Buzz. 'I' Soft. Extended. 'S': Strong. Hiss.
78	Think	[th]1i'[nK](h)	'TH': Merged. Weak to moderate. Hiss. 'I' Soft. Extended. 'N': Weak. Nasal. 'K': Moderate to strong. Sharp. Hiss.
79	Those	[t(d)h]2(a1)O's*(Z)e*	'TH': Merged with 'D' Inserted. Weak to moderate. 'O' Hard. Extended. 'S': Replaced with 'Z'. Moderate to strong. Buzz. 'E': Silent.
80	To	T(h)(i)o2, T(h)o2, T(h)o1	'T': Moderate to strong. Sharp, Knock, Hiss. 'I' Soft: Inserted. 'O' Long.
81	Today	T(h)o1-DA'y*, T(h)o1-DAy	'T': Moderate to strong. Sharp, Knock, Hiss. 'O' Short. Pause. 'D': Moderate to strong. Pop Heavy, Knock. 'A' Soft. Extended. 'Y': Silent.
82	Tomorrow	T(h)o1-mo'-rr*O'w*, T(h)o1-mo'-rr*Ow	'T': Moderate to strong. Sharp, Knock, Hiss. 'O' Short. Pause. 'M': Weak. Hum. 'O' Soft-Flat, Extended. 'R': Weak to moderate. Rasp. 'O' Hard. Extended. 'W': Silent.
83	Too	T(i)o2'o*, To2o*	'T': Moderate to strong. Sharp, Knock, Hiss. 'I' Soft: Inserted. 'O' Long. Extended.
84	Turn	T(h)u1RN	'T': Moderate to strong. Sharp, Knock, Hiss. 'U' Short. 'R': Moderate to strong. 'N': Strong. Knock, Nasal, Hum, Lilting.
85	Under	u1N-De1R	'U' Short. 'R': Moderate to strong. 'N': Moderate to strong. Hum, Nasal. Pause. 'D': Moderate to strong. Pop Heavy, Knock. 'E' Short. 'R': Strong. Rasp.
86	Very	ve-ry*(E)	'V': Weak to moderate. Buzz. Flat. 'E' Soft. Pause. 'R': Weak to moderate. Rasp. 'Y' like 'E' Hard.
87	Was	Wa*(o)s2*(Z)	'W': Strong. Vowelish. 'A': Replaced with 'O' Soft. 'S': Replaced with 'Z'. Moderate to strong. Buzz.
88	Well	We"L'l*, WeL'l*	'W': Strong. Vowelish. 'E' Soft. Extended and Repeated. 'L': Moderate to strong. Hum, Lilting. Extended.
89	Were	We1R'e*	'W': Moderate to strong. Vowelish. 'E' Short. Vowelish. 'R': Strong. Rasp. 'E': Silent.

90	What	(h)*Wh**a*(o)'*T(h)*, *(h)*Wh*a1'T*(h)*	'H': Weak. Inserted. Hiss. 'W': Moderate to strong. Vowelish. 'H': Silent. 'A': Replaced with 'O' Soft-Round. Extended. 'T'*(h)*.
91	When	(h)*Wh**e"N', (h)*Wh**e'N'	'H': Weak. Inserted. Hiss. 'W': Moderate to strong. Vowelish. 'H': Silent. 'E' Soft. Extended and Repeated. 'N': Moderate to strong. Knock, Nasal, Hum, Lilting.
92	Which	(h)*Wh**i[*CH*]1(*h*)	'H': Weak. Inserted. Hiss. 'W': Moderate to strong. Vowelish. 'H': Silent. 'I' Soft. 'CH': (as in "Rich") Merged. Strong. Hiss.
93	Who	w**H*o2', w**H*(i)o2'	'W': Silent. 'H': Strong. 'O' Long. Extended.
94	Why	(h)*Wh**(a2)y*(I), (h)*Wh**y*(I)'.	'H': Weak. Inserted. Hiss. 'W': Moderate to strong. Vowelish. 'H': Silent. 'A' Long: Inserted. 'Y': Replaced with 'I' Hard.
95	Will	Wi"L'l*, Wi'L'l*	'W': Strong. Vowelish. 'I' Soft. Extended and Repeated. 'L': Moderate to strong. Extended. Hum, Lilting.
96	Work	Wo1R*K(h)*	'W': Strong. Vowelish. 'O': Short. 'R': Moderate to strong. Rasp. 'K': Strong. Sharp. Hiss.
97	World	Wo1'RL*D(h)*	'W': Strong. Vowelish. 'O': Short. 'R': Moderate to strong. Rasp. 'L': Moderate to strong. Hum, Lilting. 'D': Strong. Pop Heavy. Knock. Hiss.
98	Year	YE-a1*R*'	'Y': Strong. Vowelish. 'E' Hard. Pause. 'R': Strong. Rasp. Extended.
99	You	*Y*o2'u*, *Y*(i)o2u*, *Y*o1u*, Yo1u*(O)'	'Y': Strong. Vowelish. 'O' Long. Extended. 'U': Silent.
100	Your	*Y*o)'u**R*', *Y*o*u*R*, *Y*o*u1*R*	'Y': Strong. Vowelish. 'O' Soft-Round, Extended. 'U' Silent. 'R': Strong. Rasp. Extended.

*An interesting irregular way in which the word "This" is vocalized is quite often heard when combined with the word "Year" as in "This year, ...". In this particular instance, "This year,..." is vocalized {[*t*(*d*)*h*]2]is*[SH]-YE'a1*R*}, with the final 'S' in "This" being replaced by 'SH' {[SH]}. And, the two Mono-Syllabic words are combined, as if they are just a single Di-Syllabic word.

Note: As with the word "This", when used with "Year", the 'S' in the words "Last" and "Past" is also often heard replaced with 'SH' {[SH]}, vocalized {*l*as*[SH]T-YE'a1*R*} and {*p*as*[SH]T-YE'a1*R*}, respectively.

Exercise.

1. Identify which of the words in the Table above you vocalized differently than Americans. Learn the changes you need to make from the Scripted description.

2. Make sentences containing words from the Table above which you have changed. Speaking in the American Accent repeat these sentences over and over until you become comfortable with the new vocalization.

3. Read aloud anything that comes in front of you, e.g. newspapers, internet articles, road signs, advertisements, and, make sure you pronounce the words you come across that are included in the above Table, the American way.

4. Practice vocalizing the pronunciation of words you have changed in everyday conversation.

5. Revisit the list and check off words you have successfully changed, and remind yourself about the words where you have lapsed and need to consolidate in your speech.

6. Some words, like “Am”, “Can't”, “And”, “Ask”, “Here”, “Him”, “To” and words beginning with “Th” as in “The” and “This”, are both distinct and recur often. Make sure you become comfortable with pronouncing them the American way. Practice them individually and in sentences. Identify other such words from the Table and do the same.

PART 5: LANGUAGE THE AMERICAN WAY.

Chapter 17:
Using Certain Words like Americans.

There are certain ways that Americans use words that are characteristic of them. They stand out as different to those not familiar with the American way of speaking. Their meaning is contrasted with their use by English speakers globally. One should be aware of American usage for appropriate use in the American context.

Some of the most distinctive usages are listed in the Table below:

Table: Words Used The American Way

No.	Typical Americans Usages	Global Usages	Comments
1	Wearing a tee shirt in late fall got me *acclimated* real fast to the cold.	Wearing a tee shirt in late autumn got me *acclimatized* quickly to the cold.	"Acclimate" is heard more often in the US whereas "Acclimatize" seems customary where there is British English speaking tradition.
2	*I am* here. He *is not*. They *have not* come. She *has not* brought it.	*I'm* here. He *isn't*. They *haven't* come. She *hasn't* brought it.	Words are often not brought together.
3	His *attorney* reached out to them on his behalf.	His *lawyer* reached out to them on his behalf.	The word "Attorney" is often used instead of "Lawyer" though the latter is also used. Barrister and Solicitor are not used in America.
4	Did you see the *billboard* as you drive into town about the new seafood restaurant?	Did you see the *hoarding* as you drive into town about the new seafood restaurant?	Americans use the more self explanatory word, i.e. "Billboard" rather than "Hoarding", to refer to a big advertising board, along a motorway or in town, posted to catch the view of people as they drive or otherwise move about. "Hoarding" in America refers to its other more common meaning globally, i.e. to hold goods in storage to profiteer.
5	Would you like *biscuit* with your egg? You can have a *cookie* later with your milk.	Would you like a *bun* with your egg? You can have a *biscuit* later with your milk.	A "Biscuit" in America is more like a small loaf or section of bread, but outside America it is like a small "Cookie".
6	Put the bag in the *boot*. Mind the *fender* while doing so.	Put the bag in the "dickie". Mind the *bumper* while doing so.	The closed compartment at the back of the car is called a "Boot" and not a "Dickie" in America. The protective metal or fiberglass protruding, protective shields are called "Fenders" in "America, not "Bumpers".
7	Where did you get all this *candy*?	Where did you get all these *sweets*?	"Candy" in America includes all sorts of sweet bites including chocolate.
8	Can you get us the	Can you get us the	In America "Check" is two things. It can be an invoice or it

	check, please. Oh, and is it okay for me to pay with a $50 *bill*?	*bill* please. Oh, and is it okay for me to pay using this £20 *note*.	can be a bank issued form for making payments. And, a "Bill" is a unit of paper currency, and may be referred to as a "Note" elsewhere.
9	He usually has his coffee at the *coffee house* every morning.	He usually has his coffee at the *cafe* every morning.	"Coffee House" is used in some places rather than "Cafe", though "Cafeteria" is used quite often in a School or Office context in the sense of a "Mess" or "Canteen".
10	I got a great deal when I bought my *condominium* (*condo* for short) during the last market downturn. It is a great *apartment*.	I got a great deal when I bought my *flat* during the last market downturn. It's a great *flat*.	A "Condominium" is a dwelling unit in a building of many units for residential living that is owned by its occupant. Condos are "Apartments", or, "Flats" as they are often called outside America. Apartments are usually thought of as being rented out, but condos are not. A condo may be on more than one floor. A flat is usually thought of as being on one floor only.
11	Sign: "Free *dirt* for you to take away!"	Sign: "Free soil for you to take away!"	In America, "Dirt" is often used to mean soil, sand or mud. But when the word "Dirty" is used, it means "Unclean" as it does elsewhere.
12	Many young people prefer to live *downtown* in the "Heights" *neighborhood.*	Many young people prefer to live in town (or the city) in the "Heights" *residential* area, or in the "Heights" colony.	"Downtown" is in the City Center area. "Neighborhood" is typically used for residential areas but is also for an area known for a particular type of activity, e.g. this is an artist neighborhood. Elsewhere, globally, the word "Colony" is sometimes used instead of "Neighborhood" a similar sense.
13	The new *drapes* give the room a whole new look.	The new *curtains* give the room a whole new look.	"Drapes seem to be more commonly used than "Curtains" in a home environment.
14	She loves my *eggplant* quiche.	She loves my *aubergine* quiche.	"Eggplant" is the word for "Aubergine", the black or navy blue egg shaped vegetable that can be used in a savory quiche or flan like pie.
15	*Fall* is beautiful here when the trees begin to change their colors.	*Autumn* is beautiful here when the trees begin to change their colors.	"Fall" is the generally used word for the season leading into winter, rather than "Autumn".
16	People have often been *fired* from this job.	People have often been *sacked* from this position.	"Fired" is the accepted word. "Sacked" may be unfamiliar to many.
17	The *folks* here love barbecue.	The *people* here love barbecue.	In America, "Folks" can mean the "People" of a town, or a community, a family, or just one's parents
18	*Football* is the passion in this city, but *soccer* is catching on too.	Soccer is the passion in this city.	"Football" is the American game in which the ball is oval and can be carried in the hands and helmets are worn. "Soccer", also often called "Football" elsewhere but not in America, is played only with the feet with a round ball and no helmets.

19	Come *for* Coffee!	Come *to* Tea/Coffee!	"For" is usually used instead of "To", in such manner
20	They are not *gonna* like this! Or, Are you *gonna* speak about this?	They are not *going to* like this! Or, Are you *going to* speak about this?	"Gonna" is a shortened form of saying "Going to". It's heard everywhere, but even more so in casual settings. Sometimes people actually write "Gonna". It is in at least one American dictionary, which does not say it is slang, but that it is informal. It is also in at least one British dictionary but shown as primarily American. Sometimes, it is actually written. If written, unless the intent is to project informality, it may raise some eyebrows.
21	He has finally *gotten* used to working the night shift.	He has finally *got* used to working the night shift.	In America, some people say "Gotten" instead of "Got" and it is acceptable.
22	We go by the *Imperial* system in the U.S. so we say: "*Inches, Feet, Yards, Miles, Ounces, Pounds, Quarts, Liters and Gallons*", and so on.	We go by the *Metric* system across most of the world, so outside the U.S. we say: "*Centimeters, Meters, Kilometers, Grams, Kilograms, Milliliters and Liters*", and so on.	The "Imperial" tradition for measures may be more complicated for many people but in America it's what people are comfortable with.
23	Did you get my *invite* for the wedding?	Did you get my *invitation* to the wedding?	Using "Invite" in America is proper and formal but globally, the word to use is "Invitation".
24	Keep him out of the *jail house*. Or, make sure he is at the *school house*.	Keep him out of jail. Or make sure he is at school.	"House" may be added to words like "Jail", "School" or "Coffee", in more traditional areas.
25	That looks like a great hammock to *lay* in over a lazy afternoon.	That looks like a great hammock to *lie* in over a lazy afternoon.	Americans usually say "Lay" for the present tense and past tense of lying down, though others say "Lie" for the present tense.
26	It is a long *line* to the window, but it is moving fast.	It's long *queue* to the window, but it's moving quickly.	The word "Line" is often used instead of "Queue".
27	We spend most of our time in the *living room* when we are home.	We spend most of our time in the *drawing room* when we are home.	Americans are particular about being accurate in their terminology. Calling the shared lounge space in the house a "Living" room is a truer description than a "Drawing Room". "Drawing Room" seems to be losing currency in favor of "Living Room". Globally, it is often called a "Hall".
28	Has the *mail* arrived, today? I'm	Has the *post* arrived, today? I'm	The word "Mail" is usually used instead of "Post", but stamps are called "Postage stamps".

	waiting for an answer to the letter I put into the *mailbox* on Monday.	waiting for an answer to the letter I put into the *postbox* on Monday.	
29	The *medics* arrived immediately as soon as the fire broke out.	The *medical personnel* arrived immediately as soon as the fire broke out.	The term "Medics" are a quick way of referring to all medical personnel engaged in a particular situation.
30	Can we meet, Monday?	Can we meet on Monday?	The abbreviated form is very common in America. It is heard in Britain as well, but it isn't global. The more formal wording with "on" is global.
31	Go *north* for three blocks and then turn *east*.	Go straight that way, for about 200 meters and then turn right.	Not just because of heading out west as in old days and western movies, but also because highways are usually marked "North", "South", "East" or "West", Americans are very conscious of such directions. In some countries, they may not use these compass points to give directions.
32	I got this recipe *off of* the internet. I got this old book *off of* a friend in my neighborhood.	I got this recipe *from* the internet. I got this old book *from* a friend in my neighborhood.	"Off" by itself has many listed uses in dictionaries. The "Off Of" combination was not among the listed uses in one authoritative American English dictionary. But, it is still encountered in conversation. It would be okay to use in a casual context.
33	The *corporation's* "officers" set policy for the organization, at the direction of the *President*.	The *company's* board of "Directors" set policy for the organization, under the *Chairman*.	The "Officers" are the senior most executives with charge for the different functions and business areas, just below the "President" and his deputy. Vice Presidents, Directors and Managers are different levels in a corporate hierarchy.
34	*Often times*, I find myself tapping my foot unconsciously.	*Often*, I find myself tapping my foot unconsciously, or, *many times* I have found myself tapping my foot unconsciously.	"Often Times" is a characteristically American way of say "Quite Often" or "Often" or "Many Times".
35	We have had a power *outage* since yesterday.	We've had a power *cut or break* since yesterday.	"Outage" is used to describe breakdowns or disruption in utilities or other services, e.g. as with the internet, phone or television.
36	Cars can *pass* each other on separate lanes.	Cars *overtake* each other on separate lanes.	"Passing" refers to a moving vehicle or person getting ahead of another. "Overtaking" is not used in America.
37	We use the *patio* a lot in summer.	We use the *verandah* a lot in summer.	A "Patio" is an open-air deck for sitting outdoors and may be covered or open to sky.
38	I was stopped by a	I was stopped by a	"Officer" is used for any police person, and "Trooper" is

	police officer (or *trooper*) because my right side tail light was not working.	"policeman" because my right side rear light was not working.	used for those on patrol on state and county highways and roads.
39	Is there a *rest room* on this floor?	Is there a *wash room* on this floor?	"Rest Room" in America is a sensitive way of saying "Lavatory", though both are perfectly acceptable and both terms are very American. Globally, "Wash Room" seems to be gaining acceptance as people hesitate to say "Toilet". "Bathroom" is still in use but it seems odd to ask for a bathroom at a restaurant, when a bath is not the purpose.
40	I like the new *rug* in the bedroom.	I like the new *carpet* in the bedroom.	In America, "Carpet" is usually used to describe wall to wall floor cladding, whereas a "rug" is a sectional decorative piece, of a particular shape.
41	I will be going to *school* today.	I will be going to *college* today.	"School" also means "College" where you can get a degree or diploma, after finishing High School.
42	Do you have grilled *shrimp* on the menu?	Do you have grilled *prawns* on the menu?	The word "Prawns" appears little known and barely if ever used in the United States. "Shrimp" is used instead, and it usually means many "Shrimp" – it is a bit odd to say "Shrimps". "Prawns" are used in many other English speaking countries.
43	Pedestrians and cyclists must use the *sidewalk* in this area.	Pedestrians and cyclists must use the *pavement* in this area.	"Sidewalk" describes accurately the pedestrian walkways in America. And, in America "Pavement" usually refers to the road surface – e.g. concrete or macadamized. In many countries it refers to a pedestrian walkway, alongside a road.
44	She is a skill*ful* communicator.	She communicates, skill*fully*.	Adverbs ending with "-ly" are usually not used at the end of a sentence.
45	The *stores* are closed today.	The *shops* are closed today.	Americans generally say "Store" for all kinds and sizes of shops. Small specialized stores may be called "Boutiques". A "Mall' though is an enclave of stores, restaurants and different kinds of service outlets, e.g. hairdressers and optometrists. They do however use the word "Shopping" a lot.
46	He is a *tall, tall* man. There are *good, good* people here.	He is a *very* tall man, or, he is an *extremely* tall man. There are *very* good people here.	Often, an adjective is used twice for emphasis.
47	This is not much different *than* that.	This is not very different from that.	"Than" is more likely used instead of "From" for such a comparison.
48	They work Monday *through* Friday.	They work Monday *to* Friday.	When American use "Through" in this way, Friday is included. It is generally understood that Friday is included if "To" is used, but by using "Through", ambiguity is removed. Sometimes Americans casually spell "Through": "Thru".
49	I filled air in the	I filled air in the	"Tires" are spelled with an 'I' and not a 'Y' and fuel is

	"tires" at the "gas" station, before coming home.	"tyres" at the "petrol" station, before coming home.	referred to as "Gas" short for "Gasoline" in America.
50	Put the *trash* in the *dumpster.*	Put the *garbage* in the *bin.*	"Trash" is used instead of "Garbage". "Dumpster" is a big disposal container for trash. "Bin" is less heard. "Trash Can" is sometimes used.
51	I will *trade* my new car for your old motorcycle.	I'll *exchange* my new car for your old motorcycle.	"Trade" is commonly used instead of "Exchange" in such a context. It isn't just used in an economic or financial sense.
52	I will be on a cruise for this year's *vacation*. I didn't go anywhere over any long week-end *holiday.*	I'll be on a cruise for the *holidays* this year.	A "Vacation" is when you take many days off work to go on a trip somewhere. A "Holiday" in America is a reference to the days given off to everyone such as for "Labor Day" or "Thanksgiving".
53	Can I speak *with* him?	Can I speak *to* him?	"With" is usually used instead of "to" in this kind of context.
54	Four multiplied/ divided *with* three.	Four multiplied/ divided *by* three.	"With" used instead of "to" in this kind of context.

Chapter 18: Moving Ahead, From Here.

You have covered most of the way at this point in your transition to the American Accent. Learning a different Accent and way of speaking is incremental. You have to practice changes as you proceed and build on what you have learned so far. This requires continued listening, observation and practice.

There are many good speakers and media sources that you can use as models to advance your own transition. This Course tells you what to look for, helping to attune your observation, as you listen both during personal practice sessions and while on the fly. There are commercials on TV and there is endless audio-visual content on the internet. There are movies – whether at movie houses, on DVD, or on the internet. There are news readers, TV show hosts and guests. There are weather announcers, teachers, professors and actors, many who make good American Accent voice models.

It's a good idea to practice the basics explained in each of the Lanes of the Four Lane Route. Do this like musicians get warmed up as they practice going through musical scales, or like gymnasts as they warm themselves up with different kinds of stretches. There is a great deal of material within the Course to practice Syllabication, Tempo and Articulation. And the exercises suggested to shape your Voice into the American mold will help. The Vocal Pattern Bridge and Word List Tables help you focus on specific Vocal Patterns and words. All of these are there to help you get into the groove of speaking the American way. But, it is important to stretch further. A practical and quick way to do this is simply to use any written material you find, whether on a catalog, a road sign, a billboard, a magazine or a book cover, to test your wings. Read sentences and paragraphs aloud over and again to yourself to identify where you slip-up, so you can correct yourself and improve every time around.

It is important to go over the same set of words again and again, until you are comfortable vocalizing all the Basic Vocal Elements in the Vocal Patterns where change is needed. If there is a poem or song you know, recite it to yourself, speaking in the American Accent. Or, you could learn a few new poems you always admired, since repetition is needed both for Accent change practice and for memorizing pieces of writing. If you have to give a speech, repeat it over and over, making sure that the Vocal Patterns you have identified for change are vocalized the American way.

With the Vocal Pattern Bridge Table you will have learned the most Distinctive Vocal Patterns, i.e. those in the Great category. As you continue to practice all that you have learned so far, look ahead to the Vocal Patterns in the sequels that follow the Vocal Pattern Bridge:

> The second of this three Coursebook series: "The American Accent Learnway – Together, On the Road Inland" contains the Vocal Pattern Inland Table which includes 200 very Distinctive Vocal Patterns. The Vocal Patterns in the Inland Table are in the Substantial Distinctiveness category and number nearly twice as many as there are in the Vocal Pattern Bridge Table. As with the Vocal Pattern Bridge Table, you can select the Vocal Patterns in the Inland Table you need to change. The second Coursebook also provides Word List Tables with the Vocal Pattern Inland Table, as provided with the Vocal Pattern Bridge Table in this first Coursebook.

The Table at the end of this chapter contains a sample of 10 Vocal Patterns from the Vocal Pattern Inland Table.

> Compare the Vocal Patterns in the Table below, vocalized in the American and British Accents. From observation, you are likely to judge that,
>
> > -the Distinctiveness is not as great as those in the Vocal Pattern Bridge, yet,

-they are still very Distinctive with substantial contrast between Basic Vocal Elements when vocalized in American and British Accents.

Compare, also, whether you personally pronounce the Vocal Patterns in the word examples provided as Scripted in the Vocal Pattern Vocalization column. It is likely that there will be a good number that you vocalize differently. These can be targeted for change.

By extending your learning to very Distinctive Vocal Patterns, the second Coursebook with the Vocal Pattern Inland Table takes you almost all the way to your final destination of speaking with the American Accent.

The final of this three Coursebook series, "The American Accent Learnway – As One, On the Summit", contains the Vocal Pattern Summit Table with just over 300 clearly Distinctive Vocal Patterns. Not being among the more Distinctive of Vocal Patterns, it is likely that many of these may have escaped the notice of learners. They will make a difference. It is aimed at closing any remaining gap.

Table: Looking Ahead At A Few Vocal Patterns From
The Vocal Pattern Inland Table

Serial	Vocal Pattern Name	Vocal Pattern Vocalization	LP	LS	ADE	EoO	Word Example with Vocal Pattern (Pauses shown)	Change OK/C	Table
117	OW - I	o*(a)'w	II	4	B	Fre	Brown, Cow, Crowd, How, Flow-er, Now, Owl, Prow-ess, Tow-er.		Y
130	AN - IV	a'-N, a-N	II	5	B	Oft	A-nna, Ca-na-da, Ca-ni.ster, Gra-nite, Ma-nners, Pla-net, Sa-nity.		Y
141	AP - III	a'-P, a"-P	II	5	B	Oft	A-ppa-ra.tus, A-ppa-ri.tion, A-ppe.tite, Ca-pi-tal, Ha-ppen, Ra-pid, Ta-ppet.		Y
153	AUGH - I	a*(o)'u*[gh]* a*(o)u*(w) [gh]*	II	5	B	Oft	Caught, Dis-traught, Fraught, Naught, Taught.		N
172	ERN - II	e1R'-*n*	II	5	B	Oft	Er-nest, In-ter-nal, Mo.der-ni-za-tion, Wes-ter-ni-za-tion.		Y
209	ODG - I	o'-[dg]*(J)	II	5	B	Oft	Co-dger, Lo-dging, Lo-dges, Ro-dger, Sto-dgy.		N
224	OP - I	o'*P(h)*	II	5	B	Oft	Cop, Crop, Hop, Flop, Pop, Prop, Shop, Sop, Stop, Top.		Y

241	UAR - II	U-a*(e)-*r*	II	5	B	Oft	Es-tu-a.ry, Ja.nu-a.ry, Feb-ru-a.ry, Sanc.tu-a.ry.		N
258	ANCH - I	a"n[*CH*](*h*)	II	6	B	Occ	Blanch, Branch.		N
261	AR - VII	a1R	II	6	B	Occ	A-nar-chist~, A-nar-chy~, Le-thar-gy, Mo-nar-chist~, Mo-nar-chy~.		N

The Vocal Pattern Bridge, Inland and Summit Tables are extracts from the Vocal Pattern Master Table which consists of more than 840 Vocal Patterns.

Vocal Patterns in each of the Vocal Pattern Tables are presented in order of Distinctiveness and Rate of Occurrence. The Vocal Patterns in each of the Vocal Pattern Tables could be determined only after all the Vocal Patterns in the Vocal Pattern Master Table were defined.

The Vocal Pattern Bridge consists of the most Distinctive Vocal Patterns – in the Distinctiveness category of Great. These number just over 100 Vocal Patterns. This Table is provided with the first Coursebook, "The American Accent Learnway – Cross the Bridge, Over the Divide", of this three Coursebook series. By Mastering the Vocal Patterns that constitute the Vocal Pattern Bridge, learners will speak like other Americans with respect to the most Distinctive Vocal Patterns. The first Coursebook takes you most of your journey toward speaking the American way. It provides the necessary foundation with the Four Lane Route and words spoken the American way, preliminary to the Vocal Pattern Bridge Table.

The Vocal Pattern Inland Table consists of very Distinctive Vocal Patterns – in the Distinctiveness category of Substantial. These number 200 Vocal Patterns This Table is provided in the second Coursebook, "The American Accent Learnway – Together on the Road Inland". The second Coursebook takes you almost all the way toward speaking the American way, as you learn to vocalize very Distinctive Vocal Patterns.

The Vocal Pattern Summit Table consists of clearly Distinctive Vocal Patterns – in the Distinctiveness category of Significant. These number just over 300 Vocal Patterns. This Table is provided with the third and final Coursebook, "The American Accent Learnway – As One, On the Summit". This final, third Coursebook aims to close the remaining Accent gap, by changing the Vocal Patterns that are clearly Distinctive, but less recognized.

With all of the Vocal Pattern Tables, it is possible to look up almost any Distinctive Vocal Pattern, across levels of Distinctiveness, to check how it is vocalized. This will result in closing the Accent gap to merge with the American Accent.

Each of the Vocal Pattern Tables enable self-diagnosis, so that learning can be targeted at specific Vocal Patterns where change is needed.

PART 6: APPENDICES

Appendix I. A.
Vocal Fidelity Phonetic System:
Pauses & Syllables

Note: A Pause is any interruption or break in vocalization between the beginning and end of a Word. A Pause separates each Syllable from the next.

Note: Symbols used for Pauses.

Dashes, '-', are used to identify relatively longer or Major Pauses. Dots, '.', are used to identify relatively shorter or Minor Pauses.

-In single Syllable words there are no Pauses. Neither dashes nor dots are needed.
-In Di-Syllabic words, only dashes are used to show the single Pause in such words.
-In Multi-Syllabic words, dashes (for Major Pauses) and dots (for Minor Pauses) are used when contrasts are distinguishable.

Note: A Syllable is nothing other than a note or stream of vocalization from a Pause to a Pause forming an integrated, separable vocal unit.

They form the building blocks of words. Each is separated from other such units by shorter or longer Pauses between them. A Syllable may even be only a single letter, if separated by a Pause.

Some words consist of only a single Syllable of no more than one letter e.g. “A” or “I”.

Appendix I. B.
Vocal Fidelity Phonetic System:
Scripting Vowel Sounds

Table:
Vocal Fidelity Phonetic System:
Scripting Conventions For Vowel Sounds

Vowel Symbols follow the Scripting Conventions in the Table below.		
Serial No.	Script Symbols	Sound Effect
1	A lower case Vowel followed by an asterisk, as in {a*}, or {e*}. (This also applies to the letters 'H', 'W' and 'Y' as in Syllable-Middle and Syllable-End positions they are like Vowels, as in {h*-}, {w*} or {y*}.)	Silencing of a Vowel as in “Read” {Rea*d} and “Plate” {Plate*}. Using examples with 'H', 'W' and 'Y': “Sarah” {Sarah*}, “Grow” {Grow*} and “Play” {Play*}.
2	A lower case Vowel followed by the digit 1, e.g., {a1}, or, {e1}.	A *Short* Vowel Sound, e.g. as in “Festival” {Festiva1l} or “Ceremony' {Cere1mony}.
3	A lower case Vowel, as in {a}, {e}, {i}, {o}, or {u}. See row 13 below for more on the 'O' Soft Vowel Sound.	A *Soft* Vowel Sound without an Extension, e.g. as in “Jam” {Jam}, “Red” {Red}, “Big” {Big}, “Song” {Song} or “Push” {Push}.
4	A lower case Vowel with an apostrophe e.g., {a'}, or, {o'}, etc. See row 14 below for more on the 'O' Soft Vowel Extension.	A *Soft* Vowel Sound with an Extension, e.g. as in “Bag” {Ba'g}, or “Clock” {Clo'ck}.
5	Lower case Vowels of 'A', 'E' and 'I' followed by two apostrophes as in {a''}, {e''}, or, {i''}.	A *Soft* Vowel Sound with an Extension, followed by a Repetition of the Vowel Sound, causing Modulation, e.g. as in “Man” {Ma'′n), “Bed” {Be'′d) or “Kid” {Ki''d}.
6	A Vowel in regular upper case e.g. {A}, or, {I}.	A *Hard* Vowel, e.g. as in “Fate” {FAte} or “Kite” {KIte}. The Hard form of the Vowels are pronounced just as you would recite the stand alone Vowels, 'A', 'E', 'I', 'O' and 'U'.
7	An upper case Vowel with an apostrophe e.g., {A'}, {O'}, etc..	An Extended *Hard* Vowel Sound, e.g. “Brave” {BrA've} or “Cold” {CO'ld}.
8	The Vowels 'A', 'O' and 'U' in lower case followed by the digit 2 as in {a2}, {o2} and {u2}.	A *Long* form of the Vowel Sound, e.g. as in “Palm” {Pa2lm}, “Food” {Fo*o2d} and “Rude” {Ru2de}.
9	A Vowel in parentheses, Scripted in any form, e.g., {(A)}, {(i)}, {(E)}, {(u2)}, etc.	A Vowel, not in the spelling of the word inserted into the phonetic Script, to show actual pronunciation, e.g., “Gypsy” {Gy*(i)psy}, “Psychology” {Psy*(I)chology}.

10	A Vowel in lower case regular Script followed by an asterisk and then another Scripted Vowel in parentheses, e.g. {e*(A)} or {i*(e)}, etc. (This also applies to the letters 'W' and 'Y' as in Syllable-Middle and Syllable-End positions they are like Vowels, e.g. {w*(u)} or {y*(i)} etc.)	A silencing of the Vowel preceding the asterisk and its replacement with the following Vowel Sound enclosed in parentheses, e.g., as in "Fete" {Fe*(A)te}, "Said" {Sa*i*(e)d} or "Wash" {Wa*(o)sh}. Examples with an 'W' or 'Y': "Clown" {Clo*(a)w*(u)n"}, "Synopsis" {Sy*(i)-nop-sis}.
11	A Scripted Vowel in parentheses either preceding or following another Scripted Vowel, e.g. {(i)U}, {(A)O}, {(a1)o}, {I(a1)}, etc.	An audible (*External*) Vowel Sound not in the spelling of a word, that appends to, either just before or after, a (*Internal*) Vowel that is in the spelling, vocalized with a transition from the first Vowel to the second, causing Modulation, e.g. as in "Mute" {M(i)Ute}, "So" {S(A)O or S(a1)O}, "Cow" {C(a)ow} and "File" {FI(a1)le*}.
12	The letters, 'W' and 'Y', when in Syllable-Middle or Syllable-End positions in lower case followed by an asterisk and then a Scripted Vowel within parentheses, e.g. {w*(U)}, {w*(o2)}, or {y*(I)}, etc.	The vocalization of the 'W' and 'Y' in this context is like the following Scripted Vowel, shown as its replacement, in parentheses. e.g. "Few" {F(i)ew*(U)}, "Crew" {Cre1w*(o2)} or "Fly" {Fly*(I)}.
13	The Vowel 'O', in lower case regular Script, followed by a closing parenthesis Symbol and an apostrophe, e.g. {-o)'-}. The Vowel 'O', in lower case regular Script, immediately followed by an apostrophe e.g. {-o'-}.	The 'O' in *Soft-Round* form with a round character and Extended, e.g. "Bought" {Bo)'u*ght}, "Cost" {Co)'st}, "More" {Mo)'re}, and "Toy" {To)'y}. The closing parenthesis denotes roundness. The apostrophe denotes Extension. The 'O' in *Soft-Flat* form with a flat character and Extended, e.g. "Bob" {Bo'b}, "Dot" {Do't} and "Nod" {No'd}. The apostrophe denotes Extension.
14	The Vowel 'O' in lower case italic Script., e.g {-*o*-}. The Vowel 'A' in lower case followed by an asterisk and then the Vowel 'O' in lower case italic between parentheses, e.g {a*(*o*)}	The 'O' *Soft-Tall* which lifts upward as heard in the British Accent but not the American, as in words like "Boy" {B*o*y}, "Join" {J*o*in}, "Port" {P*o*rt}, Score" {Sc*o*re} and "Thought" {Th*o*ught}. Italic is used in the Scripting of only this Vowel sound to indicate that it is not in the American Accent. (Americans use the 'O' *Soft-Round* with such words which has a rounded character and is Scripted with a lower case 'O' in regular case {-o-}.) In the British Accent only, when the 'O' Soft-Tall replaces an 'A' (see Row 10) as in words like "All" {a*(*o*)ll}, "Call" {Ca*(*o*)l} and "Paul" {P{a*(*o*)u*l}. (In such words, Americans replace the 'A' with the 'O' Soft-Round which has

		a rounded character and is Scripted with a lower case 'O' in regular case {-a*(o)-}.)
Note: More information is provided on the different specific Vowel forms, such as Soft, Hard and Long, in subsequent sections. More explanation on various terms relating to Vowels, such as Extension, Repetition and Modulation is given in sections below.		

Appendix I. C.
Vocal Fidelity Phonetic System: Scripting Consonant Sounds

Table:
The Vocal Fidelity Phonetic System
Scripting Conventions For Consonant Sounds

Consonant Symbols follow the Scripting Conventions in the Table below.		
Below this table: See Note 1 for explanation about Accentuation. See Note 2 on Fundamental Phonetic Attributes. See Note 3 on Adjacent Consonants. See Note 4 on Concurrence of Conventions. See Note 5 on Pauses. See Note 6 on similar middle Consonants. See Note 7 on silencing and replacement of Consonant Sounds.		
Table Protocol: When the phonetics of a Consonant or Consonant Sequence in an example word needs to be shown the word is first shown enclosed in double quotation marks and then shown again enclosed in curly brackets with only the specific Consonant or Consonant Sequence being discussed in the Vocal Fidelity Phonetic System Script. The term – Script – means that it is represented in the manner of these conventions which show how it is to be articulated.		
Serial No.	Script Symbol	Sound Effect
1	Regular lower case, e.g., {b} or {d}.	Weak accentuation. E.g. 'B' in "Ball" {ball}, or, "Doll" {doll}. See Note 1.
2	Lower case italic, e.g., {*g*} or {*d*}.	Weak to moderate accentuation. E.g. 'D' in "Dog" {*d*og}, or, 'G' in "Gift" {gift} See Note 1.
3	Regular upper case, e.g., {K} or {T}.	Moderate to strong accentuation. E.g. 'K' in "Shark" {SharK}) or 'T' in "Soft" {SofT}. See Note 1.
4	Upper case italic., e.g., {*R*}or {*V*}.	Strong accentuation . E.g. 'R' in "Car" {Ca*R*}, or 'V' in "Shove" {Sho*Ve*}. See Note 1.
5	A Scripted Consonant Sequence enclosed in square brackets, e.g., {[ch]}, {[*ch*]},{[CH]}, {[*CH*]}, {[sh]}, {[*sh*]}, {[SH]}, {[*SH*]}.	A Merged Consonant Sequence with a distinctive, unified sound. E.g. 'SH' in "Ship" {[*sh*]ip}, or, 'CH' in "Champion" {[*ch*]ampion}. See Note 3.
6a	A Scripted Consonant followed by a number, e.g., {c1}, {*c*1}, {C1}, {*C*1}, {g1}, {*g*1}, {G1}, {*G*1}.	A particular articulation of a Consonant where there are different Versions. E.g. 'C' in "Face" {Fa*C*2e} is Version 2 of 'C', or 'G' in "Huge" {Hu*G*2e} is Version 2 of 'G'.
6b	A Scripted Consonant Sequence enclosed in square brackets followed by a number, e.g., {[ch]1}, {[*ch*]1}, {[CH]1}, {[*CH*]1}.	A particular articulation of a Merged Consonant Sequence, where there are different Versions. E.g. 'CH' in "Champion" {[*ch*]1ampion}, is Version 1, or 'CH' in "Champagne" {[*ch*]3ampagne} is Version 3. See Note 3.
7a	A Consonant in lower regular case followed by an asterisk, e.g., {k*}, or {b*}.	The written Consonant preceding the asterisk is treated as silent. E.g. the 'B' in "Debt" {Deb*t}, or, 'K' in "Knit" {k*nit}, is silenced. See Note 7.
7b	A Consonant Sequence in lower regular case	The written Consonant Sequence in square

	enclosed in square brackets followed by an asterisk, e.g., {[gh]*}.	brackets preceding the asterisk is treated as Silent. E.g. 'GH' in "High" {Hi[gh]*} is Silenced. See Notes 3 & 7.
7c	A Consonant, or a Consonant Sequence in square brackets, in lower case followed by a number and then followed by an asterisk, e.g. {s2*} or {[ch]2*} and then followed by a Scripted Consonant within parentheses e.g. {(Z)}, or Consonants within square brackets enclosed in parentheses, e.g. {([*sh*])}.	A Consonant or Merged Consonant Sequence that has different Versions, identified by the number that follows, the sound of which is shown by the inserted Consonant(s) within parentheses that follow the asterisk, e.g. as in "His" {His2*(Z)}. Whenever Consonants are shown in square brackets, they are Merged, as in "Sachet" {Sa-[ch]3*([*sh*])et}.
8a	A Scripted Consonant in parentheses, which may or may not be followed by a number, not in the word's spelling, e.g., {(f)}, {(*f*)', {(F)}, {(*F*)}, {(s1)}, {(*s*1)}, {(S1)}, {(*S*1)}. If the Consonant is followed by a number, both enclosed within parentheses e.g. {(*S*1)}, this specifies the Version of the Consonant.	An inserted Consonant Sound heard in articulation but not clearly evident in the spelling of a word, Scripted according to these conventions: Examples: -'D' in "Them" {[*t*(*d*)*h*]em} -'F' in "Laugh" {Lau[gh]*(*F*)) -The 'S' with the Hiss Attribute in "Face" {fac2*(*S*1)e} which is Version 1 of 'S' and substitutes the 'C' Consonant. See Note 7.
8b	A Scripted Consonant Sequence within square brackets, which may or may not be followed by a number, enclosed in parentheses, e.g. {([ch]1)}, {([*ch*]1)}, {([CH]1)}, {([*CH*]1)}, {([zh])}, {([*zh*])}, {([ZH])}, {([*ZH*])}. If the Consonant Sequence is followed by a number, both enclosed within parentheses e.g. {([CH]1)}, this specifies the Version of the Consonant Sequence.	A Consonant Sequence with a Merged sound heard in articulation but not clearly evident in the spelling of a word. Examples: -The 'CH' sound in "Future" {fu-t4*([CH]1)ure}, i.e. Version 1 of 'CH' is inserted to replace the articulation of the 'T' in this example, i.e. Version 4 of 'T', as a precise and distinct representation of its sound. -The 'ZH' sound in "Measure" {Meas3*([*zh*])ure}, i.e. 'ZH' is inserted to replace the articulation of the 'S' in this example, i.e. Version 3 of 'S', as a precise and distinct representation of its sound. See Notes 3 and 7.
9a	A Scripted Consonant followed by an apostrophe, e.g., {r'}, {*r*'}, {R'}, {*R*'}, {l'}, {*l*'}, {L'}, {*L*'}.	Extension of the preceding Consonant. E.g. 'R' in "Her" {He*R*'}, or 'L' in "Ball" {BalL'}.
9b	A Scripted Consonant Sequence enclosed in square brackets followed by an apostrophe, e.g., {[ch]'}, {[*ch*]'}, {[CH]'}, {[*CH*]'}, {[sh]'}, {[*sh*]'}, {[SH]'}, {[*SH*]'}.	Extension of the preceding Consonant Sequence with a Merged sound. E.g. 'CH' in "Fiche" {Fi[*CH*]3'e}, or 'SH' in "Cash" Ca[*SH*]'}. See Note 3.

10	Specific Consonant and Merged Consonant sequences, followed by a lower case 'H' enclosed in parentheses, all in italic, as in {*(h)*}.	An abrupt exhalation or release of air (sounding like an 'H') increasing emphasis of preceding Consonant or Merged Consonant sequences in certain word positions. E.g. 'P' in "Pin" {P*(h)*in} or 'CH' in "Check" {[CH]*(h)*eck}.
11	A numbered Consonant, or, a numbered Merged Consonant Sequence in square brackets, in lower case, followed by an asterisk, then another Consonant, or, Merged Consonant Sequence in square brackets, that follows enclosed in parentheses and Scripted, e.g. {g2*(j)} or {[ch]3*([*sh*])}.	A silencing of the numbered Consonant or Merged Consonant Sequence preceding the asterisk and its replacement with the inserted Consonant or Merged Consonant Sequence sound that follows enclosed in parentheses, e.g 'g2*(j)' in "Gem" {g2*(j)em} or in "Champagne" {[ch]3*([*sh*])ampagne}. See Notes 3 and 7.
12	A pair of similar adjacent Consonants at the end of a word, the first in italic upper case italic and the second in regular lower case followed by an asterisk, e.g. as in {*F*'f*}, {*D*d*}, {*S*'s*}. Observe whether the first Consonant is or is not followed by an apostrophe.	A Consonant Sound articulated just once with strong Accentuation, e.g. as in "Staff" {Sta*F*'f*} or "Bliss" {Bli*S*'s*}, with Extension – as an apostrophe follows the first Consonant. Where an apostrophe does not follow the first Consonant, e.g. as in "Odd" {O*D*d*}, the Consonant Sound is not Extended
13	For two of the same Consonants in the middle of a word: --- Option 1 – (In line with the American Syllabication Principle). See Note 6 below. A pair of similar adjacent Consonants preceded by a dash, '-', denoting a Pause, with the first Consonant Scripted to reflect actual Accentuation and the second in lower case regular Script followed by an asterisk (to silence the second Consonant), e.g. {*l* l*} ' or {Pp*}, as in the examples "Fellow" and "Apple". This course follows the convention of showing only this option in phonetic representations of such words. (An exception exists in certain word examples with two adjacent 'C' Consonants in the middle of a word.) --- Option 2 – (Used more by the British and less by Americans). See Note 6. A pair of similar adjacent Consonants both Scripted to reflect equal Accentuation of Moderate level (either Weak to moderate level or a Moderate to strong level) with a dash, {-} (denoting a Pause) between them, e.g. as with {*l*-*l*}and {P-P} in the middle of a	--- Either a minor or Major Pause preceding the sound of adjacent similar Consonants, with the first Consonant articulated at either Weak to moderate Accentuation or Moderate to strong Accentuation and the second Silent, as in "Fellow" {Fe-*l* l*ow} and "Apple" {A-Pp*le}. See Note 6. --- The sound of adjacent similar Consonants with a Pause between them, the first at the end of a Syllable and second at the beginning of the next, each Accentuated at either a Weak to moderate level or a Moderate to strong level, e.g. as in "Fellow" {Fe*l*-*l*ow} and "Apple" {AP-Ple}.

	word as in the examples "Fellow" and "Apple". As a matter of protocol, only Option 1 above will be used in this course, but for the exception provided.	See Note 6.

Note 1: Consonant Sounds vary phonetically both in their Accentuation and character. To describe just Accentuation, a scale from weak to strong is used. The slabs, and the Symbols representing them, are:
-Weak (Scripted in lower case regular)
-Weak to Moderate (Scripted in lower case italic)
-Moderate to Strong (Scripted in upper case regular)
-Strong (Scripted in upper case).

Note 2: Twelve characteristics are distinguished in terms of fundamental phonetic Attributes by name. These are:

-Pop Light
-Pop Heavy
-Sharp
-Knock
-Flat
-Rasp
-Buzz
-Hiss
-Hum
-Nasal
-Vowelish
-Lilting.

These are each described in the Table: The Consonant Sound Inherent Attribute List (Appendix III. A).

See the Sections on Consonants in the Chapter: "Lane 4: The Way Americans Articulate Vowel and Consonant Sounds" to understand the interaction of factors that influence Accentuation level in the American Accent.

Note 3: It is important to recognize that adjacent Consonants (side-by-side Consonants) relate phonetically with each other in a few different ways, for proper phonetic representation and articulation.

Adjacent Consonant pairs can Merge, Link or stand Separate from each other.

Merged Consonant pairs are relatively few and make a distinctive, unified or single Consonant Sound. Obvious Merged Consonant pairs are:
-'CH' which has several variant forms of pronunciation, all of which are Merged, as in "Champion", "Monarch", and "Champagne".
-'SH' as in "Ship" or "Cash".
-'TH' in its two alternate forms as in "Think" or "Three" which has a hiss Inherent Attribute, and "This" or "There" which has Flat and Buzz Inherent Attributes.

Others, not so obvious, adjacent Merged Consonant pairs are:
-'GH' as in "Ghoul", "Gherkin", "Ghost" or "Ghastly", this combination may also stand as separate as in "Aghast". 'GH' also Merges in words like "Rough" or "Cough" to make an 'F' sound. There is also a Silent Version of 'GH' as in words like "Bough" or "Through".
-'PH', like one Version of 'GH' above, Merges to make an 'F' sound, as in "Phone" or "Sphere", but may also stand separate as in the word "Shepherd" retaining the distinct sounds of 'P' and 'H'.
-'RH' as in "Rhyme", "Rhinoceros", "Rhapsody", "Rheumatism", "Arrhythmia" and "Myrrh".

-'WH' as in “Whistle”, “Where” and “White”.

Note: Interestingly, most Merged adjacent Consonant pairs are combinations with 'H' as the second Consonant.

Merged adjacent Consonant Sounds which are the result of a pairing with 'H' as the second Consonant, but where the 'H' is not actually in the word spelling, are:
-'G' & 'H'. as in “Beige”.
-'J' & 'H' as in “Jacque”.
-'S' & 'H' as in “Leisure” (Here, this Version of 'S' is the “Buzzing 'S'” which has a 'Z' sound).
-'S' & 'H' as in “Pressure”.
-'Z' & 'H' as in 'Seizure”.

Merged adjacent Consonant pairs where the second Consonant is not an 'H' are:
-'D' and 'G' as in “Badger”, “Edge” or “Gadget”. The Consonants in this pair may also stand separately, as in the name “Edgar”.
-'D' and 'J' as in “Adjust” or “Adjacent”.

Another Merged Consonant Sound is important to note. The 'T' in words like “Center”, “Interfere”, “Butter” and “Later” in popular spoken American English is between a 'T' and 'D', of low Accentuation. The 'D' sound is not in the spelling of such words. While, dictionaries usually identify only a 'T' or a 'D' sound of low Accentuation in their phonetic transcriptions, the audio recording they provide is likely to demonstrate the Merged 'TD' sound.

This Course covers popular American English which also encompasses Standard American English. I include within popular American English what is commonly accepted as correct. Standard American English is what is regarded as correct in a more formal sense.

The Merged Consonant Sound of 'T' and 'D' is represented {[td]} in words like “Center”, “Interfere”, “Shutter” and “Later”. Note there is a very small or, in some voices, no difference between the words “Shutter” and “Shudder”. In the former, the 'T' sound is that of the Merged 'T' and 'D', {[td]}.

Adjacent Consonant pairs are Linked when they begin with the sound of the first Consonant and transition into the second, such as with 'CR' in “Crown”, or 'GL' in “Glass”, 'TW' in “Twin” or 'ST' in “Rest” – with the identity of the constituent Consonants exhibiting their original identities in the course of transition from the first Consonant to the second.

An often heard Linked Consonant Sound occurs with the connecting of 'Q' and 'W' Consonant Sounds in words like “Quiver”, “Quiet” and “Quill”. The 'U' Vowel in the spelling of these words is best represented with the 'W' Consonant. Note that while 'W' is conventionally considered a Consonant in English grammar, in positions other than at the beginning of a Syllable it is of lower intensity and less defined making it more like a Vowel Sound.

Some adjacent Consonant pairs may Link more closely than other adjacent Linked Consonant pairs. For example, the pair 'PT', in the word “Rapt” is also Linked, but not as closely as 'CR' in “Crown”. The transition is smoother in the more closely Linked pairs. Regardless, both belong to the category of Linked Consonants.

There are some adjacent Consonant sequences that are actually Linked but as at least one of the

Consonants undergoes significant transformation in the process of Linking, giving them a distinctive character when together, they are identified and grouped with Merged pairs and similarly Scripted (between square brackets). To distinguish such sequences from truly Merged pairs in the Table Scripting Conventions Applied: Phonetic Symbols for Consonant Sounds & Sequences (Appendix III. C), the Merged label is enclosed within quotation marks, as in, "Merged". For truly Merged pairs, quotation marks are not used.

These include the sequences: 'NG' as in "Sing", 'NG' as in "Range', 'NC' as in "Uncle", 'NK' as in "Think" and 'NCH' as in "Inch".

In the above sequences the 'N' is significantly transformed by losing its Main Knock Inherent Attribute. In 'NG' as in "Sing", it is not just the 'N' but also the 'G' that is significantly transformed retaining only its Flat Internal Attribute. When Scripted, these particular Linked sequences are enclosed in square brackets as if Merged, to show their distinctive character when together, as follows: {-[*n*G]1}, {-[*n*G]2}, {-[*n*C]},{-[*n*K]} and {-[*n*CH]}. The Scripting of the Consonants in the square brackets varies, depending on how they are articulated in different words. The numbers that follow a bracketed pair is indicative of a specific Version of that pair.

Each constituent Consonant in such Consonant sequences, though marked "Merged" may be Accentuated at different levels and exhibit distinct sets of Inherent Attributes unlike a true Merged pair which, being a unified, single Consonant Sound, exhibits just one level of Accentuation with a common set of Inherent Attributes that describe it.

In contrast to the Merged and Linked Consonants explained above, whenever a Pause separates adjacent Consonants, each Consonant is articulated Separately, as with the 'LD' in "Colder" {Col-der} or 'ST' in "Western" {Wes-tern}. It does not matter whether it is a Minor ('.') or Major ('-') Pause.

Note 4: Several conventions can apply to a Consonant Symbol or Consonant Sequence concurrently. Consonants may be shown in upper or lower case with italic or regular orientation to show accentuation. They may be Extended. There may be different Versions. They may Merge with other Consonants. They may be silenced, modified, or, replaced. A number of these effects might occur together. The Course's Vocal Fidelity Phonetic System enables accurate reading of the sound. E.g. in the word "Clothes", the 'TH' has moderate to strong accentuation with a 'D' sound inserted between the 'T' and 'H' to make the resulting Merged Consonant Sound distinct from the 'TH' in the word "Sloth".

Note 5: Remember, between any two letters (whether Consonant or Vowel) Pauses are denoted as follows: A relatively longer Major Pause with a dash, '-' and a relatively shorter Minor Pause with a dot, '.'.

Note 6: For two of the same Consonants next to each other in the middle of a word there are two pronunciation options. The former option is in line with the American way of beginning Syllables with a Consonant and ending with a Vowel(American Syllabication Principle), while the latter is characteristic of the British way but also heard in the American way of speaking. This course will observe the convention of representing the pronunciation of such words the former way, though the latter can also occur.

As an exception, in certain cases when two adjacent 'C' Consonants come together, the Pause always and necessarily occurs between the two, as in words like "Access" {Ac-cess} or "Vaccine" {Vac-cine}. In these cases, the two Consonants actually have different Consonant Sounds, the first having the sound of 'C' as in "Cat" and the second, 'C' as in "Face". Where the two adjacent 'C's have the same Consonant Sound, as in the example "Occupy" {O-ccu-py} the convention will be as for other similar adjacent Consonants in the middle of a word.

Accentuation level of the similar adjacent Consonants in the middle of a word depends both upon their

Inherent Attributes (see Note 2 above) and the specific Syllable position of the two Consonants, whether Syllable-Beginning or Syllable-End.

Note 7: Consonants can represent different sounds. E.g. 'S' in "Sit" has a Hiss Attribute, whereas 'S' in "His" has the sound of the Consonant 'Z' with a Buzz Attribute. These different Versions are distinguished by a number. The former 'S' is identified 'S1' and the latter 'S2'. Any Consonant followed by a '1' is the Version that is thought to be the one with its most commonly perceived pronunciation. Thus, the 'S' which has the Hiss characteristic is identified, 'S1'. Similarly, the 'G' as in "Gift" is identified, 'G1'. There are other Versions of 'G' i.e. with different pronunciations, as in "Gem", that sounds like the Consonant, 'J', identified, 'G2', or, as in "Beige" where it sounds like a Merged 'ZH', identified, 'G3'. Consonant Versions are also numbered in order of expected frequency, e.g. G2 is less common than 'G1' and more common than 'G3'.

To make phonetic reading of a Consonant that has the sound of other Consonants easier, it is written first in lower case, then identified by its specific number identifier, then marked with an asterisk to treat it as Silent, and then substituted by the Consonant(s) that it has the sound of in phonetic Scripting. The Consonant(s) that are inserted follow the asterisk between parentheses in Script to show the level of Accentuation. If the replacement Consonants are a Merger of more than one Consonant, they are also enclosed in square brackets.

E.g.1. The 'G' in "Gem" is first identified as 'g2', then silenced with an asterisk '*', and then substituted with a (*j*) in parentheses, as in {g2*(*j*)e"*M*}. The original 'G' is in lower case according to the Scripting Conventions that state that any letter to be treated as silent is to be in lower case and then marked with an asterisk. The 'J' is shown in italics to show its level of Accentuation, in this example: Weak to moderate.

E.g. 2 The Consonant 'C' has a number of different Version. The different Versions are Scripted according to these Conventions, as shown in the following examples: It can sound like a 'K' as in "Cat" {c1*(*k*)(*h*)a"t}, the hissing 'S' as in "Fleece" {*fl*e*E'c2*(*S*)'e*}, or 'SH' as in "Gracious" {g*r*A-c3*([*sh*)]i*o*u1*S*}. These different 'C's are distinguished from each other by numbering the different Versions '1', '2', and '3'.

By showing the numbered Symbol as silent, and replacing with a Consonant Symbol of the same sound that is intuitively recognizable, the particular Version becomes readily readable. If the numbered Symbol were not replaced by a recognizable equivalent Consonant Sound as shown above, it would require that each Version be memorized. This Convention eliminates this problem.

The steps above are broken down step by step for clear understanding:

Step 1 -To show that a particular Consonant Version Symbol is not to be vocalized: it is Scripted in lower case with its number identifier, and then tagged with an asterisk.

E.g.: The 'C' in "Fleece" is shown in lower case and made silent as follows: {-c2*-}

Step 2 – Following the asterisk, the replacing Consonant Sound with its intuitively recognized Symbol within parentheses is inserted to substitute the silenced Consonant Sound.

E.g.: The sound of the 'C' in "Fleece" has the *Hissing* 'S' sound (not the *Buzzing* 'S' as in "His"), and is strongly accentuated.
Strongly Accentuated Consonant Sounds are Scripted in upper case italic as follows: '*S*'.
The '*S*', is written between parentheses, as follows: {-(*S*)-}, as the letter is not in the actual

spelling and is inserted. (Per Convention 8a of this table).

The Result of Steps 1 and 2: The word “Fleece” is therefore Scripted as follows: {Fle*E'c2*(_S_)'e*}.

The same process is followed when Merged Consonant sequences are involved, i.e. two more Consonants which are unified into a single Consonant Sound. These are identified by enclosing in square brackets. Applying the process above for a Merged Consonant Sequence is shown below:

Step 1 – To silence the Symbol: The Consonants are Scripted in lower case. Enclosed within square brackets to show they are Merged, and then together treated as silent by marking them with an asterisk.

E.g. The 'CH' in “Champagne” is identified and silenced as follows: {[ch]3*-}. 'CH' is Scripted in lower case, enclosed in square brackets because it is a Merged Consonant Sequence sound, (Per Convention 5 of this table) and then tagged with an asterisk.

Step 2 – It is substituted with an equivalent readily readable, Consonant Symbol, inserted within parentheses, Scripted to show its level of Accentuation.

E.g.: The sound of the 'CH' in “Champagne” actually has an 'SH' sound. By its position at the beginning of the word, the 'SH' has weak to moderate accentuation, shown by Scripting in lower case italic as follows: '_sh_'.
Because the 'SH' is a Merged Consonant Sequence it is enclosed within square brackets: [_sh_]. (Per Convention 5 of this table). And, because the 'SH' letters are additional to the spelling, they must be inserted into the word, by enclosing them in parentheses as follows: ([_sh_]). (Per Convention 8b of this table).

The Result of Steps 1 and 2: “Champagne” is therefore Scripted as follows: {[ch]3*([sh])a"M._p_ag*_N_'e*}.

Sometimes a Consonant Version, e.g. as in the word “Gracious”, Version 3 of 'C', must be replaced by a Merged Consonant Sequence 'SH'. Applying steps 1 and 2 as explained above, the 'C' sound in “Gracious” is Scripted up as follows: {Gra.c3*([_sh_])ious}.

Appendix II. A.
Vocal Fidelity Phonetic System: Scripting Vowel Sounds

Table:
Scripting Conventions Applied:
Phonetic Symbols For Vowel Sounds

Note 1: This Table lists the different Vowel forms which are Vowel Sounds associated with the different Vowels, including those associated with the letters 'H', 'W' and 'Y' (when these are in Syllable-Beginning and Syllable-End positions). They are listed by Symbol, then named, and then examples are provided. The Symbol is then applied in a Scripted example word.

Note 2: Sometimes you will see the same example word for two different Vowel Sounds. E.g. the word "Command" is given as an example word for an 'A' Soft with neither Extension or Repetition and also for the 'A' Soft with Extension but no Repetition. This is because the word is heard vocalized in both ways. (It is also sometimes vocalized with both Extension and Repetition, but in the Table it is not shown as an example for that Vowel Sound). This is because the Course does not provide all acceptable pronunciations, while it does often provide more than one acceptable pronunciation.

In fact, because of Accent variations, there are often a few acceptable ways of vocalizing certain Vowel Sounds in many words. The Course provides one that is more generally heard and one that is considered standard and where these are the same, just the one vocalization may be provided. Because a particular Accent vocalization is not identified, it does not mean that it does not exist or that it is incorrect. But, when an example is provided to show a particular vocalization, it is because it is generally heard and usable.

Phonetic Symbol of Vowel Sound	Corresponding Vowel Form Name and Modulation if any	Word Examples	Phonetic Spelling of Example Word
Short Short Vowel: a1,e1, i1, o1, u1.	'A', 'E', 'I', 'O' & 'U'.	Festiv*al*, Princip*al*, Riv*e*t, Myst*e*ry, Pen*i*tent, C*o*ntrol, Contr*o*versy, Cadb*u*ry.	feS-Ti1va1L
a	'A' Soft with neither Extension or Repetition.	Command, Demand, Philander, Collapse, Enchant.	c1*(K)(h)c1-l1*aPS'e*
a'	'A' Soft with Extension but no Repetition.	Command, Demand, Has, Philander, Collapse, Graph, Enchant, Track.	e*(i)N-[ch]1a'nT(h)
a"	'A' Soft with Extension and Repetition.	Bass, Cap, Dad, Hat, Has, Fan, Man, Map, Slam, Span, Van.	va"N
A	'A' Hard.	Bale, Day, Rail, Made, Spade.	mAD(h)e*
A'	'A' Hard, Extended.	Bale, Day, Rail, Made, Re-lay, Spade.	rE-lA'y*
a1	'A' Short. (Same as Short Vowel Sound.)	Acrylic, Avow, Astound, Astonish, Cola.	a1-c1*(K)(h)ry*(i)-lic1*(K)(h)
a2	'A' Long.	Balm, Blather, Calm, Father, Palm, Drama, Pasta. Shah.	Ba2l*M'

a*(i)	'A' Like 'I' Short.	Cottage, Courage, Message, Postage, Savage.	me-*ss**a*(i)g2*(*J*)(*h*)
a*(e)	'A' Like 'E' Short.	Air, Care, Mary, Parent, Stare, Fare.	Pa*(e)'-*r*a1*nT(h)*
e	'E' Soft with neither Extension or Repetition.	A-dept, Hem, Pen, When, Spent, Step.	a1-DeP*T(h)*
e'	'E' Soft with Extension but no Repetition.	A-mend, Em-ber, Lend, Transcend, Trem-ble, Deficit, Intent.	iN-T*(h)*e'*nT(h)*
e"	'E' Soft with Extension and Repetition.	Bed, Bet, Jeff, Plen-ty, Spell, Trend.	Be"*D(h)*
E	'E' Hard.	Pete, Feline, Cedar, Recent.	*r*E-c2e1*nT(h)*
E'	'E' Hard, Extended.	Been, Deed, Seek, Peach.	BE'e**N'*
e1	'E' Short. Sounds like all other Short Vowel Sounds.	Co-ver, La-tent, O-ven, Pa-tent, Ri-ver.	o1-*v*e1N
e*	'E' Silent.	Arcade, Late, Made, Plate, Quite, Wrote, Site.	P*l*A'*T'(h)e**
e*(A)	'E' Like 'A' Hard.	Fete (First 'E'), Mesa.	*m*A-*s*a1
e*(i)	'E' Like 'I' Soft.	Because (First 'E'), Begin, Serious, Require (First 'E').	*r*i-q*(*k*)u*(W)I'*R*'e*
e*(O)	'E' Like 'O' Hard.	Sew, Sewn.	*s*e*(O)'w*
e*(o2), or e*(u2)	'E' Like 'O' Long or 'U' Long.	Renewal, Screw, Sinew.	*s*c1*(*k*)*r*e*(o2)'w*
i	'I' Soft without Extension.	Cringe, Dinner, Glitter, Pick, Sink.	Pic1**K(h)*
i'	'I' Soft with Extension but no Repetition.	Fizz, Jig, His, Liz, Miss, Rig, Ridge, Sing, Which, Whiz.	Hi's*(Z)
i"	'I' Soft with Extension and Repetition.	Bid, Brim, Lid, Fit, Kid, Dim, Jim, Hill, Mint, Stint.	Ji"*M*
I	'I' Hard.	Bide, Hike, Kite, Night, Ride.	HI*K(h)*e*
I'	'I' Hard, Extended.	Isle, Nile, File, Fine, Life, Rice, Spine, Tile.	*n*I'Le*
i1	'I' Short. Sounds like all other Short Vowel Sounds.	Canister, Corridor, Gullible, Maximum, Penitent, Reticent.	*R*e-ti1-c2*(*s*1)e1*nT(h)*
i2	'I' Long Like 'E' Hard.	Fiona, Benzine, Pique, Sardine.	P*(h)*i*(E)'q*(*K*)*(h)*
o (See different forms of 'O' Soft in other rows).	O Soft-Round. Many words with sound are also articulated with Extension as in the row	Boy, Board, Core, Cost, Door, Employer, Fort, Foyer, Join, Joy, Lord, Short, Song~, Store, Storage, Strong, Toy, Thought~, Vortex, Wrong~,	T*(h)*oy*(i)

	below.	Wrought~.	
o)' (See different forms of 'O' Soft in other rows).	O Soft-Round, Extended. Many words with sound are also articulated without Extension as in the row above.	Boy, Board, Core, Cost, Cough, Door, Employer, Fort, Forest, Fort, Foster~, Foyer, Join, Joy, Lord, Song, Short, Store, Storage, Strong, Toy, Thought, Vortex, Wrong, Wrought~.	[*th*]1o)'u*g*h**T(h)*
o' (See different forms of 'O' Soft in other rows).	O' Soft-Flat, Extended.	Cot, Collar, College, Coliseum, Dot, Dollar, Hot, Honest, Not, Possible, Scholar, Shop, Stop, Tom.	Do'*T(h)*
o (Used for the British Accent and certain British Accent traditions). (See different forms of 'O' Soft in other rows).	'O' Soft-Tall.	Boy, Bored, Board, Bought, Brought, Boy, Chord, Core, Court, Door, Employer, Fore, Fort, Foyer, Join, Joy, Lord, Morning, Port, Score, Short, Sought, Sport, Store, Storage, Thought, Toy, Vortex, Wrought.	[*th*]*o*u*g*h**T(h)*
O	'O' Hard.	Bone, Cope, Crow, Folk, Hole, Stone, Road, Rose, Toast, Toll.	*st*O'N'e*
O'	'O' Hard, Extended.	A-loe, Ca-llow, Flow, Go, No, Row.	a1-*l*O'e*
o1	'O' Short.	Another, Color, Dozen, Monday, Mother, Brother, Son, Smother.	*m*o1N-DA'y*
o2	'O' Long.	Boot, Cool, Coot, Pool, Soot, Room.	c*(K)*(h)*o2o1L
o*	'O' Silent.	Subpoena.	*S*u1b*-P*(h)*o*E'*n*a1
o*(a)	'O' Like 'A' Soft. May be Extended with an apostrophe.	Cow, Dowel, How, Loud, Found, Sound, Town.	c*(K)*(h)*o*(a)w*(u)
u	'U' Soft.	Bull, Bush, Cushion, Found, Full, Loud, Out, Pulley, Push, Sound, Stout.	o*(a)u*T(h)*
u'	'U' Soft with Extension.	Bull, Push, Full.	*f*u'L'l*
U	'U' Hard.	Bugle, Cute, Fume, Fugitive, Fusion, Music, Mute, Refuge.	*f*UM'e*
U'	'U' Hard, Extended.	Im-bue, Hue.	*H*U'e*

u1	'U' Short.	But, Burn, Dumb, Fungus, Cluster, Mud, Mustard, Study, Trunk, Yogurt.	mu1D(h)
u2	'U' Long. Similar to the 'O' Long.	Assume, Dubious~, Dune, Flute, Lucid, Studio, Rude, Dude.	lu2-c2*(s)iD
u*(i)	'U' Like 'I' Soft.	Busy, Business.	Bu*(i)-s2*(z)y*(E)
u*	'U' Silent.	Ghoul, Through.	[th]1ro2'u*g*h*
u*(w) See Note below.	'U' Like 'W'. Weak to moderate, Soft sound as in the 'W' in “Sweet”.	Aqua, Equal, Quality, Squall, Quagmire, Quake, Question, Squeal, Quiver, Quite, Require, Quote.	E-q*(k)u*(w)a1L
w*(o2)	'W' Like 'O' Long.	Blew, Drew, Grew, Flew, Slew.	gre*w*(o2)
w*(U)	'W' Like 'U' Hard.	Few, Hew, Knew, Mew, Pew, Skew, View.	k*nEw*(U)
w*(u)	'W' Like 'U' Soft.	Allow, Cow, Clown, Drown, How, Now, Wow.	no*(a)w*(u)
w*(o)	'W' Like 'O' Soft.	Flaw, Law, Drawn, Raw, Straw, Tawny.	fla*w*(o)
y*(I)	'Y' Like 'I' Hard.	By, Bye, Cry, Dry, Fly, Fry, Style, Pylon.	By*(I)e*
y*(i)	'Y' Like 'I' Soft.	Boy, Toy, Symbol, Synopsis, Synchronize.	sy*(i)-no)'p-siS
y*(E)	'Y' Like 'E' Hard.	Crazy, Droopy, Fury, Jury, Sleepy, Wary, Canary, January.	Ju2-ry*(E)
In rows below: In certain words, 'H', 'W' and 'Y' is Silent with the effect that the preceding Vowel Sound prevails.			
a1h*	'A' Short Linked to 'H' Silent.	Farah, Sarah.	sa*(e)-ra1h*
a2h*	'A' Long Linked to 'H' Silent.	Brahms, Rahm, Shah.	[sh]a2h*
O'w*	'O' Hard, Extended and Linked to 'W' Silent.	Blow, Crow, Know, Slow, Show.	c1*(K)(h)rO'w*
A'y*	'A' Hard, Extended and Linked to 'Y' Silent.	Bay, Clay, Flay, Ray, Say, Stay.	sA'y*

Note: While many sounds of the Consonant 'W' can be substituted by certain Vowel forms, as may be seen in the 'W' rows of the Table above, one particular 'W' vocalization cannot be substituted by any Vowel form of 'A', 'E', 'I', 'O', or 'U'. This vocalization itself is like a Vowel in character, i.e. without edges or sharp definition. This is the 'W' sound that is heard in lieu of 'U' in words that have a Syllable beginning with 'Q', e.g. “Quantity”, “Quake”, “Question”, “Squeal”, “Acquire”, “Quite” and “Quote”. It is represented by a lower case 'W' {w}, as it has a Soft Vowel Sound. It is referred to as the 'W' Soft.

Words such as “Count”, “Round” and “Fountain”, with a 'U', have a similar sound that is well represented by a 'U' Soft but could also be represented by this very similar though not identical 'W' Soft sound. This course represents these words with the 'U' Soft, though it would also be accurate to represent them using

the 'W' Soft.

Appendix II. B.
Vocal Fidelity Phonetic System: Scripting Vowel Sequences

Table:
Scripting Conventions Applied:
Phonetic Symbols For Vowel Sequences

Note 1: Some Vowel sequences can be Scripted in different ways to represent a particular sound. E.g. in the word example "Though", the Vowel Sequence 'OU' may be Scripted {o2u*} or {o*u2}, with either one of the Vowels silenced (the asterisk marks a Vowel as Silent) as they both have forms representing the same sound – the 'O' Long {o2} has the same sound as the 'U' Long {u2}. In the Table, only one of the two ways is shown.

Note 2: Vowel sequences in certain words may be articulated in different ways: Sometimes both ways are shown in separate Vowel Sound rows, e.g. "Either" and "Neither". They are shown twice, first on row 11 and then on 12, illustrating each of the two different vocalizations each popularly used. Sometimes, only one pronunciation of such words is shown, but there could be others.

Note 3: Some Vowel Sequences are articulated with a Vowel Sound that is not in the spelling of the word. Such "External" Vowel Sounds are Scripted by inserting it between parentheses at the location in the word where it is articulated, e.g. as in the word example "Beau" where the Vowel Sequence is Scripted {Be*a*u*(O)}.

Note 4: Many of the same Vowel Sequences have different sounds. Each is Scripted distinctively. Word examples give instances of each of the different vocalizations.

Sound	Representing Vowel combinations using Script Symbols to show actual sound	Vowel Sequence	Word Example	Description of Script Symbols
1	a*e*(I)'	ae	Maestro.	'A' and 'E' Silent. 'I' Hard inserted, Extended.
2	A'i*	ai	Maid, Fail, Raid.	'A' Hard, Extended. 'I' Silent.
3	a*i*(e)"	ai	Said.	'A' and 'I' Silent. 'E' Soft inserted, Extension and Repetition.
4	a2o	ao	Taos, Laos, Tao.	'A' Long, 'O' Soft. Linked.
5	a*(o)	au	Caught, Taut, Taught.	'A' Silent. 'O' Soft inserted.
6	E'a*	ea	Beach, Lean, Neat.	'E' Hard, Extended, 'A' Silent.
7	e*a*u*(O)'	eau	Beau.	'E', 'A' and 'U' Silent, 'O' Hard inserted, Extended.
8	(i)e*a*U'	eau	Beauty.	External 'I' Soft inserted. 'E' and 'A' Silent, 'U' Hard, Extended.

9	E'e*	ee	Beet, Feet, Keen, Seed.	'E' Silent. 'E' Hard, Extended.
10	Ee1	ee	Beer, Seer, Peel.	'E' Hard. 'E' Short Vowel Sound. Linked.
11	Ei*	ei	Either@, Neither@.	'E'Hard. 'I' Silent. See 12. below.
12	e*I	ei	Feisty, Either@, Neither@.	'E' Silent, 'I' Hard.
13	E'o	eo	Eon, Leon.	'E' Hard, Extended. 'O' Soft Linked.
14	e*U'	eu	Teuton, Eunice, Eugene, Pseudo.	'E' Silent. 'U' Hard, Extended.
15	Ia1	ia	Dial, Vial.	'I' Hard, 'A' Short. Linked.
16	i*(E)a1	ia	Pianist, Enthusiast, Pediatrician.	'I' Silent. 'E' Hard, inserted. 'A' Short. Linked.
17	i*(E)a	ia	Fiasco.	'I' Silent, 'E' Hard, inserted. 'A' Soft. Linked.
18	i*(E)a2	ia	Fiat, Tiara.	'I' Silent, 'E' Hard, inserted. 'A' Long. Linked.
19	i2e1	ie	Field, Shield, Fielty, Fiend, View, Wield.	'I' Long, 'E' Short. Linked.
20	Io1	io	Ion@, Lion, Zion@.	'I' Hard, 'O' Short. Linked.
21	Io	io	Ion@, Zion@.	'I' Hard, 'O' Soft. Linked.
22	i2O	io	Fiona.	'I' Long, 'O' Hard. Linked.
23	io1	io	Union.	'I' Soft, 'O' Short. Linked.
24	io*u1	iou	Curious, Furious, Glorious Ludicrous.	'I' Soft. 'O' Silent. 'U' Short. Linked.
25	O'a*	oa	Boat, Coal, Foal, Shoal.	'O' Hard, Extended. 'A' Silent.
26	O'e1	oe	Poem, Poet.	'O' Hard, Extended. 'E' Short. Linked.
27	o*E	oe	Amoeba, Foetus, Phoebe.	'O' Silent. 'E' Hard.
28	(i)o2o*	oo	Coon, Fool, Moon, Room, Soon, Stool, Pool.	'I' Soft, inserted. 'O' Silent. 'O' Long. Linked.
29	o*o*(u)	oo	Good, Hood, Wood.	Silent 'O's, 'U' Soft, inserted.
30	(i)o2u*	ou	Wound.	'I' Soft, inserted. 'O' Long. Linked. 'U' silent.
31	o*u	ou	Could, Would, Foulard.	'O' Silent. 'U' Soft.
32	o*(a)'u	ou	Account, Bough, Found, Out, Round, Sound.	'O' Silent. 'A' Soft, inserted, Extended. 'U' Soft. Linked.
33	Ua1	ua	Dual@, Stuart@.	'U' Hard. 'A' Short. Linked.
34	u2a1	ua	Dual@, Stuart@.	'U' Long. 'A' Short. Linked.
35	Ua*(e)	ua	January, February.	'U' Hard. 'A' Silent. 'E' Soft,

				inserted. Linked.
36	u*(w)a	ua	Quagmire.	'U' Silent. 'W' Soft, inserted. 'A' Soft. Linked.
37	u*(w)a*(o)	ua	Quality, Squander.	'U' Silent. 'W' Soft, inserted. 'A' Silent. 'O' Soft, inserted. Linked.
38	u*(w)a1	ua	Equal.	'U' Silent. 'W' Soft, inserted. 'A' Short. Linked.
39	u*(w)A	ua	Equate.	'U' Silent. 'W' Soft, inserted. 'A' Hard. Linked.
40	Ue1	ue	Fuel.	'U' Hard. 'E' Short. Linked.
41	U'e*	ue	Queue, Cue, Due@.	'U' Hard, Extended. 'E' Silent.
42	U2e*	ue	Due@, Flue, Sue.	'U' Long. 'E' Silent.
43	(i)u2e*	ue	Rue.	'I' Soft, inserted. 'U' Long. Linked. 'E' Silent.
44	u*(w)i	ui	Quilt, Quiver.	'U' Silent. 'W' Soft, inserted. 'I' Soft. Linked.
45	u*(w)I	ui	Quite, Quiet, Require.	'U' Silent. 'W' Soft, inserted. 'I' Hard. Linked.
46	(i)u2i*	ui	Fruit.	'I' Soft, inserted. 'U' Long. Linked. 'I' Silent.
47	u2i	ui	Fruition, Tuition.	'U' Long. 'I' Soft. Linked.
48	u*(w)O	uo	Quote, Quotation.	'U' Silent. 'W' inserted. 'O' Hard. Linked.
@Pronounced in different ways.				
Copyright © published 2021 by Adil Rehman.				

Appendix III. A.
Vocal Fidelity Phonetic System: Consonant Inherent Attributes

Table:
The Consonant Sound Inherent Attribute List

Note 1. Purpose: This Table creates awareness of the Inherent Attributes associated with different Consonant Sounds. It describes the Inherent Attributes that specific Consonant Sounds exhibit and provides guidance on the articulation of Inherent Attributes.			
Note 2. Using this Table: In Column 1, "Inherent Attribute Name", the twelve important Inherent Attributes used to describe Consonant Sounds are listed. In Column 2, "Description", the sound of the corresponding Inherent Attribute is described. In Column 3, "Articulation", how to articulate the corresponding Inherent Attribute is explained. In Column 4, "Consonant Sounds", all the Consonant Sounds that exhibit the corresponding Inherent Attribute are identified with word examples.			
Note 3. The different Consonant Sounds (in Column 4) exhibiting the corresponding Inherent Attribute (labeled in Column 1 of the same row) are identified both with a reference to the associated Consonant(s) in apostrophe marks and with example words in quotation marks. E.g., there are three Consonant Sounds associated with the Consonant 'G', all of which exhibit the corresponding Inherent Attribute. They are presented one after the other, beginning with a reference to the Consonant 'G' followed by two or more example words to distinguish them from each other, as follows: 'G'! as in "Got", "Figs" or "Log"; 'G'! as in "Passage", "Staged" or "Gym"; 'G'! as in "Genre", "Beige" or "Massage". Similarly, the Consonants, 'TH' has two Consonant Sounds: 'TH' as in "Think" or "Math"; 'TH'! as in "Bathe", "Clothed" or "Loathe". The exclamation mark next to the Consonant(s) indicates that it exhibits other Inherent Attributes other than the corresponding one, and is therefore included on other Inherent Attribute row(s) of the Table, with which it is associated. Observe that the first of the Consonant Sounds associated with 'TH' (as in "Think" or "Math") is not flagged with an exclamation mark. This is because it does not exhibit any other of the twelve Inherent Attributes. By contrast, the second 'TH' (as in "Bathe" or "Loathe), is flagged to indicate that it exhibits other Inherent Attributes and is included on at least one other Inherent Attribute row.			
Note 4. See numbered Foot Notes elaborating on the descriptive terms used, at the end of the Table.			
Inherent Attribute Name	**Description**	**Articulation**	**Consonant sounds**
Buzz1.	Medium speed Vibration* like a buzzing bee of intermediate Tone and of medium Loudness@.	Vibration* of elements of vocal apparatus including roof of mouth, lower lip, mid to forward part of tongue, and throat.	'G'! as in "Genre", "Beige" or "Massage"; 'S' as in "Music", "His", "Closed" or "Rose"; 'S'! as in "Vision" or "Measure"; 'TH!' as in "Them", "Those" or "Leather"; 'TH'! as in "Bathe", "Clothed" or "Loathe"; 'V'! as in "Vale", "Leaves", "River" or "Save"; 'V'! as in "Leaves" or "Saves"; 'X' as heard in "Xanadu", "Xavier" or "Xenophobia", 'X'! as in "Exit" or "Exalt";

			'Z' as in "Zip", "Prized" or "Maze"; 'Z'! as in "Azure" or "Seizure".
Flat2.	Flat6, low sound with abrupt slow down or stop.	Made from chest or throat, with some part of vocal apparatus whether front or back of tongue or lips, used to choke off or cause slow down or stoppage of air.	'CH'! as in "Cheap" or "Such"; 'CH' as in "Bunched" or "Drenched"; 'DG' as in "Badge" or "Fudge"; 'DJ' as in "Adjective", "Adjunct" or "Adjust"; 'G'! as in "Got", "Figs" or "Log"; 'G'! as in "Passage", "Staged" or "Gym"; 'G'! as in "Genre", "Beige" or "Massage"; 'G' as in "Ring" or "English"; 'GH' as in "Ghoul", "Gherkin" or "Ghost"; 'J'! as in "Jet" or "Jump"; 'NCH'! as in "Inch" or "Punch"; 'NG'! as in "Range" or "Tinge"; 'S'! as in "Vision" or "Measure"; 'T' as in "Adventure" or "Culture"; 'TCH' as in "Matches" or "Fetched"; 'TCH'! as in "Clutch" or "Patch"; 'TH!' as in "Them", "Those" or "Leather"; 'TH'! as in "Bathe", "Clothed" or "Loathe"; 'V'! as in "Vale", "Leaves", "River" or "Save"; 'V'! as in "Leaves" or "Saves"; 'X' as in "Exit" or "Exalt"; 'Z'! as in "Azure" or "Seizure".
Hiss.	Begins with a certain Consonant Sound which gives way with the release of air to an Extended 'S' sound like air escaping from a tube through a small puncture hole or a 'SH' sound from a small cut or gash.	A small passage is formed in various specific ways with vocal apparatus through which the breath is allowed restricted escape.	'C'! as in "Cat" or "Record"; 'C' as in "Face" or "Rice"; 'C' as in "Delicious" or "Gracious"; 'CK'! as in "Clock" or "Pick"; 'CH'! as in "Cheap" or "Such"; 'CH' as in "Chic", "Fiche" or "Sachet"; 'CH'! as in "Chronic", "Monarch" or "Loch"; 'D'! as in "Picked", "Rushed" or "Touched"; 'F' as in "Fan", "Left" or "Safe"; 'GH' as in "Coughed" or "Rough"; 'H' as in "Had" or "Head". 'K'! as in "Kin" or "Lake"; 'NCH'! as in "Inch" or "Punch"; 'NK'! as in "Drink" or "Thank"; 'NX' as in "Lynx" or "Minx"; 'P'! as in "Pat" or "Ship"; 'PH' as in "Phone", "Sophomore" or "Sophisticated"; 'Q'! as in "Quay", "Clique", "Mystique" or "Quip"; 'S' as in "Sink", "Coast" or "Case"; 'S' as in "Mission", "Pension" or "Tension"; 'S' as in "Music", "His" "Closed" or "Rose"; 'SH' as in "Ship", "Cashed" or "Fish";

			'SS' as in "Mission" or "Session"; 'T'! as in "Tom" or "Cat"; 'T' as in "Caution" or "Motion"; 'TCH'! as in "Clutch" or "Patch"; 'TH' as in "Think" or "Math"; 'WH'! as in "When" or "Which"; 'X'! as heard in "Lax" or "Fix"; 'Z' as in "Zip", "Prized" or "Maze".
Hum3.	A high speed, smooth, Vibration* like the musical note of a tuning fork. Low Volume@.	By creating a temporary chamber or cavity of a certain shape in which Vibration* is generated using an element of the vocal apparatus.	'GN' as in "Align", "Signed" or "Benign"; L' as in "Lamp", "Cloud", "Couple", "Melon", "Fall" and "Vessel"; 'L'! as in "Belt", "Sale", "File" and "Tell"; 'M' as in "Map", "Main" or "Mall"; 'M'! as in "Lamp" or "Him"; 'N'! as in "Not", "Snack" or "Often"; 'N'! as in "Can", "Pen" or "When"; 'N'! as in "Can't", "Bend" or "Lens"; 'N'! as in "Plane", "Lunch" or "Been"; 'N'! as in "Enter" or "Center"; 'NG'! as in "Range" or "Tinge".
Knock4.	Like the sound of a door, drum or kettle being struck with a hard object.	Abrupt, hard sound. The tip of the tongue touches the front of the palate and is abruptly pushed off it by a sudden expulsion of air.	'D'! as in "Dig" or "Mad"; 'D'! as in "Picked", "Rushed" or "Touched"; 'G' as in "Got", "Figs" or "Log"; 'GN'! as in "Align", "Signed" or "Benign"; 'N'! as in "Not", "Snack" or "Often"; 'N'! as in "Can", "Pen" or "When"; 'N'! as in "Plane", "Lunch" or "Been"; 'T!' as in "Tom" or "Cat"; 'T'! as in "Stand", "Stock" or "Still"; 'T'! as in "Bits", "Melts" or "Kites"; 'T'! as in "Center" or "Later".
Lilting5.	With a Curve or bend in a Consonant Sound, transitioning over the course of its articulation. The sound of the Consonant seems to almost circle or wrap around itself.	The tongue twists or curls around.	'L'! as in "Belt", "Sale", "File" and "Tell"; 'M'! as in "Lamp" or "Him"; 'N'! as in "Can", "Pen" or "When"; 'N'! as in "Can't", "Bend" or "Lens".
Nasal6.	Resonance$, Hollowness%, as with congestion during a cold.	The nasal passage is activated during articulation by intermittently blocking off sound through the oral cavity.	'GN'! as in "Align", "Signed" or "Benign"; 'M'! as in "Lamp" or "Him"; 'N'! as in "Can", "Pen" or "When"; 'N'! as in "Can't", "Bend" or "Lens"; 'N'! as in "Plane", "Lunch" or "Been"; 'N'! as in "Enter" or "Center"; 'N'! as in "Bank" or "Sting"; 'NC'! in "Rancor" or "Uncle"; 'NCH'! as in "Inch" or "Punch"; 'NG'! as in "Range" or "Tinge";

			'NK'! as in "Drink" or "Thank"; 'NK'! as in "Ankle", "Monkey" or "Blinked"; 'NX' as in "Lynx" or "Minx".
Pop Heavy	Lower Frequency*, Hollowness%, Resonance#, Projection$.	Exhalation abruptly separates tongue from other vocal apparatus, causing sudden opening of passage and release of sound.	'D'! as in "Dig" or "Mad"; 'DG' as in "Badge" or "Fudge"; 'DJ' as in "Adjective", "Adjunct" or "Adjust"; 'G'! as in "Got", "Figs" or "Log"; 'G'! as in "Passage", "Staged" or "Gym"; 'GH' as in "Ghoul", "Gherkin" or "Ghost"; 'J'! as in "Jet" or "Jump"; 'NG'! as in "Range" or "Tinge"; 'T'! as in "Center" or "Later"; 'TH'! as in "Bathe", "Clothed" or "Loathe"; 'X'! as in "Exit" or "Exalt".
Pop Light	Middle Frequency*, Hollowness%, Resonance#, Projection$.	Begins with pursed lips. Exhalation pushes lips open.	'B' as in "Boy" or "Cub"; 'P'! as in "Pat" or "Ship"; 'P' as in "Shopped", "Rapt" or "Kept".
Rasp7.	A slow speed Vibration* with a deep Tone*. Higher Volume@. Like the sound of a rough file on metal or wood, or the rattling sound of radio static.	Grating or abrasive, sound. Using vocal apparatus, involving epiglottis, lower throat and tongue. The tongue is cupped or forms a bowl. The throat is opened wide.	'R' as in "Rock", "Mart" or "Car"; 'RH' as in "Rhombus" or "Rhodesia".
Sharp8.	Sharp8, cutting edge or piercing point.	A hard, thin edge or point of sound with a sudden start and stop of airflow.	'C'! as in "Cat" or "Record"; 'C' as in "Pact", "Secret" or "Vacant"; 'CK'! as in "Clock" or "Pick"; 'CK' as in "Locked", "Rocket" or "Sticks"; 'CH'! as in "Chronic', "Monarch" or "Loch"; 'D'! as in "Picked", "Rushed" or "Touched"; 'K'! as in "Kin" or "Lake"; 'K' as in "Bikes" or "Raked"; 'NC'! in "Rancor" or "Uncle"; 'NK'! as in "Drink" or "Thank"; 'NK'! as in "Ankle", "Monkey" or "Blinked"; 'NX' as in "Lynx" or "Minx"; 'Q' as in "Quiver", "Squat" or "Liquid"; 'Q'! as in "Quay", "Clique", "Mystique" or "Quip"; 'T!' as in "Tom" or "Cat"; 'T'! as in "Stand", "Stock" or "Still"; 'X'! as heard in "Lax" or "Fix".
Vowelish9.	Sound begins small and expands, almost Vowel like, in that it has no phonetic edges	Tongue has minimal or no contact with other vocal apparatus.	'W' as in "Wall", "Wit" or "Been"; 'WH'! as in "When" or "Which"; 'Y' as in "Yet", "Yacht" or "Yonder"; 'Y' as in or "Boy", "Coy" or "Toy".

	or corners.		

The meaning of key terms used as names of Attributes:

1. Buzz: A low, ongoing, vibrating sound.

2. Flat: A smooth, level, even surface without bumps or curves making for dullness. This also applies to flat sounds.

3. Hum: A low, steady, continuing sound note or mix of sound notes.

4. Knock: An abrupt sound caused by rapping a hard, hollow surface with another hard object.

5. Lilting: Having cadence and swing as in a rhythm, with a rise and fall of the voice.

6. Nasal: Relating to the nose. Pushing air through the nose when you speak.

7. Rasp: A grating, scraping, abrasive sound.

8. Sharp: A thin edge which can cut or a point which can make holes or pierce. Also as something sudden and abrupt. This also apples to sharp sounds.

9. Vowelish: A vocal sound similar to a Vowel Sound in that it has no hard edges.

Terms used in Description

*Frequency, Tone and Vibration: Notes of sound on a musical scale depend on frequency, tone or vibration (all refer to different aspects of the same thing). From this you can estimate low, medium or higher frequency, tone or vibration.

@ Loudness and Volume: Sounds are either more or less loud (or soft), depending on the energy or power put into them.

Resonance: A deep, bold, clear sound quality, which expands, carries, vibrates and seems to bounce back like an echo.

% Hollowness: Something not solid, or having nothing inside, an empty cavity or hole, reverberation from striking on an empty enclosure.

$ Projection: A quality of sticking out or being thrown or thrust forward.

Note: See Appendix following the last Chapter to refer to the full Table of Phonetic Symbols for Consonant Sounds.

A separate Table is provided listing each of the Consonant Sounds and all the Inherent Attributes associated with each one.

Appendix III. B.
Vocal Fidelity Phonetic System:
Inherent Attributes Of Each Consonant Sound

Table:
Consonant Sounds And Their Inherent Attributes

Note 1: This Table is an overlay of the Vocal Fidelity Phonetic System enabling Accent sensitive vocalization of Consonant Sounds in different words.

It identifies the different Consonant Sounds used when speaking the American way. Each Consonant Sound is characterized by specific Inherent Attributes.

Through examples, it identifies the kind of words where a certain Consonant Sound is applied. This depends primarily upon the Syllable position of the Consonant within the word.

Words often exhibit the same Consonant Sound when the Consonant is associated with certain Syllable positions, E.g.:

-only Syllable-Beginning position, as with the Consonant 'M' in No. 30,
-only the Syllable-End position, as with the Consonant 'C' in No. 4,
-only the Syllable-Middle position, as with the Consonant 'N' in No. 37,
-the Syllable-Beginning or Syllable-End positions, as with the Consonant 'G' in No. 19,
-the Syllable-Beginning or Syllable-Middle positions, as with the Consonant 'C' in No. 3,
-the Syllable-Middle or Syllable-End positions, as with the Consonant 'N' in No. 36
-any position – Syllable-Beginning, Syllable-Middle or Syllable-End positions – as with the Consonant 'F' in No. 16.

A word with a particular Consonant in a similar Syllable position but vocalized with a different Inherent Attribute profile may be in a different Accent or a correct irregular pronunciation. The pronunciation of such words are best verified.

Note 2: A Consonant Sound that differs with another Consonant Sound in terms of any Inherent Attribute must be considered distinct even when they are associated with the same Consonant and sound very similar.

Consonant Sounds sometimes have identical Inherent Attributes yet can still be quite distinct from each other when they possess other unspecified Inherent Attributes. (The Consonant Sound Inherent Attribute List – Appendix III.A. – is not exhaustive; it seeks to identify the main Inherent Attributes, keeping the number optimal).

The level at which a Consonant Sound is Accentuated does not make it different, it just makes it louder or more intense. Only the addition or elimination of Inherent Attributes makes it different. Accentuation of each Consonant Sound varies depending on its position with a Syllable.

Serial No.	Consonant and Consonant Sequences with a corresponding Consonant Sound	Inherent Attributes of corresponding Consonant Sound
1	'B' as in “Boy”, “Cub” or “Stubbed”.	Pop Light, Flat.
2	'C' as in “Cat” or “Record”.	Sharp, Hiss.

3	'C' as in "Pact", "Secret" or "Vacant".	Sharp.
4	'C' as in "Face" or "Rice".	Hiss.
5	'C' as in "Delicious" or "Gracious".	Hiss.
6	'CK' as in "Clock" or "Pick".	Sharp, Hiss.
7	'CK' as in "Locked", "Rocket" or "Sticks".	Sharp.
8	'CH' as in "Cheap" or "Such".	Flat, Hiss.
9	'CH' as in "Bunched" or "Drenched".	Flat.
10	'CH' as in "Chic", "Fiche" or "Sachet".	Hiss.
11	'CH' as in "Chronic", "Monarch" or "Loch".	Sharp, Hiss.
12	'D' as in "Dig" or "Mad".	Pop Heavy, Knock.
13	'D' as in "Picked", "Rushed" or "Touched".	Sharp, Knock, Hiss.
14	'DG' as in "Badge" or "Fudge".	Flat, Pop Heavy.
15	'DJ' as in "Adjective", "Adjunct" or "Adjust".	Flat, Pop Heavy.
16	'F' as in "Fan", "Left" or "Safe".	Hiss.
17	'G' as in "Got", "Figs" or "Log".	Pop Heavy, Knock, Flat.
18	'G' as in "Passage", "Staged" or "Gym".	Flat, Pop Heavy.
19	'G' as in "Genre", "Beige" or "Massage".	Flat, Buzz.
20	'G' as in "Ring" or "English".	Flat.
21	'GH' as in "Ghoul", "Gherkin" or "Ghost".	Pop Heavy, Flat.
22	'GH' as in "Coughed" or "Rough".	Hiss.
23	'GN' as in "Align", "Signed" or "Benign".	Nasal, Knock, Hum.
24	'H' as in "Had" or "Head".	Hiss.
25	'J' as in "Jet" or "Jump".	Flat, Pop Heavy.
26	'K' as in "Kin" or "Lake".	Sharp, Hiss.
27	'K' as in "Bikes" or "Raked".	Sharp.
28	'L' as in "Lamp", "Cloud", "Couple", "Melon", "Fall" and "Vessel".	Hum.
29	'L' as in "Belt", "Sale", "File" and "Tell".	Lilting, Hum.
30	'M' as in "Map", "Main" or "Mall".	Hum.
31	'M' as in "Lamp" or "Him".	Nasal, Lilting, Hum.
31a	'M' as in "Game", "Seem" or "Time".	Nasal, Hum.
32	'N' as in "Not", "Snack" or "Often".	Knock, Hum.
33	'N' as in "Enter" or "Center". (When pronounced with Pause after 'N'). See Note F below.	Nasal, Hum.
34	'N' as in "Can", "Pen" or "When".	Nasal, Lilting, Knock, Hum.
35	'N' as in "Can't", "Bend" or "Lens".	Nasal, Lilting, Hum.
36	'N' as in "Plane", "Lunch" or "Been".	Nasal, Knock, Hum.
37	'N' as in "Bank" or "Sting".	Nasal.
38	'NC' in "Rancor" or "Uncle".	Nasal, Sharp.
39	'NCH' as in "Inch" or "Punch".	Nasal, Flat, Hiss.
40	'NG' as in "English" or "Sting".	Nasal, Flat.

41	'NG' as in “Range” or “Tinge”.	Nasal, Flat, Pop Heavy, Hum.
42	'NK' as in “Ankle”, “Monkey” or “Blinked”.	Nasal, Sharp.
43	'NK' as in “Drink” or “Thank”.	Nasal, Sharp, Hiss.
44	'NX' as in “Lynx” or “Minx”.	Nasal, Sharp, Hiss.
44a	'NX' as in “Anxious”. See Note G below.	Nasal, Sharp – Pause – Hiss.
44b	'NX' as in “Anxiety”. See Note G below.	Nasal, Flat – Pause – Buzz.
45	'P' as in “Pat” or “Ship”.	Pop Light, Hiss.
46	'P' as in “Shopped”, “Rapt” or “Kept”.	Pop Light.
47	'PH' as in “Phone”, “Sophomore” or “Sophisticated”.	Hiss.
48	'Q' as in “Quiver”, “Squat” or “Liquid”.	Sharp.
49	'Q' as in “Quay”, “Clique”, “Mystique” or “Quip”.	Sharp, Hiss.
50	'R' as in “Rock”, “Mart” or “Car”.	Rasp.
51	'RH' as in “Rhombus” or “Rhodesia”.	Rasp.
52	'S' as in “Sink”, “Coast” or “Case”.	Hiss.
53	'S' as in “Music”, “His”, “Closed” or “Rose”.	Buzz.
54	'S' as in “Vision” or “Measure”.	Flat, Buzz.
55	'S' as in “Mansion”, “Pension” or “Tension”.	Hiss.
56	'SH' as in “Ship”, “Cashed” or “Fish”.	Hiss.
57	'SS' as in “Mission” or “Session”.	Hiss.
58	'T' as in “Tom” or “Cat”.	Sharp, Knock, Hiss.
59	'T' as in “Stand”, “Stock” or “Still”.	Sharp, Knock.
60	'T' as in “Bits”, “Melts” or “Kites”.	Knock.
61	'T' as in “Center~” or “Later”.	Knock, Pop Heavy.
62	'T' as in “Caution” or “Motion”.	Hiss.
63	'T' as in “Adventure” or “Culture”.	Flat.
64	'TCH' as in “Matches” or “Fetched”.	Flat.
65	'TCH' as in “Clutch” or “Patch”.	Flat, Hiss.
66	'TH' as in “Think” or “Math”.	Hiss.
67	'TH' as in “Them”, “Those” or “Leather”.	Flat, Buzz.
68	'TH' as in “Bathe”. “Clothed” or “Loathe”.	Pop Heavy, Flat, Buzz.
69	'V' as in “Vale”, “Leaves”, “River” or “Save”.	Buzz, Flat.
70	'W' as in “Wall”, “Wit” or “Won”.	Vowelish.
71	'WH' as in “When”, “Which” or “White”.	Vowelish, Hiss.
72	'X' as in “Xanadu”, “Xavier” or “Xenophobia”.	Buzz.
73	'X' as in “Lax” or “Fix”.	Sharp, Hiss.
74	'X' as in “Exit” or “Exalt”.	Pop Heavy, Flat, Buzz.
75	'Y' as in “Yet”, “Yacht” or “Yonder”.	Vowelish.
76	'Z' as in “Zip”, “Prized” or “Maze”.	Buzz.
77	'Z' as in “Azure” or “Seizure”.	Flat, Buzz.
Note A: There are 80 Consonant or Consonant Sequences listed above that are associated with 54 distinct		

Consonant Sounds that recur in different words. More than a few of these have distinctive American English vocal characteristics in terms of their specific Inherent Attributes when compared with the British Accent. See Note H below.
Note B: There are 15 Consonant Sounds that are shared by 43 Consonant or Consonant Sequences. Each of the following Consonant or Consonant Sequences share a Consonant Sound with other sequence(s): -'C' in "Cat" or "Record"; 'CK' in "Clock" or "Pick"; 'K' in "Kin" or "Lake"; and, 'Q' in "Quay", "Clique", "Mystique" or "Quip". -'C' in "Pact", "Secret" or "Vacant"; 'CK' in "Locked", "Rocket" or "Sticks"; 'K' in "Bikes" or "Raked"; and, 'Q' in "Quiver", "Squat" or "Liquid". -'CH' in "Bunched" or "Drenched"; 'T' in "Adventure" or "Culture"; and 'TCH' in "Matches" or "Fetched". -'CH' in "Cheap" or "Such"; and, 'TCH' in "Clutch" or "Patch". -'D' as in "Picked", "Rushed" or "Touched"; and, 'T' in "Tom" or "Cat". -'DG' in "Badge" or "Fudge"; and, 'DJ' in "Adjective", "Adjunct" or "Adjust". -'F' in "Fan", "Left" or "Safe"; 'GH' in "Coughed" or "Rough"; and, 'PH' in "Phone", "Sophomore" or "Sophisticated". -'G' in "Genre", "Beige" or "Massage"; 'S' in "Vision" or "Measure"; and, 'Z' in "Azure" or "Seizure". -'G' in "Got", "Figs" or "Log"; and, 'GH' in "Ghoul", "Gherkin" or "Ghost". -'N' in "Plane", "Lunch" or "Been"; and, 'GN' in "Align", "Signed" or "Benign". -'NC' in "Rancor" or "Uncle"; 'NK' in "Ankle", "Monkey" or "Blinked"; and, 'NX' in "Anxious" (See Note G - this is the Pre-Pause Sound). -'NG' as in "English" or "Sting"; and, 'NX' in "Anxiety" (See Note G – this is the Pre-Pause Sound). -'R' in "Rock" "Mart" or "Car"; and, 'RH' in "Rhombus" or "Rhodesia". -'S' in "Music", "His" "Closed" or "Rose"; 'NX' in "Anxiety" (See Note G – this is the Post-Pause Sound); 'X' in "Xanadu", "Xavier"; and, 'Z' in "Zip", "Prized" or "Maze". -'SH' in "Ship", "Cashed" or "Fish"; 'S' in "Mansion", "Pension" or "Tension"; 'SS' in "Mission" or "Session"; 'T' in "Caution" or "Motion"; and, 'NX' in "Anxious" (See Note G – this is the Post-Pause Sound). See Note H below.
Note C: Silent variants of Consonants are not included in the Consonant Sound list above, as with: 'B' in "Comb", "Tomb", "Debt" or "Doubt". 'G' in "Gnat". 'H' in "Herb". 'K' in "Knit" or "Knock". 'L' in "Could", "Palm", "Holmes", "Solder" and "Salmon". 'P' in "Cupboard" or as in the name "Campbell". 'W' in "Wreck" or "Wrench".
Note D: Also not included in the Consonant Sound list above are any Consonant or Consonant sequences that are in effect Silent because a preceding Vowel yields the required vocalization (with or without Extension), as with: 'GH' in "Hugh" is Silent as the preceding 'U' yields the required 'U' Hard vocalization. 'GH' in "Through" is Silent as the preceding 'U' yields the required 'U' Long vocalization. 'GH' in "Bough" or "Drought" is Silent as the preceding 'U' yields the required 'U' Soft. 'GH' in "Dough" is Silent as the preceding 'O' ('U' is Silent) yields the required 'O' Hard vocalization. 'H' in "Sarah" is Silent as the preceding 'A' yields the required 'A' Short vocalization. 'H' in "Shah" is Silent as the preceding 'A' yields the required 'A' Long vocalization. 'H' in "McGahn" is Silent as the preceding 'A' yields the required 'A' Soft vocalization.

'H' in "Stihl" is Silent as the preceding 'I' yields the required 'I' Long Like 'E' Hard vocalization. 'W' in "Blow", "Crow", "Know" or "Slow" is Silent as the preceding 'O' Hard yields the required vocalization. 'Y' in "Bay, "Ray" or "Say" is Silent as the preceding 'A' Hard yields the required vocalization.
Note E: Versions of 'H', 'W' and 'Y' in a Syllable-End or Syllable-Middle position exhibiting Vowel Sounds are not included in the Consonant list above. These are: 'W' in "Blew" or "Flew" has the 'O' Long sound. 'W' in "Few", "Hew", "Knew", Mew", or "Pew" has the 'U' Hard sound. 'W' in "Clown", "How" or "Now" has the 'U' Soft sound. 'W' in "Flaw", "Law" or "Draw" has the 'O' Soft sound. 'Y' in "By", Bye", "Style" or "Pylon" has the 'I' Hard, Extended sound. 'Y' in "Synopsis" or "Synchronize" has the 'I' Soft sound. 'Y' in or "Boy", "Coy" or "Toy" has the 'I' Soft sound Linked to a preceding 'O' Soft.
Note F: There is another popular option for pronouncing words like "Enter" {En-ter} and "Center" {Cen-ter}, where an 'N' occurs before a 'T'. Here, the Pause occurs before the 'N' with the 'T' Silent {E-*nt**er} and {Ce-*nt**er}. Vocalized in a Syllable-Beginning position it exhibits the Hum and Knock Inherent Attributes, losing the Nasal Inherent Attribute. As these are the same Inherent Attributes exhibited by 'N' as in "Not", "Snack" or "Often", it is not a distinct Consonant Sound. And, in this Syllable position, it is Accentuated at a Weak to moderate level (consistent with Consonant Accentuation Norms). (See Table, "Consonant Position Accentuation Norms").
Note G: The Consonant Sounds shown on rows 31a, 44a and 44b above were added after the First Edition of Coursebook One. 44A and 44b are associated with the Consonant Sequence 'NX'. Both of these latter two contain a Pause, separating each into two Sounds. The Pre-Pause and Post-Pause Sounds are shared with other Consonant Sounds. The 'NX' Sound in "Anxious" Pre-Pause (like the 'NK' in "Ankle") is shared with two other Consonant Sequences on rows 38 and 42. And, Post-Pause (like the 'SH' in "Ship"), it is shared with four other Consonant Sequences on rows 55, 56, 57 and 62. The 'NX' Sound in "Anxiety" (like the 'NG' in "English), Pre-Pause is shared with one other Consonant Sequence on row 40. And, Post-Pause (like the 'S' in "Music"), it is shared with three other Consonant Sequences on rows 53, 72 and 76. Though these 'NX' Consonant Sequences are each broken into two different Consonant Sounds, as they are included in the above list each as an integrated Consonant Sequence, they are counted once each in the total figure of Consonant Sequences. In the count of Shared Consonant Sequences, their Pre-Pause and Post-Pause Sounds are each counted separately as they are actually linked but separate Sounds.
Note H: After the inclusion of the three additional Consonant Sequences (rows 31a, 44a and 44b) following the First Edition of Coursebook One, the total number of Consonant or Consonant Sequences has been increased from 77 to 80. Of these, the number of Consonant Sequences that do not share a Consonant Sound is 39 and those that share a Consonant Sound are 43. Together, these add up to 82 rather than to the total number of 80 Consonant & Consonant Sequences listed - because the two added 'NX' Consonant Sequences feature twice each in the counting of Consonant Sequences sharing a common Consonant Sound - as each is divided into two Sounds by an intervening Pause. The total number of Consonant Sounds has increased by 1 to 54 on account of the added distinct Consonant Sound associated with the Consonant Sequence on row 31a. Of these, those associated with only a single Consonant or Consonant Sequence are 39 while those that are shared is now 15. These numbers portray this updated Table.

Note: The Inherent Attribute profile of a particular Consonant Sound is limited to identifying the presence of certain defined properties, i.e. the Inherent Attributes. Each Consonant Sound contains other undefined properties that make it unique. This is why there can be and are some Consonant Sounds that have the same Inherent Attributes but remain distinct from each other.

While, the Inherent Attribute List yields a distinctive Inherent Attribute profile for most Consonant Sounds, to make each profile unique would require a significantly longer, less convenient to use Inherent Attribute List.

For example, the Hiss Inherent Attribute sound could be separated from a "Rush" sound. They both sound like escaping air, the first e.g. from a small puncture, the second from a wider gash. The Hiss sound has the sound of the 'S' in "Hiss" and the Rush sound has the sound of the 'SH' in "Rush". The List used combines both 'S' and 'SH' sounds under the Inherent Attribute "Hiss" as a compromise.

Similarly, certain Consonant Sounds associated with some Versions of 'G' involve a closing of the back of the throat with a movement of the epiglottis to produce an abrupt glottal stop sound. E.g. compare the 'G' Consonant Sound in "Big" in contrast with other 'G' Consonant Sounds in "Beige","Sting", or "Message". Only the 'G' in "Big" has the abrupt glottal stop sound, but was thought too specific to include in the List. This property if included would have further distinguished the 'G' in "Big" from the other 'G' Consonant Sounds.

Note: Though the Inherent Attribute profile of a Consonant Sound alerts one to certain aspects of its vocalization, it cannot be a complete description of the sound. There are yet other qualities that make it unique. To learn the Consonant Sounds you find difficult, after becoming aware of their Inherent Attributes, listen for the specific Inherent Attributes with the Consonant in different Syllable positions in different words as articulated by model speakers (On TV commercials, or an Online Dictionary for example), and make the distinctions between their Inherent Attribute profiles.

Note: Though there are often different Consonant Sounds associated with a particular Consonant, the overall difference is not always enough to necessitate a different Version of a particular Consonant. 'N' is an example of this. It has five different Consonant Sounds associated with it. In one of the five associated Consonant Sounds it has four Inherent Attributes, in two of the five it has three, in another two it has two, and in one it has just a single Inherent Attribute. Despite this range of differences in Inherent Attributes associated with the different 'N' Consonant Sounds, it has only one Consonant Version. By contrast, for example, 'S' has 'S1', 'S2', 'S3' and 'S4', and 'C' has 'C1', 'C2' and 'C3', to correspond with their associated Consonant Sounds. See the table, "Vocal Fidelity System: Phonetic Symbols For Consonant Sounds" (Appendix III. C). Also, see the table, "Consonant Sounds and their Inherent Attributes" (Appendix III. B).

Note: The Intrinsic Accentuation levels, (when isolated from other sounds and unaffected by Positional Accentuation), of different Inherent Attributes of Consonant Sounds are as follows:

- -Inherent Attributes that exhibit a High level Intrinsic Accentuation are:
  - Pop Light, Pop Heavy and Sharp.
- -Those that exhibit a Medium level of Intrinsic Accentuation are:
  - Flat, Hiss, Knock, Rasp and Vowelish.
- -Those that exhibit a Low level of Intrinsic Accentuation are:
  - Buzz, Hum, Lilting and Nasal.

Note: Certain other Consonant Sounds are also heard in American English but have been left out of the Consonant Sound list above, because their application is of limited scope. These include:

'C' as heard in the name of the "Luciano", as in the name of the Italian Tenor opera singer icon, "Luciano Pavarotti" and in the high end Italian Fashion Designer, "Guccio Gucci". It is articulated by Americans after a Pause both when there is a single 'C' as in "Luciano", Scripted {-c*([*ch*])} and when there are two 'C's' as in "Gucci", with one 'C' in effect Silent, Scripted {-c*([*ch*])c*}.

'J' as in the well known French names "Jacque" and "Jaqueline" that have recognition across the West, is articulated as if 'J' is replaced with a 'Z' and Merged with an 'H' Scripted {j*([*zh*])}, similar to the sound of the 'G' in "Genre", Scripted {g3*([*zh*])}; 'S' in "Vision" or "Measure", Scripted {s3*([*zh*])}; and, 'Z' in "Azure" or "Seizure", Scripted {z2*([*zh*])}.

Another Consonant Sound associated with the Consonant 'X' has emerged relatively recently. This is heard in the way 'X' is articulated in the Chinese name "Xi" as in the name of the President of China, "Xi Jinping". The Consonant Sound is articulated by the media in two ways: Either the 'X' is replaced with a Merged 'Z' and 'H' with the Buzz Inherent Attribute, Scripted {x*([*zh*])} – also similar to the sound of the 'G' in "Genre", Scripted {g*([*zh*])}; 'S' in "Vision" or "Measure", Scripted {s*([*zh*])}; and, 'Z' in "Azure" or "Seizure", Scripted {z*([*zh*])}. Or, it is replaced with a Merged 'S' and 'H' with the Hiss Inherent Attribute, Scripted {x*([*sh*])}, similar to the sound of 'SH' in "Ship"; 'C' as in "Delicious" or "Gracious", Scripted {c*([*sh*])}; or, 'CH' in "Chic" or "Sachet", Scripted {[ch]*([*sh*])}.

Then, there is the double 'Z" in "Pizza" articulated with the first 'Z' replaced by a 'T' of Low Accentuation (despite its position at the end of the first Syllable) followed by a Pause and the second 'Z' replaced with an 'S' with Hiss, articulated at a Low to moderate level of Accentuation, Scripted {z*(t)-z*(*s*1)}.

Appendix III. C.
Vocal Fidelity Phonetic System: Phonetic Symbols For Consonant Sounds

Table:
Scripting Conventions Applied:
Phonetic Symbols For Consonant Sounds & Sequences

Note 1: Scripted Symbols do not need to be memorized for each Consonant Sound. All of the Symbols are constructed according to the Scripting rules in the Table: Construction Conventions for Scripting of Consonant Sounds (Appendix I.C). The rules are logical and simple to understand and remember. Once you become familiar with them, you will be able to read the Symbols and vocalize Consonant Sounds accurately. You will also be able to use the rules to Script any English Consonant Sound yourself. Using the Script will help you understand how a particular Consonant Sound is to be articulated, to remember it well, and to communicate it.
Note 2: The level of Accentuation is associated with the position of a Consonant Sound in the Syllables of words. Consonants are located in Syllable-Beginning, Syllable-End or Syllable-Middle positions. The Accentuation level of a Consonant tends to be consistent with its position: In general, Consonant Sounds that are at or toward the beginning of a Syllable tend to exhibit weaker Accentuation and Consonants at or toward the end of a Syllable tend to exhibit stronger Accentuation.
Note 3: The Accentuation level of each Consonant Symbol is included under the Description column below. The level of Accentuation is a product of both the Inherent Attributes of a Consonant Sound, (Intrinsic Accentuation) and its position in a Syllable (Positional Accentuation). Depending on the Syllable position and Inherent Attributes, most Consonant Sounds are Accentuated at either a Weak to moderate, Moderate to strong or a Strong level. However, there are a few regularly used specific Consonant Sounds that are Accentuated at a Weak level.
Note 4: The same Consonant can be associated with different Consonant Sounds. Where a Consonant is associated with Consonant Sounds that are fundamentally different from each other, each is identified as a distinct Version with a number tag. E.g. 'G' in the word "Big" is Version 'G1' but in "Huge" is Version 'G2' But, other than such distinct Consonant Versions, some Consonants have associated Consonant Sounds that resemble each other but have slight dissimilarities in terms of their Inherent Attributes. Despite these dissimilarities, they are similar enough to be represented by the same Script Symbol. They are distinguished from each other in terms of their specific Inherent Attributes included under the Description column. The example words exhibit the Inherent Attributes included in the Description when articulated in the American Accent. A list of Consonant Sounds and their Inherent Attributes is provided in the Table: Consonant Sounds and their Inherent Attributes (Appendix III. B)
Note 5: In the Table, there are some instances where successive rows begin with identical Symbols. This happens when the same Consonant Symbol is either associated with a different Syllable position or with a slightly different Consonant Sound associated with a difference in Inherent Attributes as identified in the Description column. The corresponding examples under the Word example column illustrate the distinctive Description on each row.
Note 6: Pauses are shown in the word examples. In a two Syllable word, the Pause is always represented by a dash, i.e. '-'. If there are more than two Syllables, a '-' represents a Major Pause and a Dot, i.e. '.' represents a Minor Pause. Where Pauses are of equal length, the Pauses are shown using only the Dash, '-' Symbol.
Note 7: In the last column, only the Consonant Sound under consideration in the specific row is Scripted. The first letter is in upper case according to the Course writing protocol, however, when the Consonant

Sound under consideration is the first letter of the word, it is Scripted to show articulation.

Note 8: While the most of the Symbols below represent single Consonant Sounds, several short composite sequences of Consonant Sounds that span the End of a Syllable, an intervening Pause and the beginning of the next Syllable which function like Consonants are also included.

Note 9: This Table attempts to represent most Consonant Sounds. The Table: Construction Conventions for Scripting of Consonant Sounds provides you with the means of reading and constructing any Consonant Sound heard in English with accuracy.

Consonant Sound Symbol	Location in Syllable	Description: Pause shown if applicable, Consonant, Accentuation, Inherent Attribute(s), Extension shown if applicable.	Word Examples. Pauses shown.	Example word with Consonant Sound Scripted. Pauses shown.
b*	Middle, End.	'B': Silent.	Comb, Tomb, Debt, Doubt.	Deb*t
b	Beginning.	'B': Weak to moderate. Pop Light.	Ball, Bend, Begin, Ves-ti-bule, Cu-pboard.	*be*-gin
B	Beginning.	'B': Moderate to strong. Pop Light.	A-ban-don, Belt, Bin, Em-ber, Ca-bin, Ru-by.	A-*b*an-don
B	End.	'B': Strong. Pop Light.	Abe, Lab, Fib, Rob, Rib, Club, Lube.	LaB
-*b*b*	Beginning.	Pause precedes. 'B': Moderate to strong. Pop Light. 'B': Silent.	Stu-bborn.	Stu-*b*b*orn
B'b*	End.	'B': Strong. Pop Light. 'B': 'B' Silent.	Drubb, Stubb.	Dru*B*'b*
b*	Middle.	'B'. Silent.	Debt, Doubt.	Deb*t
c1*(*k*)	Middle.	'C': Replaced with 'K' sound. Weak to moderate. Sharp.	Scale, Scan, Scout, Scrub.	Sc1*(*k*)out
c1*(K)	Middle.	'C': Replaced with 'K' sound. Moderate to strong. Sharp.	Fact, Per-fect, Pro-tect, Sect.	Per-fec1*(K)t
c1*(K)*(h)*	Beginning.	'C': Replaced with 'K' sound. Moderate to strong. Sharp; Hiss.	Cane, Cat, Cot, Crude.	c1*(K)*(h)*ot
-c1*(K)c1*	Spans: End, Pause, Beginning.	Pause precedes. 'C': Replaced by 'K' Sound: Moderate to strong. Sharp; Hiss. 'C': Silent.	O-ccur, O-ccult, O-ccu-py.	Oc1*(K)c1*-u-py
c1*(*K*)(*h*)	End.	'C': Replaced with 'K' sound. Strong. Sharp; Hiss.	Arc, Marc, Mic, Tic.	Mic1*(*K*)(*h*)
c1*(*k*)	Beginning.	'C': Replaced with 'K' sound. Weak to moderate. Sharp.	Ba-con, Se-cond, Fo-cus, Rau-cous.	Se-c1*(*k*)ond

c2*(*s*1)	Beginning.	'C': Replaced with 'S' sound. Weak to Moderate. Hiss.	Ce-dar, I-cing, La-cy.	c2*(*s*1)e-dar
c2*(*S*1)	End.	'C': Replaced with 'S' sound. Strong. Hiss.	Face, Fleece, Dance, Mice.	Danc2*(*S*1)e
c3*([*sh*])	Beginning.	'C': Replaced with 'SH' sound. Moderate to strong. Hiss.	An-cient, Au-da-cious, Fa-cial, Spe-cial.	Fa-c3*([*sh*])ial
[*CH*]1*(h)*	End.	'C' & 'H' Merged: Strong. Flat; Hiss.	Much, Such, Starch.	Su[*CH*]1*(h)*
[CH]1	Middle	'C' & 'H' Merged: Moderate to strong, Flat.	Latched, Fetched, Stitched.	Lat[CH]1ed
[CH]1*(h)*	Beginning.	'C' & 'H'. Merged: Moderate to strong. Flat; Hiss.	Cham-pion, Chap-ter, Check.	[CH]1*(h)*ap-ter
[*ch*]1	Beginning.	'C' & 'H'. Merged: Weak to moderate. Flat.	Bran-ches, Fran-chise, Lun-ching, Wren-ches.	Bran-[*ch*]1es
[ch]2*(K)	Beginning.	'C' & 'H': Replaced with 'K' sound. Moderate to strong. Sharp.	Ar-ch-itect.	Ar-[ch]2*(K)i-tect
[ch]2*K*(h)*	Beginning.	'C' & 'H' Merged: Replaced with 'K' sound. Moderate to strong. Sharp; Hiss.	Chord, Choir.	[ch]2*K*(h)*ord
[ch]2**K(h)*	End.	'C' & 'H' Merged: Replaced with 'K' sound. Strong. Sharp; Hiss.	Mo-narch.	Mo-nar[ch]2**K(h)*
[ch]3*([*sh*])	Beginning.	'C' & 'H' Merged: Replaced with 'SH' sound. Weak to moderate. Hiss.	Cham-pagne, Ca-chet, Sa-chet.	Sa-[ch]3*([*sh*])et
[ch]3*([*SH*])	End.	'C' & 'H' Merged: Replaced with 'SH' sound. Strong. Hiss.	Cache, Fiche.	Ca[ch]3*([*SH*])e
c**K(h)*	End.	'C': Silent. K: Strong. Sharp; Hiss.	Back, Deck, Lick, Rock, Tuck.	Roc**K(h)*
[ck]*(*K*)*(h)*	End.	'C' & 'K' Merged: Replaced with 'K' sound. Strong. Sharp: Hiss.	Back, Deck, Lick, Flick, Stock, Duck.	Du[ck]*(*K*)*(h)*
-[ck]*(K)	Beginning.	Pause precedes. 'C' & 'K' Merged: Replaced with 'K' sound. Moderate to strong. Sharp.	Mi-ckey, Pi-ckle, Sti-cking, Tri-cky.	Sti-[ck]*(K)ing
d	Beginning.	'D': Weak to moderate. Pop Heavy.	Dart, Dent, Dish, Doll, Dune, Dull.	*d*ish
D	Beginning.	'D': Moderate to strong. Pop Heavy.	Ca-det, Mo-dest, La-dy, Woo-den.	Mo-Dest
D	End.	'D': Strong. Pop Heavy.	Bad, Could, Rid, Fond, Mud, Road.	BaD
-Dd*	Beginning.	Pause precedes. 'D':	La-dder, Fo-dder.	La-Dd*er

		Moderate to strong. Pop Heavy. 'D': Silent.		
*Dd**	End	D: Strong. Pop Heavy. 'D': Silent.	Odd.	O*Dd**
[dg]*[*dj*]	Beginning.	'D' & 'J' Merged: Weak to moderate. Pop Heavy; Flat.	A-djec-tive, A-djust, A-djoin.	A-[dg]*[*dj*]ust
[dg]*(J)	Beginning.	'D' & 'G' Merged: Moderate to strong. Pop Heavy; Flat.	Cu-dgel, Ga-dget, Mi-dgit.	Ga-[dg]*(J)et
[dg]*(*J*)(*h*)	End.	'D' & 'G' Merged: Strong. Pop Heavy; Flat; Hiss.	Badge, Hedge, Fudge, Ridge.	Ri[dg]*(*J*)(*h*)e
f	Beginning.	'F': Weak to moderate. Hiss.	Fit, Friend, Fly.	*f*riend
F	Beginning.	'F': Moderate to strong. Hiss.	Fan, Fe-llow, De-fer, Re-fer, De-fe-rence.	De-Fer
F	Middle.	'F': Moderate to strong. Hiss.	Craft, Left, Gift, Soft, Tuft.	CraFt.
F	End.	'F': Strong. Hiss.	Half, Safe, Life.	Li*F*e
-*f* f*	Beginning.	Pause precedes. 'F': Weak to Moderate. Hiss. 'F': Silent.	Cli-fford, Di-ffer, Sta-ffing, Su-ffice.	Di-*f* f*er
F'f*	End.	'F': 'F': Strong. Hiss. Extended. 'F': Silent.	Cliff, Staff, Whiff.	Sta*F*'f*
g*	Beginning.	'G': Silent.	Gnat.	g*nat
G1	Beginning, Middle.	'G': Moderate to strong. Knock; Pop Heavy; Flat.	Go, A-gree, Bags, Flagged.	A-G1ree
*G*1(*h*)	End.	'G': Strong. Knock; Pop Heavy; Flat.	Bag, Ig-loo, League, Rag, Stag.	Sta*G*1(*h*)
g2*(*j*)	Beginning.	'G': Replaced with 'J' sound. Weak to moderate. Flat; Pop Heavy.	A-gent, Gen-tle, Gel, Gem, Gi-ant, Pa-geant, Ri-gid.	g2*(*j*)en-tle
g2*(*J*)	End.	'G': Replaced with 'J' sound. Strong. Flat; Pop Heavy.	Cage, Sage, Wage, Huge, Ma-nage, Pa-ssage,	Ma-nag2*(*J*)e
g3*([*zh*])	Beginning.	'G': Replaced with 'ZH' Merged sound. Weak to moderate. Flat; Buzz.	Gen-re, Lar-gesse.	Lar-g3*([*zh*])esse
g3*([ZH])	End.	'G': Replaced with 'ZH' Merged sound. Moderate to strong. Flat; Buzz.	Beige, 2nd 'G' in Ga-rage, Ma-ssage.	Beig3*([ZH])e
-G1g*	Beginning.	Pause precedes. 'G': Moderate to strong. Knock; Pop Heavy; Flat. 'G': Silent.	Ba-ggage, Di-gging, Stru-ggle, Wri-ggle.	Ba-G1g*age
*G*1'g*	End.	'G'. 'G': Strong. Knock; Pop Heavy; Flat. 'G': Silent.	Hogg.	Ho*G*1'g*
[gh]1*(*g*)	Beginning.	'G' & 'H' Merged. Replaced with 'G' sound. Weak to Moderate. Pop Heavy; Flat.	Gha-stly, Gher-kin, Ghost, Ghou-lish.	[gh]1*(*g*)as-tly
[gh]2*(F)	Beginning,	'G' & 'H' Merged: Replaced	Cou-ghing, Laughs.	Lau[gh]2*(F)s

	Middle.	with 'F' sound. Moderate to strong. Hiss.		
[gh]2*(*F*)'	End.	'G' & 'H' Merged: Replaced with 'F' sound. Strong. Hiss. Extended.	Cough, Rough, Trough.	Rou[gh]2*(*F*)'
[gh]3*	End.	'G' & 'H' Merged: Silent.	Bough as in "Cow", Dough, Fur-lough, High, Sigh, Thigh.	Hi[gh]3*
[gh]3*	Middle.	'G' & 'H' Merged: Silent.	Caught, Drought as in "Shout", Fought.	Cau[gh]3*t
[gn]*(*N*)	End.	'G' & 'N' Merged: Replaced with 'N' sound. Strong. Knock; Hum; Nasal.	A-lign, A-rraign, Be-nign, Reign, Sign.	Si[gn]*(*N*)
[gn]*(N)	Middle.	'G' & 'N' Merged: Replaced with 'N' sound. Moderate to strong. Knock; Hum; Nasal.	Aligned, A-rraigned, Reigned, Signed.	A-li[gn]*(N)ed
H	Beginning.	'H': Moderate to strong. Hiss.	Had, Hem, Hill, Hop, Hub, Be-hind, Be-have.	Be-Have
h*	Beginning.	'H': Silent.	Herb, Hum-ble.	h*erb
'h*	End.	'H': Silent. Preceding Vowel Extended.	Ah, Shah.	Sha'h*
j	Beginning.	'J': Weak to moderate. Flat; Pop Heavy.	John, Jim, Jug, Jet, Je-lly, Jog, Jig.	*J*im
j*([zh])	Beginning.	'J': Replaced with 'Z' & 'H' Merged sound. Weak. Buzz.	Jacque.	j*([zh])accue
k*	Beginning.	'K': Silent.	Knob, Knock, Knot.	k*not
K	Beginning.	'K': Moderate to strong. Sharp.	Ba-ker, Li-ken, Ta-ken, Spea-ker.	Ta-Ken
K	Middle.	'K': Moderate to strong. Sharp.	Bikes, Rakes, Takes, Sticks, Tricked.	BiKes
K*(h)*	Beginning.	'K': Moderate to strong. Sharp. Hiss.	Keep, Kid, Kind, King, Kit, Kiss.	K*(h)*ing
K(*h*)	End.	'K': Strong. Sharp. Hiss.	Bake, Fluke, Like, Look, Pink, Speak, Wake.	Loo*K*(*h*)
l*	Middle.	'L': Silent.	Could, Holmes, Palm, Would.	Pal*m
l	Beginning.	'L': Weak. Hum.	Lamp, Lip, Me-lon, Zea-lot.	lamp
l	Middle.	'L': Weak to moderate. Hum.	Blimp, Cloud, Clip, Flame, Glow, Plod.	F*l*ame
L	Middle.	'L': Moderate to strong. Hum; Lilting.	Built, Delve, Elf, Melt, Old, Colt, Salt.	MeLt.
L	End.	'L': Moderate to strong. Hum.	A-ble, Ca-bal, Ca-mel, Cou-ple, Fo-ssil, Ve-ssel.	Ca-meL

L'	End.	'L': Moderate to strong. Hum; Lilting. Extended.	Bale, Keel, File, Mail, Smile, Tool.	FiL'e
-*l* l*	Beginning.	Pause precedes. 'L': Weak to Moderate. Hum. 'L': Silent.	Ba-lloon, Do-llar, Fe-llow, In.sta-lla-tion, Lo.lli-pop.	Do-*l* l*ar
L'l*	End.	'L': Moderate to strong. 'Hum. Extended. 'L': Silent.	Call, Doll, Mall, Poll, Roll, Toll, Wall.	WaL'l*
m	Beginning.	'M': Weak. Hum.	Ca-me-ra, Man, Mat, Mend, Mist, Must.	mend
m	Beginning.	'M': Weak to moderate. Hum.	Main, Meet, Mind, Mole, Mu-sic.	*mu*-sic
M	End.	'M': Moderate to strong. Hum.	Came, Come, Lime, Sum, Sum, Team, Tim-ber.	TeaM
M	End.	'M': Moderate to strong. Hum; Lilting.	Am, Sam, Hem, Dim, Him, Ram, Sum, Swim, Jim.	HiM
M	Middle.	'M': Moderate to strong. Hum; Lilting.	Clamp, Em-pty, Lamb, Stamp, Tempt.	ClaMp
-*m*m*	Beginning.	Pause precedes. 'M': Weak to Moderate. Hum. 'M': Silent.	Su-mmer, Swi-mming, Tri-mmer, To-mmy.	Su-*m*m*er
M'm*	End.	'M': 'M': Moderate to strong. Hum; Lilting. Extended. 'M': Silent.	Grimm.	GriM'm*
n	Middle.	'N': Weak. Nasal.	Blank, Rung, Sing, Range, Ranc-or, Tongs, Think, Unc-le.	Sing
n	End.	'N': Weak. Hum, Nasal. *See row above.*	En-ter~, Cen-ter~, In-te-rest~, Ven-ti-late~.	Cen-ter~
n	Middle.	'N': Weak to moderate. Knock; Hum.	Snack, Snail, Snide, Snort.	S*n*ort
n	Beginning.	'N': Weak to moderate. Knock; Hum.	Nag, Name, Na-tion, Nest, Next, Near, Di-ner, Fi-nal, Note.	*n*a-tion
n	Middle	'N': Weak to moderate. Hum; Nasal; Lilting.	Can't, Hand, Kind, Lend, Mind, Slant, Taunt, Tenth.	Le*n*d
N	Middle, End.	'N': Moderate to strong. Knock; Nasal; Hum; Lilting.	Main-tain, San-dal, Ten-der, Win-ter.	HaNd
N	End.	'N': Strong. Knock; Nasal; Hum; Lilting.	Can, Van, Hen, When.	Ca*N*
[*n*c2***S*1]	End.	'N' & 'C': "Merged", (See Footnote iii). 'N': Weak to moderate. Nasal. 'C' Strong. Flat; Hiss.	Dance, Lance, France, Ro-mance	Ro-ma[*n*c2***S*1]e
[*n*[*CH*]1] *(h)*	End.	'N', 'C' & 'H': "Merged", (See Footnote iii). 'N': Weak	Blanch, Bench, Inch, Crunch, Hench-man,	Cru[*n*[*CH*]1]*(h)*

		to moderate. Nasal. 'C' & 'H': Strong. Flat; Hiss.	Punch, Wrench.	
N-[*ch*]1	Spans: End, Pause & Beginning.	'N': Moderate to strong. Knock; Nasal; Hum. Pause. 'C' & 'H' Merged: Weak to moderate. Flat.	Lun-cheon, Pen-chant, Trun-cheon.	LuN-[*ch*]1eon
[nC]-(K)	Spans: End, Pause & Beginning.	'N' & 'C' "Merged" (See Footnote iii): 'N': Weak. Nasal. 'C': Moderate to strong. Sharp. Pause. 'K' Inserted: Moderate to strong. Sharp.	An-chor, Ranc-or, Unc-le, Sync-hronize.	U[nC]-(K)le
[*nD*]*(h)*	End.	'N' & 'D': "Merged", (See Footnote iii). 'N': Weak to moderate. Nasal. 'D' Strong. Pop Heavy; Hiss.	Band, Bond, Lend, Fund, Round, Send, Wind.	Wi[*nD*]*(h)*
[ng]1	End.	'N' & 'G' "Merged" (See Footnote iii): 'N': Weak. Nasal. 'G': Weak; Flat.	Ring, Song, Lung.	Sc[ng]1
[ng]1-(G)	Spans: End, Pause & Beginning.	'N' & 'G' "Merged" (See Footnote iii): 'N': Weak. Nasal. 'G': Weak. Flat. Pause. Additional 'G' inserted. Moderate to strong. Knock; Pop Heavy; Flat.	Ang-us, Ang-er, Fing-er, Ling-er, Mang-o, Hung-er.	Fi[ng]1-(G)er
[ng]2*([n*J*])*(h)*	End.	'N' & 'G' "Merged" (See Footnote iii): Replaced with 'N' & 'J' 'N': Weak. Nasal. 'J': Pop Heavy; Flat.	Flange, Range Sy-ringe, Tinge.	Ra[ng]2*([n*J*])*(h)*e, Ti[ng]2*([n*J*])*(n)*e
[nK]	Middle.	'N' & 'K' "Merged" (See Footnote iii): 'N': Weak. Nasal. 'K': Moderate to strong. Sharp.	Banks, Blinked, Links, Sinks, Tanks, Winks.	Bli[nK]ed
[n*K*]*(h)*	End.	'N' & 'K' "Merged" (See Footnote iii): 'N': Weak. Nasal. 'K': Strong. Sharp; Hiss.	Ink, Rank, Sink, Monk.	Mo[n*K*]*(h)*
[nk]-(*k*)	Spans: End, Pause & Beginning	'N' & 'K' "Merged" (See Footnote iii): 'N': Weak. Nasal. 'K': Moderate to strong. Sharp. Pause. 'K' Inserted: Weak to moderate. Sharp.	Ank-le, Blank-et, Ink-ling, Sink-ing, Rank-ing, Tank-er, Twink-le, Wrink-le.	Ta[nk]-(*k*)er
-*n*n*	Beginning.	Pause precedes.'N': Weak to moderate. Knock; Hum. 'N': Silent.	Ta-nning, To-nnage, Cu-nning, Di-nner.	Di-*n*n*er
[*n*S1]	End.	'N' & 'S' "Merged", (See	Res-ponse.	Res-po[*n*S1]e

		Footnote iii). 'N': Weak to moderate. Nasal. 'S1' Strong. Hiss.		
[*nS*2]	End.	'N' & 'S': "Merged", (See Footnote iii). 'N': Weak to moderate. Nasal. 'S2' Strong. Buzz.	Cans, Lens, Pins. Runs, Tons.	Pi[*nS*2]
[*nT*1]*(h)*	End.	'N' & 'T': "Merged", (See Footnote iii). 'N': Weak to moderate. Nasal. 'T1' Strong. Sharp, Knock, Hiss.	Can't, Flaunt, Plant, Print, Tent, Went.	Te[*nT*1]*(h)*
*nt**	Beginning.	'N': Weak to moderate. Knock; Hum. *See row below.*	E-nter~, Ce-nter~, I-nte-rest~, Ve-nti-late~.	Ce-nt*er
[nx]*([nK]*S*1)	End.	'N' & 'K' "Merged" (See Footnote iii): 'N': Weak. Nasal. 'K': Moderate to strong. Sharp. 'S': Linked sound. Strong. Hiss.	Jinx, Lynx, Manx, Minx.	Ly[nx]*([nK]*S*1)
[nx]*(nK)-(*sh*)	Spans End & Beginning.	'N' & 'X': Replaced with 'N' & 'K' sound. "Merged", (See Footnote iii). 'N': Weak; Nasal. 'K': Moderate to strong. Sharp. Pause. 'SH': Inserted. Weak to moderate. Hiss.	Anx-ious.	A[nx]*(nK)-(*sh*)ious
[nx]*([ng]1)-(z)	Spans End & Beginning.	'NX': Replaced with 'N' & 'G' "Merged", (See Footnote iii). 'N': Weak; Nasal. 'G': Weak to moderate. Flat. Pause. 'Z': Inserted. Weak. Buzz.	Anx-ie.ty.	A[nx]*([ng]1)-(z)ie.ty
p*	Beginning.	'P': Silent.	Cupboard.	Cup*-board
P*(h)*	Beginning.	'P'. Moderate to strong. Pop Light; Hiss.	Pe-ter, Pen, Pat, Pick, Pool, Puck.	P*(h)*ool
P(h)	End.	'P'. Strong. Pop Light; Hiss.	Ape, Cap, Step, Clip, Hip, Rope, Stop, Up.	Ste*P(h)*
P	Middle.	'P'. Moderate to strong. Pop Light.	Lapse, E-llipse, Script, Scrapes.	LaPse
p	Middle.	'P'. Weak to moderate. Pop Light.	Spill, Spot, Spied, Spin, Spade.	S*p*ot.
-Pp*	Beginning.	Pause precedes. P': Moderate to strong. Pop Light. 'P': Silent.	Cla-pping, Pu-ppy, Ra-pping, Su-pper.	Cla-Pp*ing
[*ph*]	Beginning, Middle.	'P' & 'H' Merged: Replaced with 'F' sound. Weak to moderate. Hiss.	Phone, Phi-llip, Pro-phet, Sphinx, So-phis-try.	[*ph*]one

[PH]	End.	'P' & 'H' Merged: Replaced with 'F' sound. Moderate to strong. Hiss.	Soph-more.	So[PH]-more.
q*(*k*)	Beginning, Middle.	'Q': Replaced with 'K' sound. Weak to moderate. Sharp.	A-qua, Li-quid, Mes-quite, Qui-ver, Squat, Squirt.	Li-q*(*k*)u*(*w*)id
q*(K)	Beginning.	'Q': Replaced with 'K' sound. Moderate to strong. Sharp; Hiss.	Queue, Quill, Quip, Quit, E-qua-tor.	q*(K)u*(w)it
q*(*K*)	End.	'Q': Replaced with 'K' sound. Strong. Sharp; Hiss.	Clique, Mys-tique.	Mys-tiq*(*K*)ue
r	Beginning.	'R': Weak to moderate. Rasp.	Ran, Red, Ride, Di-rect, Rob, Ru-by.	Di-*r*ect
R	Middle, End.	'R': Moderate to strong. Rasp.	A-sser-tive, Bird, Fern, Fur-tive, Herd, Word.	BiRd
R	Middle, End.	'R': Strong. Rasp. Extended.	Car, Girl, Dear, Farm, For, Her, Occur, Sir, Star, World.	Ca*R*
-*r* r*	Beginning.	Pause precedes. 'R': Weak to Moderate. Rasp. 'R': Silent.	Ba-rrel, Fe-rret, Wo-rry To-mo-rrow, Fu-rrow.	Fe-*r* r*et
R'h*	Beginning.	'R': Moderate to strong. Rasp. Extended. 'H': Silent.	Rhodes, Rho-de-sia, Rhom-bus.	R'h*om-bus
*s*1	Beginning.	'S': Weak to moderate. Hiss.	Sam, Send, Su-per, In-spire, Re-search.	*s*1u-per
*S*1	Middle.	'S': Strong. Hiss.	Best, Brisk, Lost, Lus-ter, Must, Res-ting.	LoS1t
*S*1'	End.	'S': Strong. Hiss.	Case, Greets, Loose, Hats, Ob-tuse, Use-ful, Writes.	CaS1'e
s2*(*z*)	Beginning.	'S': Replaced with 'Z' sound. Weak to moderate. Buzz.	Ea-sel, Mi-ser, Plea-sant, Rea-son.	Rea-s2*(*z*)on
s2*(Z)	Middle.	'S': Replaced with 'Z' sound. Moderate to strong. Buzz.	Posed, Closed, Dogs, Miles, Pleased, Raised.	Pleas2*(Z)ed
s2*(*Z*)'	End.	'S': Replaced with 'Z' sound. Strong. Buzz. Extended.	Amuse, Close, Has, Phase, Please, Rose, Vase.	Phas2*(*Z*)'e
s3*([*zh*])	Beginning.	'S': Replaced with 'Z' & 'H' Merged sound. Weak to moderate. Flat; Buzz.	Mea-sure, Plea-sure, Trea-sure, Vi-sion.	Mea-s3*([*zh*])ure
s4*([*sh*])	Beginning.	'S': Replaced with 'S' & 'H' Merged sound. Weak to Moderate. Hiss.	In-sure, Man-sion, Pen-sion, Ten-sion.	Ten-s4*([*sh*])ion
[*sh*]	Beginning.	'S' & 'H' Merged: Weak to moderate. Hiss.	Cu-shion, Fa-shion, Share, Ru-shing.	Cu-[*sh*]ion
[SH]	Middle.	S' & 'H' Merged: Moderate to strong. Hiss.	Crashed, Fished, Rushed, Wished.	Wi[SH]ed
[*SH*]'	End.	S' & 'H' Merged: Strong.	Bush, Cash, Fresh, Fish,	Fre[*SH*]'

		Hiss.	Hush, Wash.	
-*s*1s*	Beginning.	Pause precedes. 'S': Weak to Moderate. Hiss. 'S': Silent.	A-ssume, E-ssence, Di-sso-lute, Mi-ssing, Po-ssi-ble.	A-*s*1s*ume
-s4*([*sh*])s*	Beginning.	Pause precedes. 'S': Replaced with 'S' & 'H' Merged sound. Weak to moderate. Hiss. 'S': Silent.	A-ggre-ssion, Fi-ssure, Fi-ssion~, Mi-ssion, Pa-ssion, Se-ssion.	Mi-s*([*sh*])s*ion
-s3*([*zh*])s*	Beginning.	Pause precedes. 'S': Replaced with 'Z' & 'H' Merged sound. Weak to moderate. Flat; Buzz. 'S': Silent.	Fi-ssion~.	Fi-s3*([*zh*])s*ion
S's*	End.	'S': Strong. Hiss. Extended. 'S': Silent.	Bless, Class, Dress, Fuss, Miss, Press, Toss.	Pre*S*'s*
t1	Middle.	'T': Weak. Knock.	Dates, Eats, Kites, Wits.	Eat1s
T1*(h)*	Beginning.	'T'. Moderate to strong. Sharp; Knock; Hiss.	Tame, Tea, Tin, Tom, Tub, Re-tain, Train.	T1*(h)*rain.
*T*1(*h*)	End.	'T'. Strong. Sharp; Knock; Hiss.	Bat, Boot, Date, Goat, Hot, Kite, Front, Shut, Went.	Da*T*1(*h*)e.
t2*([td])	Beginning.	'T': Replaced with 'T' & 'D'. Merged sound. Weak. Pop Heavy; Knock. *See row below.*	Cen-ter~, Coun-ty~, Hun-ter, Wa-ter, Pe-ter, Plen-ty~, Wri-ter, La-ter.	Cen-t2*([td])er
t*	Beginning.	'T': Silent. One of other alternatives.	Ce-nter~, Cou-nty~, E-nter~, Ple-nty~, Ve-nti-late~.	Ce-*nt**er
t2*([td])t*	Beginning.	Pause precedes. 'T': One 'T' Silent. 'T': Replaced with 'T' & 'D' Merged sound. Weak. Pop Heavy; Knock.	Bu-tter, Ca-ttle, Ma-tter, Jo-tter, Ke-ttle, Sea-ttle.	Ma-t2*([td])t*er
t3*([*sh*])	Beginning.	'T': Replaced with 'S' & 'H' Merged sound. Weak to moderate. Hiss.	A-ddi-tion, Cau-tion, Frui-tion, Men-tion, Ra-tion, Re-la-tion, Sta-tion.	Cau-t3*([*sh*])
t4*([CH]1)	Beginning.	'T': Replaced with 'C' & 'H' Merged sound. Moderate to strong. Flat.	Ad-ven-ture, Den-ture, Fu-ture, Ma-ture, Su-ture,	Fu-t4*([CH])ure
t4*[CH]1	Middle.	'T': Silent. 'C' & 'H' Merged sound: Moderate to strong. Flat.	Clutched, Fetched, Hatched.	Fet4*[CH]1ed
t4*[*CH*]1	End.	'T': Silent. 'C' & H' Merged sound: Strong. Flat; Hiss.	Batch, Catch, Clutch, Fetch, Glitch, Retch.	Fet4*[*CH*]1
-t2*([td])t*	Beginning.	Pause precedes. 'T': Replaced with 'T' and 'D' Merged sound. Weak. Pop Heavy; Knock. 'T': Silent.	A-ttic, Ba-tty, Ca-tty, Ra-tty.	A-t2*([td])t*ic

-T t*(h)	Beginning.	Pause precedes. 'T': Moderate to strong. Sharp; Knock; Hiss. 'T': Silent.	A-ttend, A-ttri-bute (as in the verb), A-ttain.	A-T t*(h)ain
[th]1	Beginning.	'T' & 'H' Merged: Weak to moderate. Hiss.	Thanks, Three, Think, Thought.	[th]1anks
[TH]1	End.	'T' & 'H' Merged: Moderate to strong. Hiss.	Both, Cloth, Lathe, Math, Myth, Sloth.	Bo[TH]1
[t(d)h]2	Beginning.	'T' & 'H': Replaced with 'T', 'D' & 'H' Merged sound. Weak to moderate. Flat; Buzz.	This, That, There, Mo-ther.	Mo-[t(d)h]2er
[T(D)H]2	End.	'T' & 'H': Replaced with 'T', 'D' & 'H' Merged sound. Moderate to Strong. Pop Heavy; Flat; Buzz.	Bathe, Clothe, Loathe.	Ba[T(D)H]2e
v	Beginning.	'V': Weak to moderate. Buzz.	Re-vere, Ri-ver, Vane, Vic-tor, View, Vo-lume.	Ri-ver
V	End.	'V': Moderate to strong. Buzz.	A-bove, Brave, Drive, Grove, Move, Save, Shove.	MɔVe
v*(F)	End.	'V': 'Replaced with 'F' sound. Moderate to strong. Hiss.	Have (Often used with “To” as in “...have to..”).	Hav*(F)e
W	Beginning.	'W': Moderate to strong. Vowelish.	Was, Wax, Wet, Win, Woe, Won.	Win
'W' in other Syllable positions: See Footnote 2 of this Table, below.				
[WH]	Beginning.	'W' & 'H' Merged: Moderate to strong. Vowelish.	When, White, What, Where, Which.	[WH]en
x1*(K)(S1)	End.	'X': Replaced with 'K' & 'S' Linked sound. K: Moderate to strong. Sharp. S: Moderate to strong. Hiss.	Ex-tra~, Ex-tort~, Ex-co-ri.ate.	Ex1*(K)(S1)-tra
x1*(K)(S1)	End.	'X': Replaced with 'K' & 'S' Linked sound. K: Moderate to strong. Sharp. S: Strong. Hiss.	Ax, Box, Flax, Fox, Fix, Flex, Mix, Six, Tax, Wax.	Six1*(K)(S1)
x1*(K)-(s1)	Spans End & Beginning.	'X': Replaced with 'K' & 'S' Separated sounds. K: Moderate to strong. Sharp. Pause. S: Weak to moderate. Hiss.	Ex-it~, Ex-tra~, Ex-tort~, Ex-treme~, Re-lax-es, Tax-es.	Ex1*(K)-(s1)tra
x1*(K)-(s1)c*	Spans End & Beginning.	'X': Replaced with 'K' & 'S' Separated sounds. K: Moderate to strong. Sharp. Pause. S: Weak to moderate. Hiss. C: Silent	Ex-cel~, Ex-ce-llent~.	Ex1*(K)-(s1)c*ɛl

x2*(G)-(z)	Spans End & Beginning.	'X': Replaced with 'G' sound. Moderate to strong. Knock; Pop Heavy; Flat. Pause. 'Z': Inserted. Weak. Buzz.	Ex-alt, Ex-it~, Ex-ist, Ex-haust, Ex-ert.	Ex2*(G)-(z)it
x3*(z)	Beginning.	'X': Replaced with 'Z' sound. Weak. Buzz.	Xe-no-pho-bia.	x3*(z)e-no-pho-bia
Y	Beginning.	'Y': Moderate to strong. Vowelish.	Cra-yon, Yacht, Year, La-yer.	Year
'Y' in other Syllable positions: See Footnote 2 of this Table, below.				
z1	Beginning.	'Z': Weak. Buzz.	La-zy, Ze-bra, Zip, Li-zard, Zone.	z1ip
Z1	End.	'Z': Moderate to strong. Buzz.	Craze, Doze, Maze, Haze.	DoZ1e.
z2*([*zh*])	Beginning.	'Z': Replaced with 'Z' & 'H' Merged sound. Weak to moderate. Flat; Buzz.	A-zure, Fra-zier, Sei-zure.	A-z2*([*zh*])ure
-zz*	Beginning.	Pause precedes. 'Z': Weak. Buzz. 'Z': Silent.	Bli-zzard, Di-zzy, Fi-zzing, Mi-zzen.	Di-zz*y
Table Footnotes:				

(i) While Consonant Sounds which are silent are not technically "sounds", they also included in the table above to show how they are Scripted.

(ii) The letters 'W' and 'Y' in Syllable positions other than in the Syllable-Beginning position are more like Vowel Sounds and so are described in the Table: Scripting Conventions Applied – Phonetic Symbols for Vowel Sounds. (Appendix II. A). Also, in the Table: Consonant Sounds and their Inherent Attributes (Appendix III. B) Foot Note D, the different 'W' and 'Y' sounds are identified and associated with the Vowels sounds that they are similar to.

(iii) Though the adjacent Consonant sequences: 'NG' as in "Sing", 'NG' as in "Range', 'NC' as in "Uncle", 'NK' as in "Think" and 'NCH' as in "Inch" are actually Linked, they are identified with Merged pairs as they undergo significant transformation in the process of Linking and acquire a distinctive character together, and are therefore included in this Table of Consonant Sounds. (Linked Consonant Sounds are covered as part of Vocal Pattern Tables).

> They are Scripted like other Merged pairs between square brackets as follows: {-[*n*G]1}, {-[*n*G]2}, {-[*n*C]}, {-[*n*K]} and {-[*n*CH]}. The Scripting of the Consonants in the square brackets varies, depending on how they are articulated in different words. The numbers that follow a bracketed pair is indicative of a specific Version of that pair.

They are labeled "Merged" within quotation marks to distinguish them from truly Merged Consonant Sounds where the label Merged is without quotation marks. Each constituent Consonant in such Consonant sequences may be Accentuated at different levels and exhibit distinct sets of Inherent Attributes unlike a true Merged pair which, being a unified, single Consonant Sound, exhibits just one level of Accentuation with a common set of Inherent Attributes that describe it.

See Note 3 in Table: The Vocal Fidelity Phonetic System – Scripting Conventions for Consonant Sounds (Appendix I. C), for more information on adjacent Consonants.

Appendix IV.
Words with Irregular Vowel Consonant Sequences

When a particular vocalization of a Vowel Consonant Sequence is found in a word, and this vocalization seems unique without other word examples, such a vocalization cannot be considered a Vocal Pattern or a Vocal Pattern Variant which by definition recur in different words. It is simply called an Irregular Vowel Consonant Sequence. It is associated with an Irregular vocalization.

Such Irregular Vowel Consonant Sequences are not uncommon. Be careful not to extrapolate such a vocalizations to any other word with the same Vowel Consonant Sequence because it is unique or near unique which is why it is identified as "Irregular".

Many words with such an Irregular vocalization may be heard frequently or often, but they are nevertheless Irregular. These words have not been included in the Vocal Pattern Master Table and you will not therefore find them listed in the Vocal Pattern Bridge, the Vocal Pattern Inland, or the Vocal Pattern Summit Tables.

Some words with such Irregular Vowel Consonant Sequences are identified in the Table below so that you can make sure you pronounce them with the proper Irregular vocalization, as done by Americans. Some of these may be similarly articulated by the British.

Table:
Vocalizing Words With Irregular Vowel Consonant Sequences

This Table identifies some words with Vowel Consonant Sequences which are not Vocal Patterns. Each of these appear to be uniquely vocalized in single word. If you are looking for a word with a possible Irregular Vowel Consonant Sequence with a unique vocalization, you may find it here. This is a list of some Irregular Vowel Consonant Sequences I encountered as I went about identifying Vocal Patterns. It is a not an attempt to identify and list all words with such Irregular Sequences.

No.	Vowel Consonant Sequence	Vocalization	Words With Irregular Vocalization with Syllable breaks
Note 1. The list below is a bi-product of the search for Vocal Patterns across the language spectrum. It is not a list of all words with Irregular Vowel Consonant sequences.			
Note 2. By recognizing that a word has an Irregular Vowel Consonant Sequence, you can vocalize it in its unique way yet avoid applying such a vocalization to any other word with the same Sequence.			
Note 3. A Vowel Consonant Sequence with the same Irregular vocalization for a different conjugation of the same word has been shown on the same row.			
Note 4. A Vowel Consonant Sequence may have different Irregular vocalizations for different conjugations of a word. These have been shown on different rows.			
Note 5. A Vowel Consonant Sequence may have more than one Irregular vocalization for the very same word. Such instances are shown on separate rows.			
1	ACH	a-[*ch*], a'-[*ch*]	Ba-che-lor
2	AD	a"d*g*(*J*)(*h*)	Badge
3	ADJ	a-[DJ], a'-[DJ]	A-djec-tive
4	AF	a*(o)'-*f*	Wa-ffle, Wa-ffling
5	AF	a*(o)'F	Waft, Waf-ting
6	AG	A'*G(h)*, A(i)*G(h)*	Plague

7	AG	a2g*-*n*(Y)a1	La-sa-gna
8	AL	a2L	Ca-bal, Mis-tral
9	ALM	a2-l**m*	A-lmond
10	AN	a1N	An
11	ANC	a"N-c*[*sh*]	Fi-nan-cial
12	ANC	A'N-c3*([*sh*]), A(i)N-c3*([*sh*])	An-cient
13	ANCH	a2n[ch]*([*SH*])	Tranche
14	AND	a*(o)*nD(h)*	Wand
15	ANG	a*(i)*ng**(J)(h)*, a1*ng**(J)(h)*	O-range
16	ANG	a*(i)*ng**(J), a1*ng**(J)	O-ran-ges
17	ANG	a"*nG2(h)*, a'*nG2(h)*	Flange
18	ANG	a"*n*G2, a'*n*G2	Flan-ges
19	ANS	a"N-s4*([*sh*]), a'N-s4*([*sh*])	Ex-pan-sion
20	ANS	a"*nS*1', a'*nS*1'	Ex-panse
21	ANT	a*(o)'*nT(h)*	Want
22	ANT	a"*n*-t*[*sh*]	Sub-stan-tial
23	AQ	aq*(K)-u*(w)	A-qua~, A-qui-fer~
24	AQ	a2q*(K)-u*(w)	Aqua~, A-qui-fer~
25	AQ	a1q*(K)-u*(w), a1-q*(K)u*(w)	A-qua-tic, A-qua-rium
26	ARCH	a2R[ch]**K(h)*	Mo-nar-ch
27	ARCH	a1r-[ch]**k*, a1r-[ch]**k(h)*	Mo-nar-chy
28	ARCH	a2R-[ch]**k*	Ar-chi-tect
29	ART	a*(o)R*T(h)*	Wart
30	ART	a*(o)RT	Warts
31	AS	a*(o)'s2*(Z)'	Was
32	ASH	a*(o)'[*SH*]	Wash
33	ASH	a*(o)-[*sh*]	Washing
34	AT	a*(o)'*T(h)*	What
35	AT	a*(o)'T	Watts
36	AT	a'-t3*([*sh*])	Ra-tion
37	ATCH	a*(o)'t3*[*CH*]*(1h)*	Watch
38	ATH	A-([*th*]), A'-([*th*])	Na-then
39	ATH	a'-B	Sa-bbath
40	ATH	A'[*TH*]1'	Lathe
41	AUGH	a'u*[gh]**F'*	Laugh
42	AV	a"*V*, a'*V*, a"v*(*F*), a'v*(*F*)	Have
43	EACH	e'a*-[*ch*]1	Trea-che-ry
44	EAR	e*a2R'	Heart
45	EAR	e*a1R	Search
46	EATH	E'a*[*T*(*D*)*H*]2'	Breathe
47	EAUT	e*(i)a*U'-T*(h)*	Beau-ty

48	EC	i-K(h), e1-K(h)	E-co-no-my~
49	ECH	e'[ch]2*([SH]')	Creche
50	ECH	e'-[ch]2*([sh])	Cre-ches, E-che-lon
51	EETH	E'e*[TH]1'	Teeth
52	EETH	E'e*[T(D)H]2	Seethe
53	EIZ	E'i*Z'	Seize
54	EIZ	e*I'Z	Seis-mic
55	EJ	e*(i)-J, E-J	De-jected, Re-ject
56	EL	e*(A)'-l	E-lan, Me-lee
57	EN	e'n, en	Length, Strength
58	ENG	e*(i)'[ng]1	Eng-land, Eng-lish
59	ENG	e[ng]1-(G)	Beng-al
60	EOD	e*(a)'o*(u)D, e*(a)'o*(w)D	Mc-Cleod
61	EOR	e*o)'R	George
62	EOT	E'O'-T(h)	Leo-tard
63	EPH	e*(i)-p*h*(f)	E-phe-me-ral
64	EPH	E'-[ph]*(v)	Ste-phen
65	ER	e"R, e'R'	There
66	ER	e*-r	Eve-ry
67	ES	e*(A)'-s	Me-sa
68	ES	E-s1, e*(i)s1, e*(i)s2*(z), E-s2*(z)	Re-source~
69	ES	e1-S	Me-ssiah
70	ES	es2*(Z)', e"s2*(Z)'	Les, Wes
71	ESS	e*(i)-s	E-ssen-tial
72	ESS	e1S's*	Prow-ess
73	ETH	e1-[th]	Me-tho-di-cal
74	EUD	e*U'D(h), e*(Y)UD(h), e*(i)UD(h)	Feud
75	EUR	e1'u*R	A-ma-teur
76	EZ	e'-z	Me-zza-nine
77	IATH	I'a1[TH]'	Go-liath
78	IBUTZ	i-Bu2tz*(S)	Ki-butz
79	ICH	i[ch]3*([SH]', i'[ch]3*([SH]'	Fiche~
80	IG	i*(E)'G(h)	In-trigue
81	INS	iN-s4*([sh])	In-sure, In-su-rance
82	INTH	i'n[TH]1	Plinth
83	INTH	iN-[th]1	Co-rin-thian
84	IOL	i*(E)'o1L	Vi-triol
85	IQ	i*(E)'q*(K)(h)	Clique~
86	IS	i's2*(Z), i"s2*(Z)	His, Ms.
87	IS	I-s2*(z)	Di-ssolve
88	IUMPH	I-u1m[PH]*F'	Tri-umph, Tri-um-phant

89	OATH	O'a*[TH]1, (a1)Oa*[TH]1	Oath
90	OATH	O'a*[T(D)H]2, (a1)Oa*[T(D)H]2	Loath
91	OATH	O'a*-[t(d)h]2, (a1)Oa*-[t(d)h]2	Loa-thing
92	OCH	o'-C2(h)h*	Loch
93	OD	o1-D	Me-lo-dy
94	OF	o1f*(V), o'f*(V)	Of~
95	OF	O'-f, (a1)O-f	Pro-forma, So-fa
96	OIC	O-iC(h), O'-iC(h), (a1)O-iC(h)	He-ro-ic
97	OK	o'K, o'K(h)	Spring-bok
98	OL	o)'-l*d, o-l*d	Solder
99	ONC	o'n-C(h), o*(a2)n-C(h)	On-co-lo-gist
100	ONCH	o'n[CH]1(h), o*(a2)n[CH]1(h)	Conch
101	ONCH	o'n-[ch]1, o*(a2)n-[ch]1	Hon-cho
102	ONG	o1'[ng]	A-mong
103	ONG	o1'[ng]2*(nJ)(h)	Sponge
104	ONK	o1'[nK](h)	Monk
105	ONK	o1'[nk]-k	Monk-ey
106	OOCH	O'o*[CH]1(h), o1O[CH]1(h)	Brooch
107	OOTH	o2o*[TH]1, (i)o2o*[TH]1	Booth
108	OOTH	o2o*[TH]1, (i)o2o*[TH]1	Booths
109	OPH	o'[ph]*F'	Soph-o-more
110	OTH	o1-[th]	No-thing
111	OUG	o2u*-G, (i)o2u*-G	Mac-dou-gall
112	OUP	o*U-P(h), (i)o*U-P(h), (i)o2u*-P(h)	Cou-pon
113	OUTH	o2u*[TH]1, (i)o2u*[TH]1	Un-couth
114	UC	u2-c2*(s1), (i)u2-c2*(s1)	Lu-cy
115	UC	U-c2*(s1)	Bu-ce-pha.lus
116	UG	u-G, u'-G	Su-gar
117	UG	U'G(h), (i)UG(h)	Fugue
118	UG	u2-G, (i)u2-G	Lu-ger, Kru-ger
119	UG	U'[gh]*, (i)U[gh]*	Hugh
120	UGN	U'g*N', (i)Ug*N'	Im-pugn
121	UICH	u*i*(E)'[ch]3*([SH])	Quiche
122	UL	U'L', (i)UL'	Mule
123	UL	U'-l, (i)U-l	Mu-ling, Mu-lish
124	UNS	u1N-s4*([sh])	Un-sure
125	UP	u2P, (i)u2P, U'P, (i)UP	Dupe
126	US	u1S1	Mus-lin
127	UT	u'T(h)	Put~
128	UT	u-[t(d)]	Putting (as in placing, not as in golf)
129	UT	u'[CH]1'(h)	Butch

130	UT	u-[*CH*](*h*)	Bu-tcher

Appendix V.

The Development of this Course: Knowledge Creation and Quality

The creation of knowledge.

This Course is based on newly created knowledge. This includes:

-Fundamental Principles and Norms, namely:
  - The American Syllabication Principle.
  - The American Consonant Accentuation Principle.
  - The Consonant Position Accentuation Norms.

-Tools, including:
  - The Vocal Fidelity Phonetic System.
  - The Vocal Pattern Tables.
  - The Word List Tables.

Context and purpose.

This Course has been created out of the recognition that Accents can be a barrier to self advancement and social acceptance.

The main aim of this Course is to enable English speakers who speak in non-American ways to speak the American way, achieving the best result for effort and time put in, by providing the precise knowledge required, presenting it in priority order, and by enabling customization to individual needs.

It has been designed to fill the void in Accent training arising from general underestimation of all the challenges involved.

The approach.

During the creation of this work, I intentionally avoided other works on the teaching of spoken American English so as to build a custom solution, uninfluenced by other approaches. It is based on observation.

For the development of each Principle and Norm, I began with a hypotheses. I then expanded my observation to collect more facts for verification. This sometimes led to a rejection, or it led to a refinement of the original hypothesis. Finally, I came up with a model that closely reflected the observed facts, while also noting exceptions. This is a scientific process. It took much rework as I had to discard ideas that proved inadequate. Ideas that showed initial promise were refined and improved. The products are strongly based in fact. Both, conceptual framework and tools reflect factual observations of pronunciation and Accent.

The focus and scope.

The primary focus of the Course is on Accent. However, it also includes words that are used differently by Americans, so that it covers more broadly, the way Americans speak.

This Course is focused on learning the American English Accent as it is spoken the popular way. This encompasses standard American pronunciation. It focuses on a core Accent that is common and widely accepted across the country. It leaves out sub-Accent traits that are characteristic of and confined to specific demographic groups and smaller geographic areas.

Scripting of pronunciations is accurate and reliable.

The Vocal Fidelity Phonetic System uses Accent sensitive features to capture pronunciation with the nuances of Accent. As the name suggests, it seeks to be phonetically true with fidelity, i.e. sensitive to detail and nuance.

Note: When pronunciation is Scripted at a deeper level of detail, it captures the nuances of Accent. This is what is done in this Course. The words "Pronunciation" and "Accent" are often used interchangeably in the Course.

Note: Local American Accents share certain features in common despite their differences. Fundamental Principles and Norms that distinguish the broad American Accent are identified in the Course. These apply widely across local Accents.

Great care has been taken to ensure that the assessment of pronunciation is highly reliable. Throughout the development of the Course, the pronunciation of words were checked and rechecked to minimize the possibility of error. Not even the pronunciation of the simplest words, such as "And" or "To" were taken for granted.

The pronunciation of a word or Vocal Pattern was usually determined as follows. I would confirm my knowledge of the pronunciation of particular words or of words with a particular Vocal Pattern from direct observation of:

-Everyday conversation with people at work and recreation.
-American news and other television channels and radio stations.
-Excellent communicators in commercials.
-Recordings of spoken American English available on the internet in the public domain.

I would then look at the phonetic transcription of the word or words with a particular Vocal Pattern in reputed dictionaries, and listen to their on-line model voice recordings provided. In case of any inconsistency, I would finally base my transcription on the model voice recording. This could involve adding or otherwise adjusting phonetic elements not included in the dictionary provided phonetic transcription.

Note: Using voice model recordings as an object for direct observation is ideal for the development of knowledge concerning the spoken language because it provides speech samples of the way the language is vocalized by those who speak it well. It is particularly appropriate for the development of a Course that is focused on the spoken language.

Sometimes, when a particular pronunciation is pervasive, I would include this as a pronunciation option, usually in addition to the pronunciation based on the voice model recording.

Note: Words can have a number of different ways in which they can be pronounced with Accent variations, several of which are considered acceptable. The Course most often identifies both a standard and a widely accepted popular pronunciation in the Vocal Pattern Tables showing pronunciation. Sometimes the standard and the most popular are more or less equally common, or are the same, in which case just one pronunciation may have been provided. There could be

other acceptable pronunciations not mentioned.

Great care has been taken during the development process to eliminate error. Other than the fact that different phonetic systems produce outcomes with some variation of little significance, the reason for differences between pronunciation shown in dictionaries and this Course. is most likely because:

-Additional phonetic information is included, (consistent with the Accent sensitive features of the Vocal Fidelity Phonetic System).

Note:
Sometimes certain vocal elements often heard in a set of words are not shown. For example, the words “Do”, “Room” and “Scoot” commonly exhibit the 'I' Soft (a form of the Vowel 'I') before the 'O' Vowel Sound begins. Interestingly, audio recordings were found of these words confirming this observation, though the sound is not included in the phonetic transcriptions. This 'I' articulation is so prevalent in these words that it is included in the phonetic transcriptions in this Course (though may not be shown in dictionary transcriptions).

-A different popular pronunciation has been accepted.

Note:
Standard American English pronunciation is sometimes not very popular, even in formal settings:

E.g. Pronounced one popular American way, the 'T' in the word “Center” is silent with the preceding 'N' being the first Consonant Sound of the second Syllable, It sounds very like “Ce-ner”. This vocalization is pervasive, acceptable and respectable. Pronounced another popular way, the 'N' ends the first Syllable and the 'T' after the Pause is clearly accentuated but sounds as if were merged with a 'D'. This way it sounds very like “Cen-der”. The standard American way is to articulate both the 'N' and the 'T' very clearly with the Pause between them, as do the British, yet this is not heard that often. (There are other differences in the way the British articulate the word as a whole when contrasted even with the standard American way.)

Note:
For cross referencing of American pronunciation, I recommend the Merriam-Webster Dictionary. and, for additional cross referencing, I recommend the Cambridge Dictionary which provides both American (USA) and UK (United Kingdom) pronunciations. In case of discrepancy between them as regards American pronunciation, I recommend the Merriam-Webster. For verification of the British Accent, I recommend the Cambridge Dictionary.

Assessment of Vocal Patterns.

As part of the development of this Course, Vocal Patterns across the spectrum of the English language were identified and assessed. A near complete list of Vocal Patterns have been identified and are separately recorded in a Vocal Pattern Master Table. Only after this was done could each Vocal Pattern be fully assessed, compared and appropriately categorized. Distinctive Vocal Patterns have been categorized, according to their assessment, in either the Vocal Pattern Bridge, Inland or Summit Tables. Indistinct Vocal Patterns are recorded separately, only in the Vocal Pattern Master Table.

Objective criteria for the assessment of Vocal Patterns have been defined and used, as explained in the Course.

Appendix VI.
Table:
Glossary

No.	Word or Term	Description
1	Accent	When pronunciation is Scripted to a deeper level of detail it captures the nuances of Accent. This is what is done in this Course. While this approach is followed, the words "Pronunciation" and "Accent" are often used interchangeably in the Course.
2	Accentuation	Accentuation is the level of intensification and amplification (volume or loudness) of a Consonant Sound and its Attributes. Accentuation is the final result of two types of Accentuation, Intrinsic Accentuation and Positional Accentuation.
3	American Consonant Accentuation Principle	This states: In the American Accent, Syllable-End Consonants tend to be more Accentuated than Syllable-Beginning Consonants.
4	Accentuation scale and levels	Accentuation is quantified on a scale with four levels between Weak to Strong, as follows: Weak; Weak to moderate; Moderate to strong; Strong.
5	American Pronunciation Distinctiveness Estimate (APDE)	The American Pronunciation Distinctiveness Estimate (APDE) is a scale for assessing the extent of audible difference between American and British Accents in the way any Vocal Pattern is articulated.
6	American Pronunciation Distinctiveness Estimate levels	The American Pronunciation Distinctiveness Estimate is a scale that shows the level of audible difference between American and British Accents in the articulation of Vocal Patterns. It categorizes Vocal Patterns into the following levels: Great, Substantial, Significant and Insignificant. Vocal Patterns are prioritized for learning based on this ranking in separate Vocal Pattern Tables.
7	American Syllabication Principle	Syllabication is identified as one of the two most influential underlying tendencies that shape the American Accent. Americans have a tendency to begin Syllables within words with a Consonant (the first Syllable doesn't count – it begins with the first letter whatever it is) and where possible, except in a few contexts, they end them with a Vowel (including the first Syllable).
8	Basic Vocal Elements	The Basic Vocal Elements are features of vocal sounds. They include Pauses, Vowel forms, Vowel Modulations, Consonant Sounds, Consonant Accentuation levels, Consonant Extension and Consonant Inherent Attributes.
9	Beginning Consonant	This refers to the first Consonant of a Syllable.
10	Consonant	A 'Consonant' is an alphabet or letter (e.g. B, C, D, F, etc..) which is not a Vowel (e.g. A, E, etc.) and which has more pronounced vocal lines, edges, features and structure than those of Vowels. Consonants form the structure or hard bones of a word. They have harder edges.
11	Consonant position	The position of a Consonant within a Syllable, whether Beginning, Middle or End.
12	Consonant Sequence	Any sequence of Consonants within a word.
13	Consonant Sound	Specific Consonants often have a number of different sounds associated with them, heard in different kinds of words. Each such sound associated

		with each Consonant is separately identified as a Consonant Sound. These are listed in the Table: Consonant Sounds And Their Inherent Attributes, in the Appendix.
14	Consonant Version	Some Consonants have more than one Version, e.g. 'S' in "Sit" or 'S' in "Has". Merged Consonant Sequences like 'TH' can also have different Versions, e.g. the 'TH' in "Think" is different than the 'TH' in "This".
15	Conventions	Scripting rules for Vowels and Consonants in the Vocal Fidelity Phonetic System have been called Conventions and are shown in separate Tables in the Appendix.
16	Distinctiveness	This word is specially used to refer to the level of difference between the American Accent and the British Accent in the vocalization of different Vocal Patterns in words.
17	Dual Vowel Modulation	This type of Modulation involves two different Vowel Sounds with the first Linked to the next. Sometimes a Vowel that is not in the spelling of the Word is inserted in its vocalization adjacent to a Vowel that is within the spelling of the word.
18	End Consonant	The last Consonant of a Syllable.
19	Extension	Extension is the name given to describe a Modulation of a Vowel or Consonant Sound where the sound is lengthened.
20	Extension and Repetition	Extension and Repetition is the name used to describe a common Single Vowel Modulation which often occurs with Soft Vowel Sounds. It may be described as an initial Extended articulation of the Vowel Sound followed by a volume and tone dip followed then by a rise back to the original volume and tone.
21	External Vowel	A Vowel Sound inserted into the vocalization of a word that is not in its spelling. It is often adjacent to a Vowel that is within the spelling of the word.
22	First Part	A "Part" is a section of a word separated from other sections by a long or Major Pause. It may consist of one or more Syllables. The First Part is the First Part of a word in a word that has two or more Parts.
23	Inherent Attributes of Consonants	Each Consonant Sound can be described in terms of its own properties (just as weather can be distinguished in terms of properties such as "Cold", "Windy", "Wet", etc.). The properties of Consonant Sounds are referred to, in this Course – as part of the Vocal Fidelity Phonetic System, as their Inherent Attributes. Twelve distinct Inherent Attributes are identified.
24	Internal Vowel	Any Vowel in the spelling of a Word in contrast to a Vowel Sound heard in its vocalization but not included in its spelling.
25	Intrinsic Accentuation	When a Consonant Sound is articulated in isolation, its Accentuation comes from its Inherent Attributes and may be thought of as stand-alone Accentuation. This is Intrinsic Accentuation.
26	Intrinsic Accentuation scale and levels	Intrinsic Accentuation contributes to Accentuation. A different scale is used for Intrinsic Accentuation than the scale for Accentuation so it can be discussed separately without confusion. On the Intrinsic Accentuation scale, the different levels are: Low, Medium & High.
27	Irregular Vowel Consonant Sequence	When a Vowel Consonant Sequence in a word seems to have a vocalization that seems unique, it cannot be considered a Vocal Pattern or a

	vocalization	Vocal Pattern Variant which by definition must recur in different words. Such a vocalization and the Vowel Consonant Sequence with which it is associated is called Irregular because it is applicable to a single word.
28	Lane	The word, Lane, is used to describe separate learning areas, each focused on different factors underlying the American Accent. The different Lanes are: Lane 1: Syllabication; Lane 2: Tempo; Lane 3: American Voice; Lane 4: Articulation.
29	Last Part	A "Part" is a section of a word separated from other sections by a long or Major Pause. It may consist of one or more Syllables. The Last Part is the Final Part of a word in a word that has two or more Parts.
30	Learning Priority group and levels	Vocal Patterns have been divided into Learning Priority groups I to IV, based on their Distinctiveness level according to the American Pronunciation Distinctiveness Estimate (APDE). In the Vocal Pattern Bridge, Learning Priority group I is covered, within which there are 3 Learning Sequence subgroups.
31	Learning Sequence subgroup and levels	Vocal Patterns are categorized into Learning Sequence subgroups numbered according to their Rate of Occurrence Estimate (RoOE), within each Learning Priority group (which corresponds to the American Pronunciation Distinctiveness Estimate (APDE) level). The lower the Learning Sequence number within each Priority Group, the higher the Vocal Pattern Rate of Occurrence – therefore, the higher the learning priority. In the Vocal Pattern Bridge, 3 Learning subgroups are listed.
32	Learnway	The word, Learnway, is used as the overarching title of this Course, because it is designed to expedite and reduce effort to learn to speak the American way. Course content is presented in order of learning priority, so you learn first what matters more. It enables the learner to diagnose and focus learning effort on their specific Accent gaps.
33	Like	When a Vowel used in the spelling of a word is articulated like another Vowel Sound, the name given to it uses the word "Like" to show that the former is vocalized like the latter, e.g. 'I' Like 'E' Hard as in "Iodine".
34	Linked adjacent Vowels or adjacent Consonants	Consecutive Vowels or consecutive Consonants, each with its own sound that connect from the first to the next, without any intervening Pause, are referred to as Linked Vowels or Linked Consonants.
35	Major Pause	Any relatively long break in the vocalization of any word is called a Major Pause.
36	Merged adjacent Vowels or adjacent Consonants	When consecutive Vowels or Consonants Merge into a single sound, they are said to be Merged and may be called "Merged" Vowels (e.g. 'O' and 'A' in "Boat"), or, "Merged" Consonants (e.g. 'S' and 'H' in "Ship").
37	Mid Part	A "Part" is a section of a word separated from other sections by a long or Major Pause. It may consist of one or more Syllables. The Mid Part (or Parts) refers to any Part(s) between the First and Last Part.
38	Mid-Word Consonant	This refers to a Consonant that is more or less in the middle of a word, without regard to Syllables.
39	Middle Consonant	This refers to a Consonant in the middle of a Syllable.
40	Minor Pause	Any relatively short break in the vocalization of any word is called a Minor Pause.
41	Modulation	A Modulation is a certain kind of modification of a Vowel Sound or a

		Consonant Sound. It could involve the Extension, or the Extension and Repetition of certain forms of Vowel Sounds. It could be an insertion of an External Vowel Sound (not in the word's spelling) preceding or following a Vowel in the word's spelling. It could involve the Extension of a Consonant Sound.
42	Norm	The word, Norm, is used to refer to the tendency of Americans to decrease or increase Accentuation of Consonants depending on their position within a Syllable, according to the American Consonant Accentuation Principle.
43	Occurrence	This is the term used to indicate how often a Vocal Pattern is likely to be heard in spoken English.
44	Part	A "Part" is a section of a word separated from other sections by a long or Major Pause. It may consist of one or more Syllables.
45	Pause	Breaks that divide words into Syllables are called Pauses. They may be relatively long in which case they are called Major Pauses or relatively short in which case they are called Minor Pauses.
46	Positional Accentuation	An increasing or decreasing process that effects the Intrinsic Accentuation of a Consonant Sound, when it is part of a Syllable, depending on its position in a Syllable.
47	Pronunciation	When pronunciation is Scripted to a deeper level of detail it captures the nuances of Accent. This is what is done in this Course. The words "Pronunciation" and "Accent" are often used interchangeably in the Course.
48	Prefix	A Vocal Pattern in the middle of a word has some letters preceding it, called a Prefix. (Note: the word Prefix is given a different meaning in this Course from its general meaning, as it is relative to a Vocal Pattern.)
49	Rate of Occurrence Estimate (RoOE)	A scale to categorize the rate that a particular Vocal Pattern is heard in spoken English.
50	Rate of Occurrence Estimate levels	The Rate of Occurrence Estimate for Vocal Patterns distinguishes between the following levels, in decreasing order: Frequent, Often, and Occasional. Objective criteria are used to distinguish between each level.
51	Script and Scripting	Symbols from the Vocal Fidelity Phonetic System introduced in this Course are used to communicate how a Word, Vocal Pattern or some element within a word is vocalized. These Symbols are referred to as Script and their use is referred to as Scripting.
52	Separation of adjacent Vowels or adjacent Consonants	Separation contrasts with Linking or Merging of either adjacent Vowels, or, adjacent Consonants. It is the result of an intervening Pause. The Pause prevents linguistic effect of adjacent Vowels on each other, or, adjacent Consonants on each other.
53	Silent	When Scripting pronunciation, to show that a particular Consonant or a Vowel in the spelling of a word is not articulated, it is marked Silent with a following asterisk {*}. When a Consonant or Vowel is given a sound that is associated with another Consonant or Vowel Sound, it is similarly marked Silent but following the asterisk Symbol, the Scripted Symbol of the actual Vowel or Consonant Sound is inserted between parentheses into the spelling of the word.
54	Single Vowel Modulation	This type of Modulation involves a single Vowel Sound. It is either only an Extension or an Extension followed by a Repetition of the Vowel Sound.

55	Suffix	A Vocal Pattern in the middle of a word has some letters following it, called a Suffix. (Note: the word Suffix is given a different meaning in this Course from its general meaning, as it is relative to a Vocal Pattern.)
56	Syllable	A Syllable is a note or stream of vocalization from a Pause to a Pause forming an integrated, separable vocal unit.
57	Symbol	The Vocal Fidelity Phonetic System uses simple and familiar Symbols. They are limited to English letters, numbers and punctuation marks.
58	Tempo	This refers to one of the Four Lanes that has to be learned to speak the American way. It refers to the way different Syllables are combined into distinct Parts by cascading Syllables separated only by Minor Parts together. There are no Major Pauses in a Part.
59	Variable Consonant	The '^' Symbol represents "Variable Consonant". A Variable Consonant is any of different Consonants which can be joined to immediately preceding Vowel(s) so long as the preceding Vowel or Vowel Sequence vocalization remains unchanged.
60	Vocal Fidelity Phonetic System	A Phonetic System with enhanced Accent sensitive features enabling an objective and accurate representation of how words are vocalized, true to the features of different Accents.
61	Vocal Pattern	A Vocal Pattern: -Is a readily recognizable recurring sound sequence heard in different words. -Comprises of at least one Vowel and Consonant Sound. -Begins with a Vowel and ends with a Consonant. -Contains Vocal Elements in which the differences between Accents exist.
62	Vocal Pattern Bridge Table	The Vocal Pattern Bridge is the name given to a language-wide tool, in the form of a table, that identifies Vocal Patterns across the span of the English language. It consists of Vocal Patterns that exhibit "Great" Distinctiveness, as vocalized by Americans. These are the most Distinct Vocal Patterns. These Vocal Patterns are ordered both in terms of their Distinctiveness and in terms of their Rate of Occurrence in the language. These Vocal Patterns could only be identified after identifying, assessing and transcribing most English Language Vocal Patterns, in a separate Vocal Pattern Master Table. The Vocal Pattern Bridge is provided in this first Coursebook, of this three Coursebook series. It is followed by "Substantially' Distinctive Vocal Patterns in "The Vocal Pattern Inland Table" in the second Coursebook, and, "Significantly" Distinctive Vocal Patterns in the "Vocal Pattern Summit Table" in the third Coursebook.
65	Vocal Pattern Family	Vocal Patterns that comprise a common beginning Vowel or Vowels and vocalization, but end with a different Consonant or Consonants can be grouped into one Vocal Pattern Family.
66	Vocal Pattern Master Table	The Vocal Pattern Master Table is the comprehensive list of Vocal Patterns spanning the English Language. The assessed level of Distinctiveness and Rate of Occurrence is shown for each Vocal Pattern. The Vocal Patterns are prioritized based on these assessed levels. The pronunciation of each Vocal Pattern is shown in the Script of the Vocal Fidelity Phonetic System. Word examples are provided for each Vocal Pattern. It is from this Master Table that the Vocal Pattern Bridge, the Vocal Pattern Inland and the Vocal Pattern Summit Tables have been extracted.

67	Vocal Pattern Summit Table	The Vocal Pattern Summit Table is the name given to a language-wide tool, in the form of a table, that identifies Vocal Patterns across the span of the English language. It consists of Vocal Patterns that exhibit a Significant level of Distinctiveness (below the higher Distinctiveness levels of Great and Substantial), as vocalized by Americans. These are clearly Distinctive Vocal Patterns. Not being among the more Distinctive of Vocal Patterns, it is likely that many of these may have escaped the notice of learners. These Vocal Patterns are ordered both in terms of their Distinctiveness and in terms of their Rate of Occurrence in the language. These Vocal Patterns could only be identified after a comprehensive identification, assessment and phonetic representation of Vocal Patterns across the English Language, as compiled in the Vocal Pattern Master Table. The Vocal Pattern Summit Table is in the final of three Coursebooks ("The American Accent Learnway – As One, On the Summit").
68	Vocal Pattern Inland Table	The Vocal Pattern Inland Table is the name given to a language-wide tool, in the form of a table, that identifies Vocal Patterns across the span of the English language. It consists of Vocal Patterns that exhibit a Substantial level of Distinctiveness (below the higher Distinctiveness level of Great and above the lower Distinctiveness level of Significant), as vocalized by Americans. These Vocal Patterns are ordered both in terms of their Distinctiveness and in terms of their Rate of Occurrence in the language. These Vocal Patterns could only be identified after a comprehensive identification, assessment and phonetic representation of Vocal Patterns across the English Language, as compiled in the Vocal Pattern Master Table. The Vocal Pattern Inland Table is in the second of three Coursebooks ("The American Accent Learnway – Together, On the Road Inland").
69	Vocal Pattern Variant	Many Vocal Patterns have more than one way of being vocalized, each of which recur with some frequency. Each of these vocalizations represents a Vocal Pattern Variant. A Vocal Pattern Variant is also a Vocal Pattern.
70	Vocalization	How a sequence of Vocal sounds are articulated.
71	Vowel	Vowels are the softer vocal sounds. They are like connective tissue or padding between the harder edged vocal sounds in a word.
72	Vowel forms	Each Vowel has several different articulations or forms, each of which are named, described and given a phonetic Symbol. E.g. the 'A' as in "Fan" and "Far" are two of several different Vowel forms of the 'A' Vowel. Different Forms of each Vowel are given names such as "Soft", "Hard", etc. 50 separate Vowel Forms are listed.
73	Vowel Sequence	Any set of adjacent Vowels in the spelling of a word is a Vowel Sequence
74	Word List Table	Vocal Patterns with more word examples than can be accommodated in the Vocal Pattern Tables, i.e. the Bridge, Inland and Summit Tables, are accommodated in a separate compilations of Word List Tables, each compilation corresponding with the Vocal Pattern Table provided with each of the three Coursebooks.
75	Word Type	A Word Type is any set of words which share some pattern of sound in common, and are therefore pronounced in an analogous way.

Appendix VII.
Bibliography

From the outset of this work, it was my intent to develop an independent solution addressing the objective of this Course. I decided therefore on the approach of forming conclusions based on direct observation of English as it is spoken by Americans – and by the British, for comparison. I corroborated these observations with on-line audio recordings of model pronunciations by authoritative dictionaries. I avoided the influence of other work on this subject. For these reasons, the Bibliography listed below is limited to the following:

Two of my three sources listed are dictionaries. The first is taken as authoritative for American English and the second for British English. Wikipedia was my third source.

1. Merriam-Webster, Retrieved 2015 to 2020. *Dictionary.* https://www.merriam-webster.com/dictionary
2. Cambridge, Retrieved 2015 to 2020. *Dictionary.* https://dictionary.cambridge.org/dictionary/english
3. Wikipedia, Retrieved 2016. *Rhoticity in English.* https://en.m.wikipedia.org/wiki/Rhoticity_in_english
4. Wikipedia, Retrieved 2017. *Language family.* https://en.m.wikipedia.org/wiki/Language_family
5. Wikipedia for information to provide a simple picture of how America was gradually settled by different peoples of different language backgrounds.

About the Author

It is relevant to share a bit about my own language development, my education and career – the context that led me to devote myself full-time, for many years, to the creation of this Course.

I grew up in India where I went through most of my education. Though my parents came from different language backgrounds, the language spoken at home was English. My mother learned English at a Convent School in Bombay from Irish teachers. My father qualified at Cambridge University in the United Kingdom, becoming, in his career, the Legal Director for a multi-national organization, and later, the Principal of a Law College. Other influences included schooling at British schools for expatriates in India and subsequent schooling in the Indian Public School system.

My mind was opened to the subject of Linguistics while at college. After a Bachelor's degree in English & Psychology, and then, a Master's degree in Sociology, both from Bombay University, I went on to have a career in Human Resource Management & Consulting with well known companies in India, the Middle East and the United States.

I continued my education, along with my profession. In India, my learning from a two year foundation course for a doctoral level program in Human Resource Development contributed greatly to the scientific approach underlying the development of the American Accent Learnway™. After moving to the United States in 2003, I earned a Master of Science Degree in Human Resource Management from Golden Gate University, in San Francisco.

Over the course of my life, exposure to the diverse Accents of English across the world, the phonetics of other languages, and subsequently, to the English spoken in America, also provided relevant background for this work.

I see that the present work called upon all that I have learned as a student in the areas of Human sciences and Language, and as a Human Resource Development professional. It required learning about what is knowledge, – and how to create it. The excitement of this pursuit was also important. From the beginning, I saw the purpose as bold. It was actually a much bigger adventure than I anticipated, with many unknowns to consider along the way. What has been most personally satisfying is that it all conforms with fact.

I believe it will be useful for many people. I am keen that everyone who is interested in speaking the American way see what has been learned. For me, both the journey and what it revealed has been fascinating.

www.ingramcontent.com/pod-product-compliance
Lightning Source LLC
Chambersburg PA
CBHW080839120626
46553CB00009B/2489
9798985085501